Contents

TopGear
Quiz Book

TopGear Quiz Book

BBC BOOKS

1 3 5 7 9 10 8 6 4 2

Published in 2013 by BBC Books, an imprint of Ebury Publishing.
A Random House Group Company.

Foreword by Matt Master
Main text by The Puzzle House

The Random House Group Limited Reg. No. 954009

Addresses for companies within the Random House Group can be found at www.randomhouse.co.uk
A CIP catalogue record for this book is available from the British Library.

ISBN: 978 1 849 90585 5

MIX
Paper from responsible sources
FSC® C016897

The Random House Group Limited supports the Forest Stewardship Council® (FSC®), the leading international forest-certification organisation. Our books carrying the FSC label are printed on FSC®-certified paper. FSC is the only forest-certification scheme supported by the leading environmental organisations, including Greenpeace. Our paper procurement policy can be found at www.randomhouse.co.uk/environment

Commissioning editor: Lorna Russell
Managing editor: Joe Cottington
Project editor: Steve Tribe
Production: Antony Heller

Printed and bound by CPI Group (UK) Ltd, Croydon, CR0 4YY

Foreword

In your hands is the key to the vast and dusty catacombs of utterly useless motoring knowledge, compiled over literally days by some of the greatest minds in uselessness. Them and Google.

Learn even a quarter of what lies within and you will have become an invaluable member of any pub quiz team, or at least one where no other member knows anything much about cars.

But go carefully. In delving further you will also unlock the potential to bore anyone to death in a matter of minutes. A little knowledge is a dangerous thing, so they say. A lot of knowledge about cars can be truly lethal. Use this knowledge wisely. Keep it to yourself. Never, ever reveal it to the elderly or infirm. Or someone you really fancy.

Contained herein is a detailed chronological quizathon through the whole noisy history of motoring, missing out as many of the boring bits as we could get away with while still cobbling together nearly 3,000 questions about one thing. You don't get that too often in a lifetime, for obvious reasons.

Covering the birth of the car, world wars, Germany, racing, rallying, Sixties America, supercars, green cars, tiny cars, massive cars, brilliant inventions and catastrophic balls ups, we'd like to think this book has it all. There's even a chapter about motorbikes. We were seriously winging it on that one.

You'll also find a chapter or two on *Top Gear* telly, the presenters and their fondness for a gigantic cock-up. We couldn't leave any of that out. And besides, things were getting desperate by about Chapter 30.

We hope you enjoy this, probably the biggest and most comprehensive *Top Gear* quiz book to be published this year. There's something for everyone, from nerdy F1 knowledge to stalker-level recall of James and Richard's almost constant television presence. If this book fails to leave the most ardent petrolhead sated then we give up. See what your GP can recommend instead. Challenging at times, usually slightly daft and guaranteed to be of no actual use in real life, this is the ultimate driving test…

1 The Horseless Cart

Swerving the steaming piles of equine excrement, Car Version 0.1 shared its primitive road network with all manner of ancient transport. Not so far removed from the carriages and carts it sought to leave behind, Man's early efforts to ditch the nag were giant leaps of imagination, early uptake for eccentric horse haters only.

But in no time the car proper was born, with recognisable bits like bonnets and steering wheels. Soon the only horses worth mentioning would be driving your pistons. This was tomorrow, today, and its appetite was for oil, not oats.

1 The first engine powered road vehicle was built in which century?
   a) 18th
   b) 19th
   c) 20th

2 Messrs Carless, Capel & Leonard of Hackney Wick patented which term in 1896?
   a) Oil
   b) Petrol
   c) Motor

3 What name was given to the very first vehicle designed to be propelled by a motor?

4 Were the Renault family originally manufacturers of buttons or bottles?

5 In the late 19th century the first speed records went to vehicles powered by which fuel?
   a) Gas
   b) Electricity
   c) Petrol

6 These were followed by records using which fuel?

7 Who am I?
   - In 1883 I built the world's first light petrol engine
   - In 1886 I patented my Motorwagen which had a two stroke petrol engine
   - Later my business name was linked to Mercedes and I worked with Daimler

8 In 1887 Daimler equipped a workshop for 23 people to build his engines in which German city? Stuttgart or Frankfurt?

9 How fast was the first person in the UK to be successfully charged with speeding actually driving?
   a) 8mph
   b) 18mph
   c) 80mph

10 The Daimler 35hp, the prototype for the motor car at the start of the 20th century, was given a new brand name. What was it?

11 Traffic lights today are red, amber and green. Which of these colours was not present in the world's first traffic lights?

12 Dutch company Bikkers made a steam car in 1907, but what were they most famous for making? Bicycles or fire engines?

13 How many wheels did the first patented motor car have?

14 In what means of transport did Rudolf Diesel, who was granted a patent for the internal combustion engine, die in mysterious circumstances?

15 The Grenville steam carriage was built by Robert Neville Grenville of Glastonbury. What was his 'day job'? A railway engineer or a music entrepreneur?

16 Peugeot was a family company that was originally part of which trade? Was it farming or ironmongery?

17 The first engine powered road vehicle included a log basket and a haystack boiler among its component parts. True or false?

18 Where did Daimler establish its first factory in the UK?
a) Coventry
b) Dagenham
c) Luton

19 In the early 20th century most pioneering cars were run on petrol. Columbia made cars run on electricity. True or false?

20 What was the top speed of the 1880 steam powered Grenville Steam carriage?
a) 10mph
b) 15mph
c) 20mph

21 Bicycle manufacturers Adler made components for Benz, but what else did they make? Was it sewing machines or typewriters?

22 Herbert Austin and Frederick Wolseley first met in Australia where Wolseley was a manufacturer of kangaroo farm equipment. True or false?

23 In which city did trams first appear?
a) Amsterdam
b) Berlin
c) San Francisco

24 Why could the person who financed Benz's motorwagen not apply for the patent?

25 The Bordino Steam Carriage of 1854 had wooden wheels and wooden spokes. What were its tyres made from, iron or more wood?

26 Where were Lanchester cars made?
   a) The US
   b) The UK
   c) France

27 Citroen's 2CV was originally planned to replace a traditional horse and cart in rural France. True or false?

28 In the late 19th century Daimler and his engineering partner Maybach fitted their engines into what types of vehicle? Stagecoaches or ploughs?

29 The Goddu Tandem had a very high top speed for its time when it was built in 1897. What was the speed?
   a) 20mph
   b) 30mph
   c) 40mph

30 Frenchman Adolphe Clement was a pioneer of the motor industry but was already a magnate in which area of transport?

31 Arnold & Sons fitted their cars with electric self start dynamotors which also helped in which terrain? Clue: Useful in Switzerland, Austria and parts of Italy but less so in Holland!

32 In 1902 the Mercedes name was established for which company's cars?
   a) Daimler
   b) Benz
   c) Adler

33 Did Henry Ford build his first car in the 19th or 20th century?

34 Where was the first British-built car built?
a) England
b) Scotland
c) Wales

35 Which of the following was not found on Benz's 1888 Motorwagen – a spark plug, a clutch, a radiator or a windscreen wiper?

36 Armand Peugeot's first 'horseless carriages' were designed to run on what?

37 Which company built the first four wheeled vehicle to reach 10mph?

38 Belgian manufacturer FN built their 3.5HP in 1900 and gave it a name which, coincidentally, was shared by a British queen. What was the name?
a) The Matilda
b) The Elizabeth
c) The Victoria

39 French motoring pioneer Albert de Dion had which title?
a) Prince
b) Count
c) Marquis

40 Before it became a fuel for cars 'gasoline' was used as what, and where was it sold?

41 Name the year
- The British Labour Party won its first two seats
- The world's first motor show opened in New York City
- The Daimler Motor Company was founded

42 Rolls Royce founder Charles Rolls died in a car crash. True or false?

43 From being used for leisurely drives about town, the Bikkers Steam Car of 1907 had a particularly dirty job to do. What was it?

a) Working in coal mines
b) Transporting barrels of oil
c) Cleaning out cesspits

44 Which was the first manufacturer to equip its cars with pneumatic tyres?

a) Citroen
b) Daimler
c) Peugeot

45 Who am I?

- I married motoring pioneer Karl
- I cashed in my dowry to finance his invention
- A tourist route in southern Germany is named after me, acknowledging when I 'borrowed' my husband's car (the first ever) and drove 60 miles from Mannheim to Pforzheim to see my mum!

The Answers

1 a) 18th
2 b) Petrol
3 Motorwagen
4 Buttons
5 b) Electricity
6 Steam
7 Karl Benz
8 Stuttgart
9 a) 8mph (Legend has it he was chased by a police officer on a bicycle!)
10 Mercedes
11 Amber
12 Fire engines
13 Three
14 Ship (It was the SS Dresden)
15 Railway engineer
16 Ironmongery
17 True (It also had a chimney and a carrying fork!)
18 a) Coventry
19 True
20 c) 20mph
21 Typewriters
22 False (He made sheep shearing machines)
23 b) Berlin

24 This was Mrs Benz and married women could not apply for patents
25 Iron
26 b) The UK
27 True
28 Stagecoaches
29 b) 30mph
30 Bicycles
31 Helped the engine on hills
32 a) Daimler
33 19th (1896)
34 b) Scotland
35 A windscreen wiper
36 Steam
37 Daimler
38 c) The Victoria
39 b) Count
40 Cleaning product sold in pharmacies
41 1900
42 False (He perished in a flying accident)
43 c) Cleaning out cesspits
44 c) Peugeot
45 Bertha Benz

2 The Only Way is Aristocracy

The single greatest hurdle to early motoring was the need to be richer than Croesus. Cars were cutting edge in a way that our nano-tech age takes for granted, and the only way to get behind the wheel if you didn't have blue blood in your veins was to chauffeur someone who did.

This was the era of louvered bonnets longer than ocean liners and ermine fur in lieu of window rubber. It was extravagance beyond comparison, then and now.

1 Where was the classic Bugatti Type 35B first built?
   a) Italy
   b) France
   c) UK

2 What is the background colour of the classic Bugatti badge, seen on all Bugatti's from 1910 until the early 1950s?

3 The 1924 Hispano Suiza H6C had a chassis made from what?
   a) Tulip wood
   b) Cast aluminium
   c) Stainless steel

4 In which decade of the 20th century did coachbuilding and design consultancy Bertone begin, which was still in business well into the 21st century?
   a) 1920s
   b) 1930s
   c) 1940s

5 In 1905 the Darracq 200HP broke the world land speed record at what speed?
   a) 44mph
   b) 88mph
   c) 110mph

6 Which Bugatti clocked up over a thousand competitive victories between 1924 and 1931 when it ceased production?

7 In which London area were luxury coach builder Park Ward based?
   a) Belsize Park
   b) Richmond
   c) Willesden

8 Whose initials appear on the original Bugatti badge, seen on all Bugattis from 1910 until the early 1950s? Was it Ettore Bugatti or Jean Bugatti?

9 The Brooke Swan had a swan's neck at the front which did what?
a) Sprayed the road
b) Sounded a warning bell
c) Steered the car

10 The name Aston in the famous Aston Martin comes from the Aston area of Birmingham. True or false?

11 F.H. Royce & Company, which later became Rolls Royce was established in which city?

12 Name the year
- Cadillac produced the Model 30, the first production car with a self starter as standard
- The first Keystone Kops movies were made
- *Titanic* sank on its maiden voyage

13 Where was the 1906 Motor Exhibition held?
a) Crystal Palace
b) Olympia
c) Royal Albert Hall

14 Which British monarch was the first to buy a Daimler?
a) Victoria
b) Edward VII
c) George V

15 The Rolls Royce Silver Ghost had a high roof so that men in top hats could sit inside in comfort. True or false?

16 What is the logo of the prestigious Alvis company, founded in 1919?

17 Which was the first motor company founded in Britain specifically to make cars?

18 One of the Bugatti brothers, shared his first name with the surname of which famous painter?
   a) Rembrandt
   b) Monet
   c) Cezanne

19 Lawrence of Arabia praised his Rolls Royce Silver Ghost for helping him win the desert campaign of the First World War. True or false?

20 Who am I?
- I raced to my first victory in a Bugatti in 1930
- I was honoured at the end of WWII for my work with the French Resistance
- The new Bugatti superior sports car of the 21st century is named after me

21 In the 1950s Rolls Royce advertised that the loudest thing you could hear in their new cars was what?

22 From the early 1930s Park Ward became the coachbuilder of choice for which luxury manufacturer?

23 The US Hudson Terraplane was launched by which aviation celebrity in 1932?
   a) Amy Johnson
   b) Amelia Earhart
   c) Orville Wright

24 The Talbot Lago was built in which style?

a) Art Nouveau
b) Art Deco
c) Pop Art

25 In 1937 the transport minister of the time was offended by the Lagonda V12 as he said the horn outlet grilles resembled what?

26 Name the year

- The Alfa Romeo 40–60 HP was developed in Milan
- The RAC announced it would revive the motor car Tourist Trophy after a six year gap
- The First World War broke out

27 What does 'goutte d'eau' refer to in the name of the famous model from Talbot Lago?

a) The waterfall
b) The teardrop
c) The rainstorm

28 How many Bugatti Royales were made?

a) Six
b) Twelve
c) Twenty

29 In 1924 Raymond Mays was driving a Bugatti in the Shelsley Walsh Mountain race in Wales when what fell off – although the driver continued?

a) Wheel
b) Windscreen wiper
c) Headlamp

30 Sir Henry Royce's first patent was for a bayonet lamp socket. True or false?

31 Talbot Lago was based in which country?
 a) USA
 b) France
 c) UK

32 Which maker boasted they had 'the best car in the world'?

33 Which motor pioneer was the first aviator to complete a double crossing of the English Channel?

34 In which luxury car did dancer Isadora Duncan meet her death when her scarf got caught up in its wheels?

35 Which items were not included in the price list of early luxury cars, by Mulliner for example?
 a) Seats
 b) Windscreen wipers
 c) Tyres

36 In 2010 a Talbot Lago T23 fetched how many pounds at auction?
 a) Just under a million
 b) Just under two million
 c) Just under three million

37 Which Bugatti model sported the Park Ward, the Binder and the Double Fiacre?

38 Which manufacturer made the Barker Tourer?

39 The Silver Ghost had a letterbox slot in the windscreen so you didn't have to open the door to give someone a message and the car stayed warm. True or false?

40 The Hispano Suiza was a Spanish company based where?

41 Name the year
- King George VI was crowned
- The emergency 999 telephone service began
- The first motor show was held at Earl's Court in London

42 In 1930 Rolls Royce bought which other very prestigious UK motor company?

43 In the 1907 Rolls Royce Silver Ghost what was the 'sprinting gear'?

44 In 1987 a Bugatti Royale, a 60+ year old car was sold for how much?
   a) 2.5 million
   b) 3.5 million
   c) 5.5 million

45 Who am I?
- I was the first Cambridge undergraduate to own a car
- I founded my famous company over a lunch with my business partner Henry
- Our names have been synonymous with luxury cars for over a century

The Answers

1 b) France
2 Red
3 a) Tulip wood
4 a) 1920s
5 c) 110mph
6 Type 35
7 c) Willesden
8 Ettore Bugatti
9 a) Sprayed the road
10 False (It refers to a hill climb at Aston Clinton in Buckinghamshire which the car conquered with ease in 1914)
11 Manchester
12 1912
13 b) Olympia
14 b) Edward VII
15 True
16 Inverted red triangle with the Alvis name on it
17 Daimler
18 a) Rembrandt
19 True
20 Pierre Veyron
21 The electric clock
22 Bentley

23 b) Amelia Earhart
24 b) Art Deco
25 A woman's breasts
26 1914
27 b) The teardrop
28 a) Six
29 a) Wheel
30 True
31 b) France
32 Rolls Royce
33 Charles Rolls
34 Bugatti
35 c) Tyres
36 b) Just under two million
37 Royale
38 Rolls Royce
39 False (It was so it could be opened and increase visibility in stormy weather)
40 France
41 1937
42 Bentley
43 Fourth gear
44 c) 5.5 million
45 Charles Rolls

3 German Genesis

Barely had the motorcar splintered a spoke before the Germans were making far bigger, faster and more advanced versions than everyone else and racing them to ruthless effect all around the world. They barely broke stride for the next century either, goosesteps notwithstanding.

1 Auto Union evolved into which modern day group?
   a) Audi
   b) BMW
   c) Mercedes

2 Into what type of vehicle did Gottlieb Daimler first demonstrate his petrol powered internal combustion engine?
   a) A tractor
   b) A stage coach
   c) A motorcycle

3 Audi was one of the oldest German car marques but where did the factory end up after WWII because of boundary changes?

4 Which German motor company made the first production car with a diesel engine?
   a) Porsche
   b) Mercedes Benz
   c) Daimler

5 Emile Jellinek who bought the marketing rights for the Daimler car renamed the brand as Mercedes. Who or what was Mercedes that the car was named after?

6 Which were the first German cars to be built on an assembly line?

7 The BMW badge, first produced in 1917, is black, white and which other colour?

8 Herr Porsche – the first of the motoring dynasty – originally designed famous cars for which company?

9 Which company was formed by Jörgen Skafte Rasmussen in 1932, and included DKW, Horch and Wanderer?

10 The BMW factory originally built what?

11 The 'B' in BMW refers to the region where the first factory was based. What does it stand for?

12 Porsche Type 60 later became known as what?

13 Name the year

- There was a General Strike in Britain
- Princess Elizabeth was born
- The famous Mercedes Benz badge was created

14 Which designer, who went on to found a prestigious marque that bears his name, designed the Blitze-Benz racer which held the land speed record from 1909 to 1924?

15 After the Daimler Benz merger what did the Mannheim plant concentrate on building?

a) Luxury cars
b) Military vehicles
c) Trucks and buses

16 Hanomag began making cars in the 1920s but as early as 1835 they were famous for making what?

17 In 1949 Auto Union returned to the German market in which city?

a) Düsseldorf
b) Stuttgart
c) Berlin

18 In 1911 Gustav Otto established the company which evolved into

BMW in which city?

19 What was renamed the 'strength through joy' car in 1938 although later returned to its original name?

20 Who am I?

- I completed my training as a plumber but was always fascinated by electricity
- The last car I designed for Mercedes Benz was the SSK
- I went on to found my own world famous company renowned for its fast cars

21 Why did the Auto Union badge have four circles?

22 A ride in a Daimler bus inspired which British motor manufacturer famous for its luxury cars in the early 20th century?

23 Which German manufacturer won the French Grand Prix days before the outbreak of WWI?

24 Why did Daimler Benz originally not wish to make 'people's cars'?

25 Hitler introduced a savings stamp scheme so that more people could afford his 'people's car'. True or false?

26 Name the year

- The VW Beetle or people's car was due to go into full time production in September
- Germany invaded Poland
- The outbreak of WWII occurred – also in September!

27 Adolf Hitler commissioned the Volkswagen so that he could drive it on German roads reinforcing the idea of him as a man of the people. True or false?

28 What cc did the original Beetle have?

29 What was the original mock up prototype of the VW Beetle made from?

30 The Dixi 3/15PS became the first car from which now world famous German manufacturer when they took over the Dixi factory in 1928?

31 Up to the 1930s German racing cars were assigned what colour?

32 The SSK was the fastest car in the world when it first appeared. How many were produced?

a) 28
b) 38
c) 58

33 Which motoring innovation in 1930s Germany helped the popularity of cars such as the VW Beetle?

34 What type of vehicle was the Type 2 Volkswagen?

35 Why was the SSK nicknamed the Trossi?

36 To make sure they were within the legal limit for the race, what did Mercedes remove their cars at the A.V.U.S. Grand Prix in May 1934?

37 In the Mercedes 35HP the passengers and driver sat behind the engine. Where had passengers and driver sat in earlier cars?

38 The K in the Mercedes SSK is the German word for short. What is it?

39 Which racing team were linked to Mercedes and Auto Union?
a) Silver Bullets
b) Silver Arrows
c) Silver Shots

40 The original Opel 4/12 nicknamed the Laubfrosch or tree frog was a two seater, a three seater or a four seater?

41 What nickname was given to the small light engine produced by Daimler and Maybach due to its distinctive shape? Was it the cuckoo clock or the grandfather clock?

42 In which decade of the 20th century did rivals Daimler-Mercedes and Benz merge? 1920s or 1930s?

43 In 1928 BMW took over the factory which was building which iconic British car?

44 Which manufacturer produced the 60HP, the most advanced car on the market at that time?

45 The brief from Adolf Hitler for the people's car was that it should carry how many people?

The Answers

1 a) Audi
2 c) A motorcycle
3 East Germany
4 b) Mercedes Benz
5 Emile's daughter
6 Opel
7 Blue
8 Volkswagen
9 Auto Union
10 Aircraft engines
11 Bayerische (Bavarian)
12 Volkswagen Beetle
13 1926
14 Ferdinand Porsche
15 c) Trucks and buses
16 Steam engines
17 a) Düsseldorf
18 Munich
19 VW Beetle
20 Ferdinand Porsche
21 Represented the four companies which amalgamated to form Auto Union
22 W.O. Bentley
23 Mercedes

24 They thought it would damage their reputation in the luxury market
25 True
26 1939
27 False (He couldn't drive)
28 985cc
29 Wood
30 BMW
31 White
32 b) 38
33 Autobahns or motorways
34 Van
35 Carlo Trossi was its first owner
36 Paintwork from the body
37 Above the engine
38 Kurz
39 b) Silver Arrows
40 A two seater
41 The grandfather clock
42 1920s
43 Austin 7
44 Mercedes
45 Five – two adults and three children

4 Cloth Cap Racing

In the days before press junkets in sponsored fireproof Y-fronts, racing drivers were loveable amateurs, chain-smoking piss artists who drove their cars to the circuit and kept optimistic that they'd be driving home at all. The only concession to safety was a slightly firmer moustache wax.

1 In which UK county was the first purpose-built race circuit built?
 a) Kent
 b) Surrey
 c) Sussex

2 Brooklands race circuit opened in 1909. What year did it close? Clue: There was a major world conflict beginning that year!

3 In which Italian city was the Alfa company founded?

4 The 1930 Bentley Speed Six became famous for beating which train between Monte Carlo and Calais? Was it the Blue Train or the Orient Express?

5 Which driver gained the first Bentley victory at le Mans?
 a) John Duff
 b) Glen Kidston
 c) Bernard Rubin

6 On which Isle did Bentley have three winners in June 1922?
 a) Isle of Dogs
 b) Isle of Wight
 c) Isle of Man

7 Who am I?
- I was apprenticed to the Great Northern Railway Locomotive Works in Doncaster when I was 16
- My cars were Le Mans 24 Hour race winners in the 1920s and my name is still associated with prestigious British cars
- My nickname came from my first name initials W.O.

8 Which F1 driver's first name sounds likethe the surname of a pair of coachbuilder brothers who built sports cars in the 1930s?

9 Which Bentley was the last of the W.O. period of Bentleys?

10 The fortune which originally financed the Aston Martin Company came from where? English China Clay pits in Cornwall or the expansion of the railways countrywide?

11 Which marque won the first ever Grand Prix Championship?

12 Which car company was known as SS Cars before WWII?

13 Name the year
- The Bentley R Type Continental could surpass 120mph
- The first scheduled flight of a comet left London for Johannesburg
- The Olympics were held in Helsinki

14 Who bought out Bentley in 1931?

15 W.O. Bentley went to work for which manufacturer in 1935 after his own company went bankrupt and he had to work for an arch rival for a short period?

16 Which twosome achieved the World 24 Hours record in 1925?

17 Part time Bentley Boy, Sydney Charles Houghton Davis, was generally known by which first name?

18 In 1929 what did Duff and Head attach to their headlight to make it easily identifiable to the pit crew?
a) Lion
b) St George's Cross
c) English Rose

19 In which county was the oldest speed hill climb in Britain?
a) Yorkshire
b) Worcestershire
c) Somerset

20 Who am I?
- My family made a fortune out of diamonds in South Africa
- I played six first class cricket matches for Surrey as a wicket keeper/batsman
- My nickname was Babe, and I was one of the leading Bentley Boys of the late 1920s

21 What was the British Grand Prix called when it was raced at Brooklands in 1926–1927?

22 Old Mother Gun and Old Number One were cars from which stable?

23 In 1929 how much was the prize money for winning the Irish Grand Prix?
a) £100
b) £500
c) £1,000

24 Who was the first driver to race a Bentley?
a) Frank Clement
b) W.O. Bentley
c) Oliver Bertram

25 What nickname was given to a group of Bentley cars in the late 1920s and early 1930s which were financed by reclusive heiress Dorothy Paget?
a) Puffers

b) Blowers
c) Breathers

26 Which world famous car was the first production car to have alloy wheels fitted as standard?

27 The British Grand Prix is the oldest in the world. True or false?

28 Eddie Hall won the JCC '200' at Brooklands in 1924, 1925 and 1926 driving which small car?

29 Which Bentley Boy proved he was a versatile racer by becoming champion National Hunt jockey in 1918?
a) Eddie Hall
b) George Duller
c) Oliver Bertram

30 Between the First and Second World Wars what was the JCC?

31 In 1929 racing Bentleys took three minutes to refuel. How long did it take the Alfas?
a) 90 seconds
b) Four minutes
c) Ten minutes

32 Why was established driver Eddie Hall not able to take part in motor racing during the winter of 1928?

33 Bentley Boy Jack Dunfee's racing career ended when his brother was killed in a race. He went on to establish what kind of agency?
a) Estate agency
b) Travel agency
c) Theatrical agency

34 Which motoring speed legend drove a Bugatti at the 1928 Ulster Tourist Trophy which caught fire and had to burn out in the pits?

35 In 1930 which manufacturer produced a specially built car for Le Mans three time winner Woolf Barnato?

36 In 1929, at which venue was the Irish Grand Prix held?

37 In a stunt worthy of *Top Gear*, where did the 'Old No 7' make a spectacular appearance at a celebration dinner after the Le Mans success of 1927?

38 In 1928 W.O. Bentley refused to race as a protest against what?

a) The class system
b) The handicapping system
c) The prize money

39 Glen Kidston's last race was at which circuit where he won with Woolf Barnato?

40 Frank Clement was unique among Bentley racers between 1919 and 1931 as he was the only professional among amateurs. True or false?

41 Name the year

- The United Kingdom had three kings
- The Olympic Games were held in Munich
- E.R. Hall came second for the third time in consecutive years in the Ulster Tourist Trophy

42 In which county was the formidable Sutton Bank climb?

43 In the late 1920s Eddie Hall had a famous collision with what?

a) His brother's car
b) A horse
c) A town hall

44 A sportsman and a racer to the very end, George Duller collapsed and died at which famous sporting event in 1962?

45 Which racing driver broke the London–South Africa flying record in a Lockheed DL-1 Special Vega in 1931?

a) Bernard Rubin
b) Glen Kidston
c) George Duller

The Answers

1 b) Surrey
2 1939
3 Milan
4 The Blue Train
5 a) John Duff
6 c) Isle of Man
7 W.O. Bentley
8 Jenson Button (Alan & Richard Jensen)
9 8 Litre
10 English China Clay pits in Cornwall
11 Alfa Romeo
12 Jaguar
13 1952
14 Rolls Royce
15 Lagonda
16 J F Dudd/W Barnato
17 Sammy
18 b) St George's Cross
19 b) Worcestershire
20 Woolf Barnato
21 RAC Grand Prix
22 Bentley
23 c) £1,000
24 a) Frank Clement

25 b) Blowers
26 Bugatti type 35
27 False (It's the French)
28 Austin 7
29 b) George Duller
30 Junior Car Club
31 a) 90 seconds
32 He was part of the Olympic Bobsleigh team
33 c) Theatrical agency
34 Malcolm Campbell
35 Bentley
36 Phoenix Park
37 London's Savoy Hotel (The car was pushed into the dining room!)
38 b) The handicapping system
39 Le Mans
40 True
41 1936
42 Yorkshire
43 c) A town hall
44 Epsom Derby
45 b) Glen Kidston

5 The Motoring Masses

Altering the social and physical landscape in a manner to rival the atomic bomb, affordable motoring was one of Mankind's great sea changes. Mass production, pioneered by Henry Ford, meant unprecedented affordability, and suddenly the average man was whisked over new horizons and back again in about the same time it took to saddle up his horse.

1 Who am I?

- I was born on a farm in Michigan in 1863
- I founded my own Motor Company, which still bears my name, in the early years of the 20th century
- Models include the Capri, the Anglia and the Mondeo

2 The Ford Model T didn't have front brakes. True or false?

3 Which French car manufacturer had his name in lights on the Eiffel Tower between 1925 and 1934, as part of a sponsorship deal?

4 The 1933 Exhibition of Progress was held in Detroit and organised by which car firm? Was it Ford or Chrysler?

5 The Essex A 1919 was one of the first cars made at Dagenham in Essex. True or false?

6 The Model T was famously available in only one colour, black. But why black? The paint was cheaper or black enamel dried more quickly?

7 Who am I?

- I was a leading figure in the British Motor industry, having my own business from 1904 until my death in 1940
- I became Lord of Longbridge
- I am associated with the car which became Britain's rival to the Model T Ford

8 What was the advantage of the 1913 Humber Humberette being termed 'cycle car'?

9 Name the year
- Production of Ford's Model T's reached 1,000 per day
- Ernest Shackleton made his third trip to the Antarctic with the ship *Endurance*
- The First World War began

10 In 1927 Andre Citroen said that 'the first words a baby should learn to pronounce are mummy, daddy and' what?

11 What was the maximum speed of the first mass produced car the Ford Model T?
a) 22mph
b) 42mph
c) 62mph

12 In the Model T what did the centre pedal operate?
a) Reverse
b) Gear change
c) Brakes

13 Name the year
- US gangster Al Capone was arrested for tax evasion
- *Star Trek*'s Leonard Nimoy was born
- The Highway Code was first published

14 Europe's first mass produced car was produced by which French manufacturer? Was it Peugeot or Citroen?

15 Which was the most successful UK manufacturer of the 1920s?

16 A record breaking number of 15 million Ford Model T's were made between 1908 and 1923. Which motor company broke that record in 1972?

17 Which tyre company took over Citroen in 1934 when the car company went bankrupt?

18 The Ford script on its logo was created by Ford's chief engineering assistant who had previously designed script on what?

a) Cinema posters
b) Visiting cards
c) Comic book covers

19 Which was the first country to have motorways, roads devoted purely to motor vehicles with at least two traffic lanes in each direction?

20 The world's first traffic lights were installed near which London landmark?

a) Buckingham Palace
b) Houses of Parliament
c) St Paul's Cathedral

21 What were the Model T's wheels made of until replaced by wire wheels in 1926?

22 What was the launch price of the Austin 7 when it burst on to the market in 1922?

a) £75
b) £165
c) £200

23 In the Model T was lubricating oil propelled around the engine by a pump or by gravity?

24 How many Austin 7s were sold between 1922 when it took the market by storm, and the outbreak of WWII in 1939?

a) Just under 100,000
b) Just under 200,000
c) Just under 300,000

25 What was Morris's answer to the Austin 7?

26 Name the year
- Scrabble was first marketed
- Mahatma Gandhi was murdered
- The Citroen 2CV went on sale

27 BMW's first cars were licensed-built Austin 7's. True or false?

28 The inventor of the disc brake in 1902 was a member of which profession?
a) Doctor
b) Train driver
c) Member of Parliament

29 In 1918 what portion of US cars on the road were Model T's?
a) A quarter
b) A third
c) A half

30 What motoring first went to Mr Beene of London in 1935?
a) First driver responsible for a multiple pile up in Great Britain
b) First to drive a vehicle that could only reverse
c) First to obtain a driving test pass certificate in Great Britain

31 What was Cadillac's first car called? Clue: Go alphabetical.

32 In 1932 a Japanese car manufacturer built the Type 10 which was almost a carbon copy of the Austin 7. Which manufacturer built it?

33 How far were the seats in a Riley Brooklands from the ground?
- a) Six inches
- b) Nine inches
- c) Eleven inches

34 What powered the Model T's lights until they were replaced by electric lamps in 1919? Was it acetylene or oil?

35 Since the Model T didn't originally have a fuel pump when fuel was low it was sometimes necessary to reverse it up hills. True or false?

36 Which company built the first ever mass produced taxi?
- a) Citroen
- b) Renault
- c) Peugeot

37 A man called Cadillac founded the city of Detroit years before the automobiles moved in. Is that true or false?

38 What was nickname of the Model T Ford?
- a) Tin Lily
- b) Thin Lizzie
- c) Tin Lizzie

39 The Ford Popular, built throughout the 1950s boasted how many windscreen wipers?
- a) One
- b) Two
- c) Three

40 In which city was the Austin Motor Company founded?

41 The affordable Ford Model Y, built for the British market, was reinvented and evolved as the Popular and which other model?

42 The wonderfully named Dodge Brothers, became car manufacturers in their own right, but initially they were subcontractors to which major US company?

43 How much did the first Highway Code cost?

a) A penny
b) Sixpence
c) A shilling

44 What was the established speed limit in the UK in 1920?

a) 15mph
b) 20mph
c) 25mph

45 What was the first car to be produced on Merseyside?

The Answers

1 Henry Ford
2 True
3 Citroen
4 Ford
5 False (It was made in the USA)
6 Black enamel dried more quickly (Speed of production wasn't lost)
7 Herbert Austin
8 Lower road tax
9 1914
10 Citroen
11 b) 42mph
12 a) Reverse
13 1931
14 Citroen
15 Austin
16 Volkswagen (with the Beetle)
17 Michelin
18 b) Visiting cards
19 Germany
20 b) Houses of Parliament
21 Wood
22 b) £165
23 Gravity

24 c) Just under 300,000
25 The Morris Minor
26 1948
27 True
28 a) Doctor (Lanchester)
29 c) A half
30 c) First to obtain a driving test pass certificate in Great Britain
31 Model A
32 Datsun
33 a) Six inches
34 Acetylene
35 True
36 b) Renault
37 True
38 c) Tin Lizzie
39 a) One
40 Birmingham
41 The Ford Anglia
42 Ford
43 a) A penny
44 b) 20mph
45 Ford Anglia (105E)

6 Warring Wonders

Nothing focuses the mind quite like a war. Needing rugged, reliable, versatile machines to go anywhere, carrying anything, while being shot at, the First and Second World Wars gave birth to all manner of motoring inspiration, including the modern day SUV. Well, it seemed like a good idea at the time.

1 Which wartime vehicle was invented by Ernest Swinton and first used in the battle of the Somme in 1916?

2 In the competition between Ford, Willys and Bantam to build a four wheel drive reconnaissance vehicle, who was first to get the US army contract?

3 Which manufacturer, whose vehicles are still made today, was the largest arms manufacturer in the Austro Hungarian Empire in WWI?

4 The engineering team at Jaguar formulated their idea for producing the company's own engine while they were on fire watch duty during WWII in their native Coventry. True or false?

5 In the early 1920s the Royal Tank Corps received its first major new tank type, the Medium, which was made by whom?
   a) Vickers
   b) Rolls Royce
   c) Sherman

6 Which military vehicle's name came about through an abbreviation of General Purpose vehicle or GP?

7 Which designer famed for classic cars designed the Volkswagen Kubelwagen, a military vehicle used from 1940 onwards?

8 Which stalwart of the British motor industry made Lancaster bombers?

9 The Humber Super Snipe, much favoured by Field Marshal Montgomery in WWII, had which nickname?
   a) Brave Banger

b) Old Faithful
c) Monty's Python

10 Which company from the north west of England, famous for its trucks, was a major producer of tanks in WWII?

11 Which truck made by Albion, which shares its name with a road out of London, was widely used in WWI when 6,000 were built for war service?

12 Liberty was not a truck manufacturer as such but its name was adopted to produce standardised designs for which country's military vehicles in WWI?

13 What did the amphibious Volkswagen Schwimmwagen have as an aid to water propulsion?

14 The 1925 Hanomag 2/10PS was nicknamed the Kommissbrot because it was said to look like a loaf of army bread rations. True or false?

15 Which French manufacturer made the FT, the first turreted tank produced in any quantity?
a) Peugeot
b) Citroen
c) Renault

16 What was the nickname of the Daimler Scout Car? (Think Australian wild dog!!)

17 During WWII, Alvis ceased car production but assisted Rolls Royce producing what?

18 What colour was the very first Land Rover, and why?

19 In WWI many Rolls Royce Silver Ghosts were built as armoured cars. True or false?

20 What does the abbreviation AFV stand for?

21 The inventor of the preselector gearbox for battle tanks towards the end of WWI in 1917 had a name with a *Dad's Army* link. What was his name?
   a) Major Pike
   b) Major Mainwaring
   c) Major Wilson

22 What were Land Rovers originally made from to bypass postwar restrictions on building with steel?

23 The threat of invasion from German and Soviet forces pushed Poland towards a tank building programme which was partly financed by which country?
   a) France
   b) The UK
   c) The USA

24 The Luftwaffe was the German airforce. The Panzerwaffe was made up of what?

25 Tactical markings on armoured vehicles in WWII were often made of symbols on playing cards. True or false?

26 What were 'Kangaroos' devised by II Canadian Corps?

27 What was a Sherman Crab used for?

28 Which maybe unexpected member of the crew was part of the team on the Sherman BARV, widely used on the Normandy beaches on D-Day?

29 The Austin 10 utility truck had which nickname?

30 In which country was the Marmon-Herrington Armoured Car Mark II produced?

31 After being captured, a number of Italian Fiat-Ansaldo M11/39 tanks were issued to the 6th Australian Division Cavalry. What recognition markings were applied to their front, side and rear?

32 Which tank shares its name with a British WWII leader?

33 Which manufacturer made the GPA Seagoing Jeep?

34 What did the BBC call Land Rovers in their attempt not to advertise a brand name?
   a) Army cars
   b) Field cars
   c) Defence cars

35 The Unic P107 Halftrack, developed by Citroen, had wheels at the front and what at the rear?

36 All US armoured divisions used the same basic badge which was which shape?

37 At which motor show was the first Land Rover put on show?
   a) Amsterdam
   b) London
   c) New York

38 In the North Africa campaign what effect did the sun and sandstorms have on the camouflage paintwork?

39 Which famous first was the Lorraine 38L?

a) First armoured vehicle with flanged wheels for use on railways
b) First fully tracked personnel carrier to go into action
c) First artillery tractor to tow light weapons

40 The tank got its name from the starter letters of Tracked, Armoured, Non civilian Kit. True or false?

41 Name the year

- The London Blitz began
- Germany invaded the Netherlands and Belgium
- The DAF M39 armoured car was entering Dutch service

42 In 1940 British vehicles were camouflaged in two shades of which colour?

43 Which famous US tank was the first to have a turret mounted 75mm gun?

44 The 11th Hussars had 30 CS9 armoured cars made by which British manufacturer? Was it Morris or Austin?

45 In WWII what was an AVRE? AV stood for armoured vehicle, what about RE?

The Answers

1 Tank
2 Willys, with the MB Jeep
3 Skoda
4 True
5 a) Vickers
6 Jeep
7 Ferdinand Porsche
8 Austin
9 b) Old Faithful
10 Leyland
11 A10
12 USA
13 Propellor
14 True
15 c) Renault
16 Dingo
17 Aero engines and other aircraft equipment
18 (Avro) Green, built from war surplus materials
19 True
20 Armoured fighting vehicle
21 c) Major Wilson
22 Aircraft-grade aluminium
23 a) France
24 Armoured vehicles, mainly tanks

25 True
26 Armoured personnel carriers
27 Mine clearing
28 Diver
29 The Austin Tilly
30 South Africa
31 White kangaroos
32 Churchill
33 Ford
34 b) Field cars
35 Tank tracks
36 Triangular
37 a) Amsterdam
38 It made it go a lot paler
39 b) First fully tracked personnel carrier to go into action
40 False (It was its code name during its development)
41 1940
42 Green
43 Sherman
44 Morris
45 Royal Engineers

➲

7 Italian Lessons

Postwar Germany wasn't allowed to manufacture a toothpick if it looked sharp, so time was ripe for a new nation to dominate the automotive industry. Enter, implausibly, the Italians. The Fifties and Sixties was a halcyon period for our spaghetti eating chums, with many of the most iconic and influential car designs in history appearing and racing to brilliant effect against far more powerful foreign fare. It didn't last of course, but the memory lives on.

1 Ferrari won the Mille Miglia in 1951. Which Italian manufacturer came second?
   a) Ferrari
   b) Lancia
   c) Alfa

2 What colour were the Alfa Romeo race cars of the 1920s?

3 Which sports car won the Mille Miglia, Spa and Le Mans in 1949? A clue? It was red!

4 Which nationality of car was the only one to beat the Italians when Grand Prix resumed in 1946?

5 Vincenzo Lancia founded his motor company in 1906 after six years of racing for which motor company?

6 What is the nickname of the 1952 Alfa Romeo Disco Volante? The Flying Saucer or The Boomerang?

7 The Lancia Flaminia is named after a road that connects Rimini to which city?

8 The Ferrari logo is called the Cavallino Rampante. True or false?

9 The 8C referred to the eight cylinder engines in which cars?

10 Which British driver, also famous for sports car racing, made his debut for Ferrari in 1968 at the Italian Grand Prix?

11 In 1954 Enzo Ferrari described which car as 'the most beautiful ever made'?
   a) A Ferrari

b) An Alfa Romeo
c) A Jaguar

12 In which decade of the 20th century did Bugatti cease production although it resurfaced some 40 years later?

13 Name the year
- Alberto Ascari won the Italian Grand Prix for the second year running in a Ferrari
- Pedestrian crossing lights were installed in New York
- Fiat launched the 8V Zagato

14 Who made its first purpose built sports car, the 166, in 1949, and won the Mille Miglia in the same year and the year after?

15 Giovanni Moretti is famous for his sports cars but his business originally made what?

16 What does SWB stand for in the Ferrari GT SWB?

17 The Alfa Romeo Alfetta 158 won every race it entered in 1950. True or false?

18 Scudo Ferrari literally means what?
a) Ferrari Company
b) Ferrari Workshop
c) Ferrari Stable

19 The Ferrari 400GT Superamerica of 1959 was left hand drive only. True or false?

20 Who am I?
- I was sacked by Enzo Ferrari who called me a tractor salesman

- I developed the Miura and Paul McCartney bought my 400GT in 1967
- My name is synonymous with fast cars from the 1960s onwards

21 Which was Alfa Romeo's first car to be built on a production line?
 a) 1900
 b) 1750
 c) 164

22 Which Spanish manufacturer, named after the mythical winged horse, was meant to rival the Prancing Horse but did not really succeed?

23 What does 'lusso' mean in the Ferrari Lusso?

24 Which Italian manufacturer won the first World Grand Prix Championship in 1925?

25 The Maserati Ghibli used so much fuel it had two fuel tanks. True or false?

26 Name the year
- The MOT was introduced
- Alfred Hitchcock's *Psycho* burst onto the movie scene
- Ferrari took the first four places in the GT class at Le Mans

27 Ferrari's first Formula 1 win was at which Grand Prix?
 a) Italian Grand Prix
 b) French Grand Prix
 c) British Grand Prix

28 Which US F1 champion drove a Ferrari to second place in the 12 hour race at Sebring in 1962?

29 The rarest Ferrari 275 GTBs were made for NART. What does NART stand for?

30 How was the Ferrari 365 GTB/4 better known after it came first, second and third in the Florida 24 Hour Race in 1967?

31 When Ferruccio Lamborghini crashed during the Mille Miglia in 1948 what did he crash into?
a) A tree
b) The scoreboard
c) A roadside restaurant

32 Which endurance race did Ferrari win in 1949?

33 What was the nickname of the Ferrari 156 which gave US driver Phil Hill the drivers' title in 1961?

34 Which Ferrari had the distinction of being the first to be reviewed in an English language journal?

35 American Masten Gregory repainted his Ferrari in US racing colours. What were they?

36 What was the nationality of Ferrari's Grand Prix winning driver at the British Grand Prix in 1951?
a) Argentinian
b) American
c) Austrian

37 What did the MM stand for in the Ferrari 166 MM?

38 Ferrari's first royal customer was king of where?
a) Great Britain
b) Belgium

c) Saudi Arabia

39 The Ferrari 166 M was nicknamed 'la barchetta' meaning what?
- a) Little bullet
- b) Little boat
- c) Little bull

40 Which Ferrari was the first road car to have an integrated spoiler?

41 In 1952 Giovanni Bracco won which race in a Ferrari which prompted Enzo to produce 32 replicas and name them after the race?

42 Who built the Ferrari 250 GT SWB as raced by Stirling Moss?

43 What was the nickname of the Maserati Tipo 61?

44 In order to buy a Ferrari 250GTO you had to have the personal approval of the mighty Enzo himself. True or false?

45 Which model's name was in honour of Alberto Ascari's two world championships in the early 1950s?

The Answers

1 b) Lancia
2 Red
3 Ferrari
4 French (Talbot-Lago)
5 Fiat
6 The Flying Saucer
7 b) Rome
8 True
9 Alfa Romeos
10 Derek Bell
11 c) A Jaguar (It was an E Type)
12 1950s
13 1952
14 Ferrari
15 Motorcycles
16 Short wheelbase
17 True
18 c) Ferrari Stable
19 False – all bar one!
20 Ferruccio Lamborghini
21 a) 1900
22 Pegaso
23 Luxury
24 Alfa Romeo

25 True
26 1960
27 c) British Grand Prix
28 Phil Hill
29 North American Race Team
30 Ferrari Daytona
31 c) A roadside restaurant
32 Le Mans
33 Sharknose
34 212
35 White and blue
36 a) Argentinian
37 Mille Miglia
38 b) Belgium
39 b) Little boat
40 250GTO
41 The MM to celebrate the Mille Miglia
42 Pinin Farina
43 Birdcage
44 True
45 Mondial

8 Cooties and Chrome

The enduring image of American motoring is a gigantic, be-winged Cadillac, top down at the drive-in, two teenagers lost in the front somewhere, sucking each other's faces off. The car offered a generation of disenfranchised adolescents unimaginable freedom, chugging about drinking milkshakes and getting felt up to a soundtrack of rock and roll drowned out by thirsty V8 engines.

1 Which 1950s Ford has a name that links with a TV series?
   a) Supercar
   b) Thunderbird
   c) Batman

2 What was distinctive about gullwing doors?

3 In the 1950s the 'big three' manufacturers were Ford, Chrysler and which other company?

4 The Cadillac Jacqueline was named in honour of Jackie Kennedy or Jackie Collins?

5 Which New York building, once the world's highest, and named after a US motor manufacturer, is decorated with hub caps, radiator caps and bonnet decorations?

6 What did the US Lincoln company take its name from?
   a) First owner Henry Lincoln
   b) English city where the founder was born
   c) US President Abraham Lincoln

7 Which Cadillac, a mass of chrome and tail fin, shares its name with a TV soap?
   a) Eldorado
   b) Chateauvallon
   c) Dallas

8 From 1954 onwards what was fitted to Cadillacs which made them more appealing to women?

9 The Buick XP 300 was fuelled by what?

10 How many wheels did the two seater Ford Gyron with its gyroscopic stabiliser have?

11 Which manufacturer had a famous ad which said 'You're lord of every highway in the luxurious Roadmaster'?
 a) Buick
 b) Chrysler
 c) Dodge

12 The Ford Mystere of 1956 could have either a conventional engine or a gas turbine at the rear. True or false?

13 Name the year
- The very first Chevrolet Corvette appeared
- Bill Haley gave the first performance of 'Rock Around the Clock'
- Sweet rationing ended in the UK

14 BAT cars designed by Alfa Romeo were used as the Batmobile in films and TV. True or false?

15 Rock icon Elvis Presley owned a motoring icon a Cadillac, which he sang about in the song 'Let's Play House'. Famously, what colour was it?

16 The Checker Marathon Limousine1963 had six doors. True or false?

17 Which was the top of the range Cadillac Eldorado of 1959?
 a) The Biarritz
 b) The St Tropez
 c) The Monte Carlo

18 The 1952 Packard Pan American had what capacity engine?
 a) 2,815cc

b) 4,638cc
c) 5,358cc

19 The 1957 Ford Edsel had its own Ford sponsored TV show. True or false?

20 On average a Cadillac or Buick would average how many mpg on the open road?
a) Less than 10
b) 10 to 20
c) Over 20

21 What was the Kaiser Darrin made from?

22 The 50 millionth car to roll off the General Motors assembly line was a Chevrolet that was what colour?
a) Black
b) Gold
c) White

23 What name was given to the Firebird II's single control which could accelerate, steer and brake?
a) Mono control
b) Unicontrol
c) Omnicontrol

24 What term is used in the US to denote a saloon car, i.e. one with a fixed metal roof?

25 Kaiser Motors were US cars built in Germany. True or false?

26 Which marque was said to be the 'standard of the world'?

27 The view to the rear in the 1956 Buick Centurion was via a TV screen. True or false?

28 What was the engine capacity of the massive finned Cadillac Eldorado?
a) Around 2,200cc
b) Around 4,500cc
c) Around 6,300cc

29 The 1953 Ford Syrtis had an electrically retractable hardtop roof. What was it called?
a) Roof-O-Matic
b) Retracto top
c) Roof O Rama

30 Which was the USA's first production sports car?

31 Why could the 1954 Ford FX Atmos really be said to 'fly the flag'?

32 Virgil Exner is a famous name in 1950s motoring. What was his role?
a) Test driver
b) Designer
c) Financial backer

33 Which part of a Cadillac reached its greatest height in 1959?
a) Its mirrors
b) Its tail fins
c) Its mudguards

34 What was distinctive about the rear window in the sporting coupe, the Oldsmobile 88 Cutlass?

35 In 1956 what did Chrysler introduce into its cars?
- a) Transistor radios
- b) Automatic windscreen wipers
- c) Cigarette lighters

36 General Motors two seater convertible Le Sabre was named after what?

37 What was the cc of the Packard Pan American of March 1952?
- a) 2,815cc
- b) 3,884cc
- c) 5,358cc

38 In 1959 Cadillac launched a model with even more massive fins, hinged glass cockpit cover and sliding doors. What was it called?
- a) The whirlwind
- b) The hurricane
- c) The cyclone

39 The Checker minibus (more like a stretch limo) was only sold to which establishments?
- a) Airports
- b) Hotels
- c) Casinos

40 How long were the tail fins of the Cadillac Eldorado?
- a) 28 inches
- b) 36 inches
- c) 45 inches

41 Name the year
- Elvis Presley had a UK No 1 with 'Jailhouse Rock'

- Pele played in the World Cup in Sweden
- General Motors unveiled its Firebird III with its masses of wings and fins

42 What were Virgil Exner's flamboyant Fifties designs for Chrysler cars called?

a) The New Look
b) The Forward Look
c) The Fantail Look

43 The body of the Lincoln XZL 500 exhibited at the Chicago Automobile Show in 1953 was made from what?

44 The 1958 Ford La Galaxie had two steering wheels. True or false?

45 Which Chevrolet with its V8 engine shares its name with a suburb of Los Angeles?

The Answers

1 b) Thunderbird
2 They opened upwards
3 General Motors
4 Jacqueline Kennedy
5 Chrysler building
6 c) US President Abraham Lincoln
7 a) Eldorado
8 Power steering (Cadillacs were very heavy motors!)
9 Petrol/methanol mix
10 Two wheels
11 a) Buick
12 True
13 1953
14 False
15 Pink
16 False (It did in fact have eight)
17 a) The Biarritz
18 c) 5,358cc
19 True
20 b) 10 to 20
21 Fibreglass
22 b) Gold
23 b) Unicontrol
24 Sedan

25 False (Kaiser were an American company)
26 Cadillac
27 True
28 c) Around 6,300cc
29 a) Roof-O-Matic
30 Chevrolet Corvette
31 The body was in the colours of the stars and stripes, red, white and blue
32 b) Designer
33 b) Its tail fins
34 Slatted
35 a) Transistor radios
36 Fighter aircraft
37 c) 5,358cc
38 c) The cyclone
39 b) Hotels
40 c) 45 inches
41 1958
42 b) The Forward Look
43 Plastic
44 False (It didn't have any!)
45 Bel Air

➲

9 Le Mans Part 1

In the pre-war years, Le Mans was a laid back affair, with larger-than-life characters taking their impossibly powerful road cars across the channel to have a gentle pop at the Bosch before driving them home again. There was a lot of champagne and a fair bit of sudden and gruesome death, possibly unrelated but in all probability not.

Le Mans Part 1

1 What colour were the D Types which won Le Mans in 1956 and 1957?
   a) Blue
   b) Green
   c) Red

2 The Le Mans 24 Hour race is run generally on public roads. True or false?

3 Which prestigious British manufacturer won at Le Mans in 1928?

4 The Aston Martin DB2 which came 5th at Le Mans in 1950 fetched how much at auction in 2009?
   a) £100,000
   b) £250,000
   c) £500,000

5 What prevented Bentley from winning its first entry to Le Mans?
   a) A burst tyre
   b) A leaking fuel tank
   c) Collision with a tree

6 Which British make of car won at Le Mans in 1951, 1953, 1956 and 1957?

7 Who am I?
   - I founded the company which bears my name producing the first car in 1919
   - After watching the inaugural Le Mans I said, 'I was quite certain that this was the best race I have ever seen.'
   - Our team won Le Mans the following year

8 How many attempts did the Jaguar C Type make before it won its

first Le Mans? Was it one, three or nine?

9 Which Aston Martin, a success at Le Mans in the mid 20th century, was the first to sport the monogram of the company's new owner David Brown?

10 In 1927 Dr J.D. Benjafield was co-driver in a 3 litre Bentley which won Le Mans. What happened to the car afterwards?

11 Which driver won Le Mans in consecutive years from 1928 to 1930?

12 Which Aston Martin shares its name with part of the UK and finished third overall in Le Mans 1935?

13 Name the year

- The UK singles chart enjoyed its first full year
- Queen Elizabeth II was crowned
- The Porsche 550 Spyder won Le Mans at its first attempt

14 Which Lotus won Le Mans six consecutive times – a name which perfectly reflected its achievements?

15 Carroll Shelby, 1959 Le Mans winner, was the man behind which racer of 1962?

16 Which Ferrari won Le Mans in 1966 and again the following year? Was it the 250LM or the 275GTB?

17 In the tragic Le Mans of 1955 Mike Hawthorn was driving for which manufacturer?

18 Which country abandoned Grand Prix racing after the 1955 crash?

a) Austria
b) Spain
c) Switzerland

19 In the first Le Mans race, Bentley driver Frank Clement went on horseback to collect emergency fuel for his car. True or false?

20 In which month of the year does the Le Mans 24 Hour race take place and why?

21 In 1924 what did Bentley protect their fuel tank with to prevent a repeat of a burst tank the previous year?
a) Woollen blankets
b) Coconut matting
c) Linoleum

22 The 1936 Le Mans was cancelled. This was due to very severe weather. True or false?

23 What size engine did the Bentleys of the mid 1920s have?
a) 1.5 litre
b) 3 litre
c) 6 litre

24 Who drove the Le Mans winning Bentley which beat the Blue Train from Monte Carlo to Calais?
a) Woolf Barnato
b) W.O. Bentley
c) Frank Clement

25 In 1931 why did Jean Bugatti paint his Le Mans racers black?
a) In memory of his late grandfather
b) In protest at the French government's refusal to sponsor them

c) To distinguish them from his father's Bugattis

26 Name the year

- Two monkeys were the first living creatures to travel into space
- *Carry On Nurse* was shown in UK cinemas
- Aston Martin had its first Le Mans win

27 How long a break did the Le Mans race take due to the outbreak of WWII?

a) 6 years
b) 8 years
c) 10 years

28 Which Bentley had back to back wins in 1929 and 1930?

29 In 1925 which make of car beat the Bentleys at Le Mans and came in second?

a) Morgan
b) Sunbeam
c) Rover

30 Which elegant French car scored a 1/2 at Le Mans in 1938 but was eventually bought out by Hotchkiss in 1954?

31 Where was the boot in the Renault 4CV, a sporty version of which was a Le Mans winner?

32 Which company which was revived from the Sunbeam Talbot Darracq marque won Le Mans in 1950 with its T26m Grand Sport?

33 Which make of car, loved by Hollywood superstars such as Humphrey Bogart, won Le Mans in 1951 and 1953 with a special C type version?

34 What did the C stand for in Jaguar's C Type, built to give Jaguar a Le Mans victory?

35 Le Mans finisher the Mini Marcos was nicknamed 'La Petite Puce' by the French, meaning what? Clue: It's tiny, jumps around and can be very irritating… but it isn't Richard Hammond!

36 In 1954 Jaguar entered four of its new D types at Le Mans but who won?

37 On which part of the car did the Jaguar XK 140 have the words 'winner Le Mans 1951–53'?

a) Bonnet lid
b) Boot lid
c) Dashboard

38 The Lotus Elite won its class at Le Mans six times. What was it made of – it was one of the first cars to be made with this?

39 Why did Mercedes Benz withdraw from motorsport for 30 years after the 1955 event?

a) There was a serious accident
b) They felt road cars would be more profitable
c) There was a shortage of skilled drivers

40 In 1924 which was the only non French car to start at Le Mans?

41 Originally the Le Mans race was going to be a three year event. True or false?

42 Which Lancia came first in class at Le Mans in 1951?

43 Which make of car was the first in the race's history to average over 100mph?

44 The Allard J2, which took third place at Le Mans in 1950, fetched how much at auction in 2008?
   a) £100,000
   b) £196,000
   c) £206,000

45 Which British team withdrew from racing, along with Mercedes, after the tragic crash of 1955, even though they had won the race?

The Answers

1 a) Blue
2 True (They are cordoned off for the occasion)
3 Alvis
4 c) £500,000
5 b) A leaking fuel tank
6 Jaguar
7 W.O. Bentley
8 One (It won at its first attempt)
9 DB2
10 Dr Benjafield used it on his patients' rounds
11 Woolf Barnato
12 Ulster
13 1953
14 Elite
15 AC Cobra
16 275GTB
17 Jaguar
18 c) Switzerland
19 False (He borrowed a bicycle from a gendarme)
20 June as it has the maximum hours of daylight
21 b) Coconut matting
22 False (There was severe political unrest in France after an indecisive election)
23 b) 3 litre

24 a) Woolf Barnato
25 b) In protest at the French government's refusal to sponsor them
26 1959
27 c) 10 years
28 Bentley Speed Six
29 b) Sunbeam
30 Delahaye
31 At the front
32 Talbot Lago
33 Jaguar
34 Competition
35 The Little Flea
36 Ferrari
37 b) Boot lid
38 Fibreglass
39 a) There was a serious accident
40 Bentley (They went on to win it)
41 True (The best of three races)
42 Aurelia GT
43 Jaguar (C Type)
44 b) £196,000
45 Jaguar

10 The Rise of the Supercar

Before the mid-Sixties, sports cars were practical things made vaguely impractical for the purposes of racing. But with the advent of the supercar – two seater mid engine road rockets – suddenly the whole thing was turned on its head. Now sports cars were purpose-built impractical, and specifically for the road. Needless to say this started in Italy where it has pretty much stayed ever since.

1 Where did the designers of the Lamborghini Miura put the petrol tank?

a) The front

b) The middle

c) The back

2 What was the significance of the 40 in the name of the Ford GT40?

a) It was 40 inches high

b) Only 40 were made

c) It was the 40th Ford in production

3 Name the year

- England beat West Germany to win the World Cup
- The Beatles had a No 1 with 'Yellow Submarine'
- Lamborghini launched the Miura, which came in yellow but could not travel underwater

4 Alfredo Ferrari gave his name to which Ferrari classic, after he tried to persuade his father to make a more affordable Ferrari?

5 In the late 1950s which GT became known as the 'superstars' supercar' after orders from Hollywood A list stars and the rulers of Iran and Saudi Arabia?

a) Ferrari

b) Alfa Romeo

c) Maserati

6 The AC Cobra was a joint venture between British firm AC and the makers of a powerful engine from which country?

7 The Lotus Elite was made from which material, very innovative in 1957, which made the vehicle much lighter?

8 How many 1962 Ferrari 250GTOs were made – 36 or 56?

9 In which country was the Iso Grifo built?

10 Which supercar appears on the San Bernardino Pass in the opening scenes of the movie *The Italian Job*?

11 The Maserati Quattroporte was ahead of its time as an Italian supercar. Apart from anything else it had how many doors?

12 The Toyota 2000GT was a joint venture between Toyota and which other Japanese manufacturer?

a) Nissan
b) Yamaha
c) Suzuki

13 Name the year

- Oldsmobile made its mark with the launch of the first car with a turbo charged petrol engine
- The football World Cup was held in Chile
- The world first had sight of the Ferrari 250

14 Which 1960s Alfa Romeo was voted in at 15 in *Top Gear*'s Sexiest Cars List?

a) Guiletta
b) Stradale
c) 1900

15 The Lamborghini Espada takes its name from what?

a) A bullfighter's cape
b) A matador's dagger
c) A picador's sword

16 How is the 1968 Ferrari 206GT more usually known?

17 Who did Lamborghini name their Islero after?
   a) A killer Spanish bull
   b) A notorious member of the Mafia
   c) A thoroughbred racehorse

18 What did Jaguar call the D Type when it was modified into a road car?

19 Which cars had an independent suspension called the Chapman Strut after the company's founder?

20 Which Mercedes Benz could make a top speed of 155mph back in 1957 and was the first to have direct fuel injection?

21 Where was the Bolwell Nagari VIII made?
   a) USA
   b) Italy
   c) Australia

22 What did SV stand for in the name of the Miura P400 SV?

23 Which company made Britain's first mid engined sports car and what was it called?

24 The Aston Martin Zagato was a joint venture between British Aston Martin and Zagato who are based where?

25 In the Mercedes 300SL were the gullwing doors introduced from a design or an engineering angle?

26 Name the year
- Ferrari produced the Ferrari 250LM, its first road car with a V12 engine
- The Great Train Robbery took place in the UK

- The ring pull was invented to open drinks cans

27 In 1962 the Aga Khan commissioned a Maserati 5000 GT with its own 45rpm record player. True or false?

28 The ZiL 112 Sports was the USSR's first sports car. How many were made?

a) 2
b) 20
c) 200

29 Back in 1957 the Jaguar XKSS achieved 1–60 in how many seconds?

a) Five
b) Seven
c) Nine

30 A 503 model by which German manufacturer boasted that it was the first to have a roof which could be lifted electronically?

a) Porsche
b) BMW
c) Audi

31 Who made the clock in the Lincoln Continental III?

a) Faberge
b) Cartier
c) Rolex

32 Which Maserati was inspired by the US racetrack where it had been successful in 1939 and 1940?

33 In which country was the 1962 Djet built, a car which was one of the first mass produced mid engined sporty numbers in the world?

34 Which company, founded by Jem Marsh and Frank Costin, revealed its 1800 model in 1964, complete with plywood chassis?

35 The Mercedes SEL could travel at 125mph with a maximum of how many people on board?
   a) Two
   b) Three
   c) Five

36 Which Royal was bought a Reliant Scimitar GTE in 1970?

37 The Facel Vega II was made where? Clue: Christian Dior was one of its fans.

38 Which company made the first production car to have butterfly doors?
   a) Lamborghini
   b) Alfa Romeo
   c) Ferrari

39 Which 'number' was shared by the Ferrari 250 LM and a later incarnation the 275GTB? Was it a V8 or a V12?

40 The Lamborghini Miura cost £6,500 when it was launched in the mid 1960s. True or false?

41 The Monteverdi 3755 was the first high performance luxury car from the Monteverdi stable in which country?

42 How much did the AC Cobra cost at its launch in the mid 1960s?
   a) £1,500
   b) £2,500
   c) £3,500

43 What was the symbol of the Gordon-Keeble, with a speed of 135mph in 1964?

a) Gazelle
b) Tortoise
c) Cheetah

44 Only 18 Alfa Romeo Stradale cars were made. What does its name mean?

a) Fast going
b) Road going
c) Track going

45 Who am I?

- I sang to celebrate the Queen's Diamond Jubilee in 2012
- I bought an orange Lamborghini in the 1960s
- In the 1970s I bought a Lamborghini Espada when I founded the band Wings

The Answers

1 a) The front
2 a) It was 40 inches high
3 1966
4 Ferrari Dino
5 c) Maserati
6 USA
7 Fibreglass
8 36
9 Italy
10 Miura
11 Four
12 b) Yamaha
13 1962
14 b) Stradale
15 b) A matador's dagger
16 Dino
17 a) A killer Spanish bull
18 XK-SS
19 Lotus
20 300 SL Roadster
21 c) Australia
22 Spinto Veloce (Tuned fast)
23 Lotus Europa
24 Italy

25 Engineering
26 1963
27 True
28 a) 2
29 b) Seven
30 b) BMW
31 b) Cartier
32 Indy
33 France
34 Marcos
35 c) Five
36 Princess Anne
37 France
38 b) Alfa Romeo
39 V12
40 True
41 Switzerland
42 b) £2,500
43 b) Tortoise
44 b) Road going
45 Sir Paul McCartney

11 The Transit and Chums

It's easy to forget, obsessed as Man is with speed and power, that the car started life as the cart, and its workaday evolution, the very fibres in the fabric of motoring, is the white van. Usually a Ford Transit, although other white vans are available, this is the workhorse that has kept us all moving, building, bank robbing and wolf whistling at women in short skirts for half a century.

1 In which decade of the 20th century was the original Ford Transit introduced?

a) 1940s
b) 1960s
c) 1980s

2 The Ford Transit was originally supplied to which clientele?

a) Builders
b) The emergency services
c) Train replacement companies

3 The Land Rover III Station Wagon had what kind of roof?

a) Soft top
b) Safari roof
c) Sun roof

4 AEC was formed originally to build what?

a) Tractors
b) Stagecoaches
c) Buses

5 What was the nickname of the Austin K2 Box van, famous in the late 1940s?

6 How was VW's Kombinationkraftswagen better known in the UK?

7 Who am I?

- I am a former British F1 racing driver from north of the border
- I set a record of F1 wins until the record was broken by Alain Prost
- I helped in the development of the Ford F150 Lightning truck

8 Which phenomenon of the 1960s increased demand for more powerful trucks?

9 What type of vehicle was the Lamborghini 22PS?
a) Taxi
b) Tractor
c) Pick-up truck

10 What was the nickname of the Subaru MV1800?
a) The urchin
b) The brat
c) The tramp

11 In 1962 AEC were taken over by which giant based in the north west of England?

12 In the 1950s Spanish built Ford trucks were called Ebro after a Spanish river. What were UK built Ford trucks called?

13 Name the year
- London hosted the Olympics and Paralympics
- Queen Elizabeth II celebrated her Diamond Jubilee
- Ford Launched its new Transit Custom which was the first van to be awarded a five star safety rating by Euro NCAP

14 The Gelandewagen or G-Wagen was Germany's answer to what?
a) Land Rover
b) Transit van
c) Ferguson tractor?

15 In which decade of the 20th century did Benz start to make diesel powered lorries?

16 What was the name of Ford's first ever pick-up truck which has been in production for six decades?

17 Which Japanese pick-up legend is also known as the 4Runner and the Surf? Clue: Think *Top Gear* destruction!

18 Which pick-up truck was launched by Dodge in 1980?
a) Bull
b) Stallion
c) Ram

19 Which GMC creation was the first pick-up to break the 200mph sound barrier?
a) Syclone
b) Whirlwind
c) Tornado

20 How is the Citroen Multispace better known?

21 The Chevrolet 3100 series of pick-up trucks could seat how many along its bench seat?

22 Which Japanese manufacturer cracked the US pick-up market with the aptly named Titan?

23 Which Shelby pick-up truck shared its name with a US state?
a) Wyoming
b) Dakota
c) Oregon

24 In 1987 the once all-powerful Leyland company was sold to which Dutch based manufacturer?

25 The Transit Connect is larger than a standard Transit. True or false?

26 Name the year
- A Holden Maloo R8 became the world's fastest pick-up
- Jeremy and James drove to the North Pole
- Car owners in Moscow were threatened with a fine if their cars were dirty

27 Who was the leading truck maker at the start of the 21st century?

28 In the late 1920s onwards Leyland's Beaver, Bison and Buffalo were part of which of their ranges?
a) The jungle range
b) The zoo range
c) The wild range

29 Chevrolet's 454 SS Pickup usually came in which shade of black?
a) Jet black
b) Onyx black
c) Charcoal black

30 Dodge launched a special edition in its D series called the Macho Power Wagon. True or false?

31 AMO began production in 1924 and marked the start of motor production in which country?

32 Which world famous truck was built in Luton and Dunstable from the 1930s and was still built over 70 years later?

33 BMC's VA truck was specially designed to deliver what?
a) Parcels

b) Refrigerated food
c) Livestock

34 In October 2012 it was announced the Transit building factory was to close in which city?

35 Which was the first truck to carry the BMC badge?

36 The Dodge L'il Red Express was obviously red but what colour was its name that appeared on either side?

37 Which company, whose name is Latin for 'I roll' grew out of a Swedish company which made ball bearings?

38 Which Citroen, launched in 1996, was later offered with an electric motor option?

39 The 'F' in ERF stood for which famous name in the world of trucks and a company which originally made agricultural machinery and steam engines?

40 Transit chassis can be converted into the *Top Gear* favourite vehicle, the motorhome. True or false?

41 Name the year
- The airbag was introduced in the US, the invention of Geoffrey L Mahon and Allen Breed
- A gallon of petrol (approx 4.5 litres) cost £2.05
- The Transit received a turbo charged diesel for the first time

42 Which company, more associated with fast cars, launched a light truck at the 1930 Milan show, and gets its name from Societa Anonima Lombards Fabbrica Automobili?

43 In 2009 Sabine Schmitz attempted to beat Jeremy Clarkson's sub-10 minute lap time of which circuit in a Transit?
   a) Silverstone
   b) *Top Gear* track
   c) Nurburgring

44 The Renault Pangea was based on which of their popular vans?

45 Ford makes the Transit but who makes the Jumper and the Jumpy?

The Answers

1 b) 1960s
2 b) The emergency services
3 b) Safari roof
4 c) Buses
5 Birmingham Bedford
6 Campervan
7 Jackie Stewart
8 The arrival of motorways
9 b) Tractor
10 b) The brat
11 Leyland Motors
12 Thames
13 2012
14 a) Land Rover
15 1920s
16 F-100
17 Toyota Hilux
18 c) Ram
19 a) Syclone
20 Berlingo
21 Three
22 Nissan
23 b) Dakota
24 DAF

25 False (It is more compact)
26 2006
27 Daimler-Chrysler (formerly Daimler-Benz AG)
28 b) The zoo range
29 b) Onyx black
30 True
31 Russia (Automobilnoe Moskowvoskoe Obshchestvo)
32 Bedford
33 a) Parcels
34 Southampton
35 701 7 tonner
36 Gold
37 Volvo
38 Berlingo
39 Foden
40 True
41 1991
42 Alfa Romeo
43 c) Nurburgring
44 Kangoo
45 Citroen

➲

12 The Full Monte

Before rallying became a multinational, multi-corporation business it was the amateurish preserve of a handful of oily-fingered nutters who thought nothing of driving at breakneck speeds up snow-covered mountain roads in cars with tyres the width of their pencil moustaches. The Monte Carlo rally challenged man and machine in an unprecedented fashion, matching mechanical know-how with balls of hardened steel.

1 The Monte Carlo rally takes place in Monaco and which other country?
   a) Italy
   b) France
   c) Sicily

2 Erik Carlsson won two Monte Carlo rallies between 1960 and 1963 in which make of car?

3 Which famous name in British motoring won the 1931 Monte Carlo Rally in an Invicta?

4 Which car, the epitome of the 1960s, won the Monte Carlo Rally in 1964, 1965 and 1967?

5 The *Top Gear* team negotiated Monte Carlo's Col de Turini when they were completing which challenge?

6 Kitty Brunell drove which make of car in October 1929?
   a) Bentley
   b) Rolls Royce
   c) Talbot

7 Who am I?
   - I only raced British cars until 1954
   - My brother in law Eric Carlsson won Monte Carlo in 1962 and 1963
   - I came second to Sydney Allard in an Allard in my first Monte Carlo Rally in 1952

8 Sebastien Loeb won his 7th Monte Carlo rally in 2013 driving which make of car?

9 The first Monte Carlo rally was in 1911 and the fourth in 1925. Why the gap?
   a) It was never designed as an annual event
   b) War years intervened
   c) There weren't enough interested parties during other years

10 What colour was the livery of the Monte Carlo winning Mini Coopers?

11 What was the name of the first British winner of the Monte Carlo rally?
   a) Bentley
   b) Healey
   c) Austin

12 Hotchkiss cars had much Monte success in the 1930s. Hotchkiss was born in the USA but where did he launch his first car in 1903?

13 Name the year
- The first Five Nations Rugby contest was held
- Norwegian explorer Roald Amudsen became the first man to reach the South Pole, beating the expedition led by Captain Scott
- The inaugural Monte Carlo rally took place

14 Monte winner the Renault 4CV was available in only one colour in austere postwar France. What was it?

15 In 1959 Pat Moss (sister of Stirling) and Ann Wisdom won Monte Carlo in which famous car within months of its launch?
   a) Mini
   b) Austin A40
   c) Ford Anglia

16 Which Irish driver, with co-driver Henry Liddon, won Monte Carlo in 1964 in a Mini Cooper S?

17 Which Ford Escort with its famous rear spoiler proved its 'worth' by coming second at Monte Carlo in 1993?

18 In 1965, out of 237 starters how many teams finished in this thrilling but hazardous event?
   a) 21
   b) 51
   c) 81

19 Sebastian Loeb's 2013 car was not be used in rallies where he was not competing. True or false?

20 Name the year
- The Mini Cooper caused a stir on its first outing at Monte Carlo
- An American astronaut orbited the Earth
- Push button 'panda' pedestrian crossings were opened in London. If you didn't use them you risked a fine!!

21 In 1981 which French marque won Monte Carlo in a Turbo?
   a) Renault
   b) Citroen
   c) Peugeot

22 Matthias Feltz and and Franz Wittman drove which VW at Monte Carlo in 1986?

23 Which car won in 1983 driven by Hannu Mikkola?

24 How many drivers entered the inaugural race?
   a) 23

b) 33
c) 43

25 After their trio of wins Hopkirk, Makinen and Aaltonen were dubbed what?
a) The three wise men
b) The three musketeers
c) The three blind mice

26 Name the year
- Margaret Thatcher won a second term as Prime Minister
- The wearing of car seat belts was made compulsory in Britain
- The Audi Quattro made its first appearance at the Monte Carlo Rally

27 1995 saw the first victory for which iconic Subaru?
a) Impreza
b) Forester
c) 360

28 Which car won the Monte Carlo Rally at its first attempt in 1981?

29 Which make of car followed Sebastian Loeb's run of three victories in 2003, 2004 and 2005?
a) Ford Escort
b) Toyota Celica
c) Mitsubishi Lancer

30 After the heyday of the Mini Coopers in the Sixties which German giant won from 1969 to 1971?
a) Porsche
b) BMW
c) Mercedes

31 Name the year

- Argentina won the World Cup in Mexico, helped by the 'hand of God'
- The Lancia Delta S4 won the Rally Argentina
- The Delta S4 also won Monte Carlo

32 In their own personal 'rally' Jeremy Clarkson raced to Casino Square in Monte Carlo in an Aston DB9, with Richard and James travelling on which form of transport?

33 How many times did the rally take place before the outbreak of WWI?

34 The rally is usually run during which month of the year?

a) January
b) June
c) December

35 What does the Rallye Monte Carlo badge show a picture of?

a) A casino
b) A rally car
c) A mountain pass

36 The Monte Carlo rally is run over which surface – in addition to the likely ice and snow?

37 Why were three Mini Coopers disqualified in the rally in 1966?

a) They broke the lighting rules
b) The drivers' registration documents were wrongly filed
c) They had the wrong type of tyres

38 To mark the centenary year of the rally the organisers announced that Liverpool would be a starting point for the rally. True or false?

39 Which destination were you unlikely to see on the Monte Carlo Rally in the 1950s?

a) Reims
b) Nice
c) Digne

40 In the 1965 rally the Porsche 904's heater all but packed in and they had to keep stopping to get hot flasks of coffee. True or false?

41 Name the year

- A Florida woman bought a Mercury Comet Caliente and still owned it 48 years later
- A famous year for 007's Aston Martin which sold 46 years later in 2010 for £2.6 million
- A Mini Cooper won the Monte Carlo Rally

42 In the late 1960s which Porsche took first and second places in three consecutive years?

43 In 1988 which manufacturer won Le Mans with Andy Wallace, Johnny Dumfries and Jan Lammers as its drivers?

44 Where is the final podium at the end of the rally?

45 Name the year

- Jim Clark was killed at Hockenheim
- Graham Hill won the Monaco Grand Prix
- Porsche came first and second at Monte Carlo

The Answers

1 b) France
2 Saab
3 Donald Healey
4 Mini (Cooper S)
5 The World's Best Driving Road
6 c) Talbot
7 Stirling Moss
8 Citroen
9 b) War years intervened
10 Red and white
11 b) Healey
12 France
13 1911
14 Blue
15 b) Austin A40
16 Paddy Hopkirk
17 Ford Escort RS Cosworth
18 a) 21
19 True
20 1962
21 a) Renault
22 Golf GTI
23 Audi Quattro

24 a) 23 (Although seven failed to meet [i.e. rally] in Monte Carlo)
25 b) The three musketeers
26 1983
27 a) Impreza
28 Renault 5 Turbo
29 a) Ford Escort
30 a) Porsche
31 1986
32 The French TGV (which goes at 200mph)
33 Twice
34 a) January
35 b) Rally car
36 Tarmac (asphalt)
37 a) Broke the lighting rules
38 False (But you could start from Glasgow!)
39 a) Reims
40 False (The heater was shot at but they reputedly had swigs of brandy to keep warm)
41 1964
42 911
43 Jaguar (XJR-9)
44 Grounds of the Place du Palais
45 1968

13 American Muscle

America's reputation for making cars that can't go round corners is hard fought and richly deserved. The odd exception making the rule is the muscle car. Uncle Sam's only truly useful contribution to motoring since the Model T Ford, these cheap, powerful and, by local standards, remarkably agile machines instantly entered automotive folklore and today command mega bucks when they come up at auctions.

1 The 1966 Pontiac GTO was said to have what look?
   a) A milk bottle
   b) A beer bottle
   c) A Coke bottle

2 Which Chevrolet, seen as a rival to Ford's Mustang, was launched in 1966 with publicity in 14 different locations at the same time?

3 Which Big 'Mercury' shares its name with an American Big Cat?
   a) Puma
   b) Jaguar
   c) Cougar

4 General Motors' 1951 two seater convertible 'Le Sabre' is named after what? A fighter aircraft or a sword?

5 The Dodge Charger was an iconic muscle car of the 1960s with an R/T option. What did R/T stand for?
   a) Rally/Tourer
   b) Road/Track
   c) Rev/Throttle

6 The 1960s Ford Comuta was powered by what?

7 Who am I?
- I worked for Pontiac and decided to design muscle cars for the road
- I invented the name GTO – Gran Turismo Omologato
- I built a car factory in Northern Ireland with UK government funding

8 Which Ford was the original Pony car?

9 The Camaro was a rival to the Ford Mustang but who manufactured it?

10 What size engine did the Dodge Viper have?
   a) 6 litre
   b) 7.5 litre
   c) 8.3 litre

11 Which General Motors coupe is credited with being the world's first muscle car?

12 Muscle Car giant Carroll Shelby's previous occupation was what?
   a) Texan oil worker
   b) Coal miner
   c) Chicken farmer

13 Name the year
- The 70mph speed limit was introduced in the UK
- The millionth Mini rolled off the assembly line
- The first song about a Mustang, 'Mustang Sally', was recorded in the USA

14 Which Oldsmobile did General Motors launch to rival the Pontiac GTO?

15 What was the original suggested name for the Plymouth Barracuda?
   a) Cub
   b) Panda
   c) Teddy

16 What nickname was given to the Mercury Cougar's front grille?
   a) Cheese grater
   b) Electric shaver
   c) Toaster

17 Did the early Mustangs, which were race cars only, have larger or smaller engines than their successor the GT500?

18 The original Pontiac GTO gained which nickname?
   a) Great
   b) Goat
   c) Goblet

19 Ford launched a Special Edition of their Mustang on the 40th anniversary of which iconic movie in which an earlier model had had a leading role?

20 Name the year
- The world's first passenger hovercraft service began
- Oldsmobile fitted turbocharged petrol engines into their road cars
- Pontiac launched their iconic muscle car the Grand Prix

21 Who made the Pontiac Firebird Trans Am?

22 The Monaro was a muscle car from another area of the globe. Where was its home? Clue: It was made by Holden.

23 Because of the rules of NASCAR the Dodge Charger had to have what added to its production version?
   a) Four doors
   b) Boot spoiler
   c) Automatic gearbox

24 Bruce Springsteen styled himself 'The Boss', but which manufacturer produced cars of the same name in the late 1960s?

25 Which long running Mercury muscle car had an advertising campaign which featured a mountain lion on its bonnet?

26 Name the year
- The first heart transplant was carried out in South Africa
- The hippie movement declared this summer was the summer of love
- Pontiac launched the Firebird Trans Am

27 The L'il Red Express could hold its own with the muscle cars of its day. What was it?
   a) Train
   b) Pick-up truck
   c) SUV

28 The Plymouth Hemi Cuda did how many miles to the gallon?
   a) 6
   b) 12
   c) 20

29 How many different engine sizes were offered with the Chevrolet Camaro?
   a) 4
   b) 6
   c) 8

30 To make its mark in the muscle car market Chevrolet launched which car in 1969?
   a) Le Mans
   b) Monte Carlo
   c) Daytona

31 A muscle car for the southern hemisphere, which rear wheel drive was styled as the Great Australian Road Car?
   a) Ford Falcon
   b) Ford Eagle
   c) Ford Kestrel

32 In 1971 Buick revamped which series?
   a) Monaco
   b) Cannes
   c) Riviera

33 Which series of Chevrolets began in 1962 and lasted until the early 1970s with the SS model?

34 The De Tomaso Pantera had the look of a US muscle car but Alejandro de Tomaso himself hailed from where?
   a) Argentina
   b) Bolivia
   c) Chile

35 Where was the Dodge Charger first shown to the public?
   a) New York Motor Show
   b) Commercial break on TV
   c) NASCAR race

36 After the launch of the Chevrolet El Camino General Motors introduced which 'green' element into its cars?

37 The Plymouth Roadrunner Superbird was built to allow Plymouth to enter which events?
   a) F1
   b) NASCAR
   c) Le Mans

38 What are copies of Shelby Cobras known as?
   a) Sniper vipers
   b) Fake snakes
   c) Smile reptiles

39 How many Ford Mustangs were sold in the first year that they

went on sale?

a) 100,000
b) 200,000
c) over 400,000

40 A top of the range Chevrolet Chavelle shared a name with a famous beach, much loved by the rich and famous. Was it Miami or Malibu?

41 Name the year

- The summer Olympics were held in Tokyo
- The Beatles had their first US chart entry and 3 months later held the top 5 places in the US singles charts
- 22,000 Ford Mustangs were ordered on the first day it was revealed at the World's Fair in New York

42 Which Alfa Romeo muscle car was named after a Canadian city?

43 Which car hire firm did Ford team up with to produce a Mustang in the mid 1960s?

44 The Ford Mustang was named in honour of what?

a) Horse
b) Aircraft
c) Rifle

45 Which macho advertising was attached to that of the 1967 Mercury Cougar?

a) Guy's car
b) Man's car
c) Boy's car

The Answers

1 c) Coke bottle
2 Camaro
3 c) Cougar
4 A fighter aircraft
5 b) Road/Track
6 Electricity
7 John DeLorean
8 Mustang
9 Chevrolet
10 c) 8.3 litre
11 Pontiac GTO
12 c) Chicken farmer
13 1965
14 442
15 b) Panda
16 b) Electric shaver
17 Smaller
18 b) Goat
19 *Bullitt*
20 1962
21 General Motors
22 Australia
23 b) Boot spoiler
24 Ford
25 Cougar

26 1967
27 b) Pick-up truck
28 a) 6 – on a good day!!
29 c) 8
30 b) Monte Carlo
31 a) Ford Falcon
32 c) Riviera
33 Nova
34 a) Argentina
35 b) Commercial break on TV
36 Unleaded petrol
37 b) NASCAR
38 b) Fake snakes
39 c) Over 400,000 (They were planning on sales of 100,000 in the first year)
40 Malibu
41 1964
42 Montreal
43 Hertz
44 b) Aircraft
45 b) Man's car

14 Formula 1 Part 1

Formula 1 first appeared in 1950, a far cry from the digital circus of today but the cutting edge of racing nevertheless. Legends like Fangio, Hawthorn and Moss came and too often went prematurely in a period that saw the life expectancy of a driver average two seasons.

1 Who was the first British F1 champion?
  a) John Surtees
  b) Graham Hill
  c) Mike Hawthorn

2 On which track did Jim Clark suffer a fatal crash?

3 Mario Andretti made his F1 debut in his adopted country. Where was this?

4 Juan Manuel Fangio won 24 Grand Prix races and five world titles, but which country did he hail from?
  a) Spain
  b) Argentina
  c) Brazil

5 Which Scottish F1 legend made his debut for Lotus at the 1960 Dutch Grand Prix and drove with them throughout his 72 race career?

6 Name the year
- Fuel rationing ended in the UK
- Car manufacturers Rover unveiled the first car powered with a gas turbine engine
- F1 Motor Racing began

7 Talking about driving skill which legend of motor racing said, 'There's a very big gap between the best amateur and the poorest professional'?
  a) Stirling Moss
  b) John Surtees
  c) Graham Hill

8 Which New Zealand driver, who made his F1 debut with Cooper, began driving the car he developed and which bore his name in 1966?

9 Who had seven world titles on two wheels before becoming World Champion on four wheels in 1964 with Ferrari?

10 How many times did Graham Hill win the Monaco Grand Prix?

11 Silverstone hosted the first F1 Grand Prix. What was Silverstone before this?

12 Who had 16 Grand Prix wins between 1955 and 1961?

13 Name the year
- It was McLaren's first year in Formula 1
- The fuel injection system was developed for cars produced in Britain
- England won the football World Cup

14 Tony Brooks had his first win in an F1 car while he was still a student of what?
  a) Engineering
  b) Dentistry
  c) Politics

15 Who was the first driver to be F1 World Champion, winner of the Indianapolis 500 and Le Mans?

16 In the 1950s which Italian had most wins (13) between 1951 and 1955?

17 No one won the British Championship prior to 1950 on more than one occasion. True or false?

18 The first woman to compete in F1 drove for Maserati in 1958 at which Grand Prix?
- a) French
- b) Italian
- c) Belgian

19 In 1955 the oldest GP driver was Louis Chiron at the Monaco Grand Prix. How old was he?
- a) 45 years 292 days old
- b) 50 years 292 days old
- c) 55 years 292 days old

20 Who am I?
- I was born in Australia in 1926 and made my debut at the 1955 British Grand Prix in a Cooper
- I was the first man to win the driver's championship in a rear engined car (in 1959)
- In 1962 I launched my own team which bore my name and drove with them until 1970

21 Stirling Moss was World Champion four times in consecutive years. True or false?

22 The British Grand Prix has been held at Brand's Hatch, Silverstone and which other track?

23 Who was the first South American to be F1 World Champion?
- a) Emerson Fittipaldi
- b) Juan Manuel Fangio
- c) Jose Froilan Gonzalez

24 Who was the first driver to win three British championships at three different venues?
- a) Jack Brabham

b) Jim Clark
c) Alberto Ascari

25 Which of the following drivers *did* win the British Grand Prix?
a) Graham Hill
b) John Surtees
c) Wolfgang Von Trips

26 Name the year
- The first F1 race was held at Silverstone England on 13 May
- The first football World Cup after WWII took place and England were beaten by the USA
- The first *Peanuts* cartoon appeared

27 Which Briton was the fast World Champion, the year Captain Slow was born?

28 Who won the inaugural Constructors' Championship in 1958?
a) Ferrari
b) Vanwall
c) Cooper-Climax

29 Which country had most World Champion runners up in the 1950s and 1960s?

30 Who am I?
- I was the first Englishman to win the British Grand Prix
- My sister was a world class rally driver
- I was also a first class sports car driver and won the Mille Miglia in Italy in 1955

31 Which Austrian was World Champion the year *Top Gear* first aired as a regional programme?

32 Who was the first New Zealander to win the World Championship, having made his debut at the 1965 Monaco Grand Prix?

33 Graham Hill was World Champion with BRM in 1962, but which team gave him his win in 1968?
  a) Brabham
  b) Lotus
  c) Maserati

34 Who was the first British runner up in F1?

35 Which Japanese team won its very first Grand Prix in 1967?

36 Which of the following racing drivers was not knighted?
  a) Jack Brabham
  b) Jim Clark
  c) Stirling Moss

37 Which driver, who had his first F1 win with Alfa Romeo, had the nickname Nino?

38 Who was the only US born driver to win the Driver's Championship in the 20th century?

39 How many Grand Prix did the Maserati 250F win?
  a) Two
  b) Eight
  c) Twelve

40 Ferrari won eight constructors' championships in the first 20 years of F1. True or false?

41 Name the year
- Jackie Stewart won the World Championship

- Richard Hammond was born
- Matra Ford won the constructors' championship

42 How many times did Graham Hill win the Monaco Grand Prix in the 1960s?

43 Who was the third F1 driver to win the Indianapolis 500 after Jim Clark and Graham Hill?

a) Mario Andretti
b) Jack Brabham
c) Phil Hill

44 What is the approximate length of a Grand Prix race? Is it 100 miles or 200 miles?

45 Who am I?

- I was born in Argentina in 1911
- I raced with Alfa Romeo in 1950 and 1951
- I had 24 victories, 29 pole positions and 23 fastest laps during my career

The Answers

1 c) Mike Hawthorn
2 Hockenheim
3 USA
4 b) Argentina
5 Jim Clark
6 1950
7 a) Stirling Moss
8 Bruce McLaren
9 John Surtees
10 Five
11 RAF base
12 Stirling Moss
13 1966
14 b) Dentistry
15 Graham Hill
16 Alberto Ascari
17 True
18 c) Belgian
19 c) 55 years 292 days old
20 Jack Brabham
21 False (He never won)
22 Aintree
23 b) Juan Manuel Fangio
24 a) Jack Brabham

25 c) Wolfgang Von Trips
26 1950
27 Jim Clark
28 b) Vanwall
29 Great Britain (11 in all!)
30 Stirling Moss
31 Niki Lauda (1977)
32 Denny Hulme
33 b) Lotus
34 Stirling Moss
35 Honda
36 b) Jim Clark
37 Giuseppe Farina
38 Phil Hill
39 b) Eight
40 False (They only won twice)
41 1969
42 Five
43 a) Mario Andretti
44 200 miles
45 Juan Manuel Fangio

➲

15 Ferrari on Top

Scuderia Ferrari dominated motorsport in the Fifties and Sixties, both on Grand Prix and endurance circuits around the world. The technology of Enzo's superlative sports cars readily translated to the public road too, establishing Ferrari as the last word in performance with provenance. If there was a race worth winning, Ferrari had won it. And usually come in second and third too.

1 In 1961 Baghetti drove his 156 to victory in the French Grand Prix which was staged where?

a) Paris
b) Nice
c) Reims

2 The magnificent Ferrari 250 GT was first shown in traditional Ferrari red in Geneva in 1962? True or false?

3 After signing for Ferrari in 1963 John Surtees won his first F1 win in which country?

a) Germany
b) Italy
c) Great Britain

4 How many times did Ferrari win Le Mans between 1960 and 1966?

a) Two
b) Four
c) Six

5 Who won the 1961 F1 Drivers' title for Ferrari?

a) Phil Hill
b) Clay Regazzon
c) Juan Manuel Fangio

6 The French Grand Prix was won by Ferrari twice in the 1960s, once by a Belgian driver. Who was he?

7 Who am I?

- I was famous as one of the original Goons
- My films included *What's New Pussycat?*
- I owned an ice blue Ferrari 275 GTB

8 Which model had the same chassis and engine as the GTB Berlinetta, although one was a coupe and the other was open topped?

9 The Dino was seen as a rival to which Porsche?

10 Around a hundred 250 GTOs were made. True or false?

11 Which model evolved from the 250 GTO and had success at Le Mans in 1966 and the following year?

12 Which car took places 1, 2 and 3 at Daytona in 1967 beating Ford at its home fixture?

13 Name the year

- Ferrari launched its FF model
- Manchester City won the Premiership in the final seconds of the season
- A 1960s Ferrari GTO was sold in the UK for an eye-watering record of £20.2 million

14 Apart from the doors, bonnet and boot lid what was the 1960 250GTE made from?

15 After whom, in 1969, did Enzo Ferrari name the Ferrari Dino?

16 Which letters were added to the 250 in the name of Ferrari's first mid engined road car?

17 In the movie *The Thomas Crown Affair*, which actress described a Ferrari as 'one of those red Italian things'?

18 In 1969 the 312P competed at Spa in a race over how many kilometres?

a) 500
b) 1,000
c) 5,000

19 In 1968 the Ferrari Daytona was the fastest production car on sale at the time with a top speed of 174mph. True or false?

20 Who am I?

- I joined Ferrari in the mid 1950s as a driver
- I abandoned my Ferrari Dino at the Portuguese Grand Prix in 1960 and retired from the race
- I was the first US F1 champion

21 Which Austrian driver partnered Masten Gregory to a Le Mans win in 1965?

a) Niki Lauda
b) Jochen Rindt
c) Jo Siffert

22 Which engine powered the Fiat Dino road car which was used in F2 competition?

23 In the proposed merger of Ford and Ferrari in the mid 1960s what would the racing team have been called?

24 An aerodynamic experiment saw one 1962 250 GT SWB given what nickname?

a) White van
b) Breadvan
c) Milk van

25 The Ferrari 312/68 had a top speed of 200mph. True or false?

26 Name the year
- Wolfgang Von Trips won the British and Dutch Grand Prix for Ferrari
- Yuri Gagarin was the first man in space
- The Berlin Wall was built

27 Ferrari only had one win at the Monaco Grand Prix during the 1960s. True or false?

28 In the 1960s which of the following is the odd one out in that it did not share the same number of constructors championships as Ferrari?
   a) Brabham Repco
   b) Lotus Climax
   c) BRM

29 In 1961 and 1962 the World Champion shared the same surname. Which one didn't race for Ferrari?

30 Who stymied the Ford Ferrari merger of the mid 1960s? Mr Ford or Signor Ferrari?

31 Which engine powered the Ferrari 330 LMB to a Le Mans victory in 1963?

32 Ferrari launched the Mistral Spider. True or false?

33 The Dino Spider of 1969 had a Ferrari badge or a Fiat badge?

34 In the name of the Ferrari 250 LM what did LM stand for?
   a) Luxury manufacture
   b) Le Mans
   c) Luigi Motoring

35 Which head of a tyre company had a variation of the 330GTC Speciale exclusively made for him?

36 A US oil heiress asked to be buried in her Ferrari Superamerica when she died. True or false?

37 How many times did Phil Hill win Le Mans with Ferrari?

38 When Ferrari had six consecutive Le Mans wins, how many were with an Italian only pair of drivers?

39 How many Italians won the Italian Grand Prix with Ferrari in the 1960s?

40 You couldn't buy a 250 GTO unless Il Commendatore approved it personally. True or false?

41 Name the year

- Ferrari won the constructors' championship for the second time in the decade
- The Beatles occupied the top five positions in the US singles chart
- The Beach Boys were having 'Fun Fun Fun' on the roads of California

42 The Dino was Ferrari's first link with which other Italian manufacturer?

a) Lamborghini
b) Fiat
c) Alfa Romeo

43 Which manufacturer put a stop to Ferrari's run of Le Mans wins in the early 1960s and dominated the 24 Hour race for the rest of the decade?

44 How many times did Ferrari win the GT championship between 1962 and 1964?

45 Who am I?

- I was famously the first man to be World Champion on two and four wheels
- I won the Belgian Grand Prix for Ferrari in 1966 and then left Ferrari
- I was runner up the same year but had signed for Cooper by then

The Answers

1 c) Reims
2 False (It was shown in marine blue)
3 a) Germany
4 c) Six
5 a) Phil Hill
6 Jacky Ickx
7 Peter Sellers
8 GT Spydor
9 911
10 False (There were in fact fewer than forty)
11 275 GTB
12 Ferrari 330P4
13 2012
14 Steel
15 His son who died in 1956
16 LM
17 Faye Dunaway
18 b) 1,000
19 True
20 Phil Hill
21 b) Jochen Rindt
22 V6
23 Ferrari-Ford (With Ford-Ferrari building road cars)
24 b) Breadvan

25 False (It fell just short at a pedestrian 193mph)
26 1961
27 False (They didn't have any in Monaco)
28 c) BRM
29 Graham Hill (Phil Hill did!)
30 Signor Ferrari
31 V12
32 False (Maserati launched the Mistral Spider, Ferrari's Spider was California)
33 A Fiat badge (It had a Ferrari engine)
34 b) Le Mans
35 (Leopoldo) Pirelli
36 True
37 Three
38 One
39 One
40 True
41 1964
42 b) Fiat
43 Ford
44 They won the lot!
45 John Surtees

➲

16 A Brief History of Porsche

Despite a dubious gene pool containing both the Volkswagen Beetle and Hitler, Porsche has for most of its life enjoyed an unshakeable reputation as the dominant global force in sports cars; in making them, in selling them, in racing them. And this despite pedalling just one idea for the best part of half a century. Throughout its long life Porsche's rear-engine 2+2 has represented an engineering pinnacle equally deserving of wide-eyed admiration and a leery mistrust of its physics-defying uber-ability. Often cheaper than its rivals, always better-made and inevitably better to drive, the 911 shouldn't be half as amazing as it unfailingly is. Nowadays brand Porsche is woven into the fabric of motoring, winning races at every level in every corner, yet as familiar a presence in the supermarket car park, running the same old errands as you, just much faster, and with a certain smugness.

1 The founder of Porsche (Herr Porsche by name) had a first name which was the same as the surname of a 21st-century England Premiership footballer. What was his full name?
   a) Terry Porsche
   b) Ferdinand Porsche
   c) Gerrard Porsche

2 In *Top Gear* series 13 episode 4, James and Richard raced a Panamera against which organisation that has Royal approval?

3 The first Porsche 356's engine was made by which manufacturer?

4 When was the famous Porsche badge first seen? Was it in 1953, when Hillary and Tenzing conquered Everest, OR was it 1969 when Neil Armstrong first stepped on to the Moon?

5 The Porsche 911 GT1 didn't come cheap. How much would you have had to stump up to buy one of these beauties?
   a) £150,000
   b) £350,000
   c) £550,000

6 The Boxster name is a mix of which two names?

7 In series 16 Richard competed in a Porsche 911 against a VW Beetle dropped from a helicopter. Where was this?
   a) South African desert
   b) North Pole
   c) The streets of Sydney, Australia

8 Which was the first all new Porsche after the Cayenne in 2002?

9 Although designed by Porsche as a leisure vehicle, what did the Kubelwagen or 'bucket seat car' become in 1939?

10 In July 1996 which landmark in the production of Porsche cars was reached?

a) The 500,000th Porsche
b) The millionth Porsche
c) The 5 millionth Porsche

11 The Porsche Panamera made its debut in 2009, at a motor show in which country?

a) India
b) Russia
c) China

12 The Porsche 1970s 911 2.7 Carrera RS offered two versions. One was the Sport, what was the other?

13 Name the year

- The Olympic Games were held in London
- The National Health Service began
- This year marks the start of the car company which sold cars under the Porsche name with the launch of the 356

14 Why did the French jail Ferdinand Porsche for two years after WWII?

15 Ferdinand Piëch (a Porsche nephew) quarrelled with the family and went on to head which other famous car company?

16 Who said, 'Hammond has a Porsche. So does May. Under the rules of the Cool Wall, this makes them as cool as plastic shoes'?

a) Jeremy Clarkson

b) Jimmy Choo
c) Simon Cowell

17 In 1964 which French manufacturer objected to the name 901 as there was an '0' in the middle which they had patented? Was it Citroen or Peugeot?

18 In 2007 the Hamster abandoned his beloved Porsche in a flooded West Country and ran all the way home to keep which date with a beloved member of his family?
a) His daughter's birthday party
b) His and his wife's anniversary
c) His brother's wedding

19 At the end of the 1940s, one of the Porsche family thought it would be impossible to sell more than 500 of Porsche's 356 model. How many were actually sold by 1954? Was it 50, 500 or 5,000?

20 Who am I?
- I was an American actor who starred in the movie *The Great Escape*
- My second wife, actress Ali McGraw, said I didn't like the women in my life to have balls
- I drove a 1970 Porsche 911S Coupe when I played the role of Michael Delaney in the movie *Le Mans*

21 What was unprecedented about the design of the Cayenne?

22 At the beginning of the 21st century which country was Porsche's biggest market, in terms of sales?

23 There would be some sense in the Cayman being named after the Cayman Islands – but it isn't! What is it named after?

24 In the *Top Gear* Challenge to find the World's Best Driving Road, who chose to drive a Porsche 911 GT3 RS on a trip which would centre on the Alps?

25 Which town name appears on the Porsche logo?

26 Name the year
- The third Bond movie, *Goldfinger* starring Sean Connery, was released in August of this year
- The *Sun* newspaper was published for the first time, replacing the *Daily Herald*
- The first Porsche 911 was made available to buy, a year after it had been shown to the world

27 Which road going Porsche grew out of the development of a new racing car whose plans never came to fruition?

28 In 2010 Porsche introduced the 918 capable of reaching 60mph in how many seconds?
  a) Three
  b) Five
  c) Seven

29 In 2012 Porsche advertised that what percentage of the cars they had ever built were still on the road?
  a) 30%
  b) 50%
  c) 70%

30 Porsche's brief to build a 'people's car', which later became the Volkswagen Beetle, was for the car to carry how many people?

31 Which transcontinental rally saw wins for the Carrera 4x4 in the 1980s?

32 What was the nickname of the Porsche RUF CTR1?

33 Butzi Porsche's father had a nickname which is also the name of a type of transport. What was it?
  a) Ferry Porsche
  b) Tug Porsche
  c) Schooner Porsche

34 In the early years of the 21st century the Carrera GT held the road-legal lap record at which famous German circuit? Was it the Nurburgring or Hockenheim?

35 Which Porsche shares its name with the US emergency phone number?

36 In 1951, the 356 SL was victorious at which 24 hour endurance race?

37 Which Portuguese and ex-Manchester United footballer owned a Porsche 911 Turbo?

38 Which motoring related reason caused the first motoring Herr Porsche to miss the birth of his first son?
  a) His car broke down
  b) He was at a race
  c) He went to the wrong hospital

39 In series 5 our intrepid trio of presenters were each given how much money to buy a Porsche?

40 Porsche's design company designed the Volkswagen Beetle. True or false?

41 Name the year
- The bikini celebrated its 60th birthday
- David Beckham resigned as England captain, after the national team failed to reach the World Cup semi finals in Germany
- The Porsche Cayman sports car was introduced

42 The 911 GT1 was designed specifically to win which race?

43 Which Porsche model had the nickname 'the sugar scoop'. Was it the 904 or the Panamera Turbo?

44 In *Top Gear*'s series 5 Porsche challenge which coastal town was the team's first destination? Was it Bangor, Blackpool or Brighton?

45 Who am I?
- I appeared in cult movies of the 1950s including *Rebel Without A Cause*
- My middle name was Byron, chosen because my mom loved poetry
- My life ended in a car accident while driving a Porsche 550 Spider

The Answers

1 b) Ferdinand Porsche
2 Royal Mail
3 Volkswagen
4 1953
5 £550,000
6 Boxer & Roadster
7 a) South African desert
8 Panamera
9 The German Jeep
10 b) The millionth Porsche
11 c) China
12 Touring
13 1948
14 For creating military vehicles for the German government
15 Audi
16 a) Jeremy Clarkson
17 Peugeot
18 a) His daughter's birthday party
19 5,000 (By the time production ceased over 80,000 had been sold)
20 Steve McQueen
21 It had four passenger doors
22 America
23 A Latin American alligator (Caiman)

24 Richard Hammond
25 Stuttgart
26 1964
27 Carrera GT
28 a) Three seconds
29 c) 70%
30 Five – two adults and three children
31 Paris Dakar rally
32 Yellowbird
33 a) Ferry Porsche
34 Nurburgring
35 911
36 Le Mans
37 Cristiano Ronaldo
38 b) He was at a race
39 £1,500
40 True
41 2006
42 The Le Mans 24 Hour Race
43 904
44 Brighton
45 James Dean

➲

17 Eastern Upstarts

It took a while for the Japanese to make an impact on the West, but impact they did. Ingenuity and reliability the likes of which an indifferent British manufacturing industry couldn't hold a candle to in the second half of the 20th century quickly saw Toyota, Nissan and Honda change the motoring landscape for good. Japan did to mass production what Henry Ford had done to normal production. It made it highly efficient, cost effective and, in a move unfamiliar outside of Germany, it actually made everything properly.

1 Which Japanese manufacturer supplied the vehicle for *Top Gear*'s first Star in a Reasonably Priced Car?

2 Which of the following was NOT a mass produced Japanese car of the 1970s?
  a) Violet
  b) Gloria
  c) Marilyn

3 In 1978 the original Honda Prelude was based on which reliable but less exciting earlier Honda?

4 Which Japanese company made the world's bestselling sports car of the 1970s? Was it Datsun or Toyota?

5 What was the unique selling point of the Honda Series III CRX launched in 1992?
  a) Electronically operated removable roof
  b) Satellite navigation
  c) Sony CD player as standard

6 Toyota is written in Japanese with eight strokes. Eight is a lucky number in Japan. True or false?

7 Name the year
- Brazil succeeded England as World Champions in football
- Austria's Jochen Rindt was F1 World Champion
- The Toyota Celica, which by the 21st century had reached its seventh generation, was launched at the Tokyo Motor Show

8 Which small car was the first front wheel drive Datsun?

9 The Infiniti brand was created by which company?

10 The Daihatsu Charade GTi, launched in 1987, made the vital 0–60mph in how many seconds?
   a) 6.9
   b) 7.9
   c) 8.9

11 The Lexus brand was launched as the luxury arm of which Japanese manufacturer?

12 Which coupe of the late 1980s was known as the Silvia in its native Japan, the 180SX in Australia, and even more confusingly the 240SX in the USA?

13 Name the year
- Elton John recorded the record breaking 'Candle in the Wind' in honour of Princess Diana
- In the movie *The Full Monty* a group of unemployed Sheffield steel workers bared all!
- The small but wonderfully powerful Daihatsu Cuore Avanzato TR-XX went on sale in the UK

14 Which 1970 Toyota was the first mass produced sports GT from Japan?

15 What was the nickname of the Suzuki SC100 GX, which was launched in the UK in 1979?
   a) The whizzbang
   b) The whizzo
   c) The whizzkid

16 Japanese firm Toyota entered their first competitive race in 1957 in the Australian rally, during which a kangaroo bounced off the car. True or false?

17 The origins of the Suzuki car company lie in which other, very different industry?

18 Toyota officially debuted their first F1 car at which Grand Prix?

19 In the early 1980s there were rumours that the tiny Suzuki SC100 would be produced by sports car manufacturer Lotus. True or false?

20 Who am I?

- I was a well known maker of textiles before going into car manufacture in 1933
- My surname is the same as my company's name – with one letter's difference
- I became a major Japanese car manufacturer with models such as the Celica, the Supra and the MR2 series

21 Which Japanese manufacturer was the first to have an F1 win?

22 In 2006 Honda had their first F1 win for four decades when Jenson Button won which Grand Prix?

23 Where was Honda's first Grand Prix victory?

24 Which car, unveiled in 1969 and on sale worldwide a year later is arguably the first Japanese car aimed at the US market?

25 Which Nissan superhatch was known as Pulsar in its native country?

26 Name the year

- The Olympic Games took place in Athens
- *The Lord of the Rings: The Return of the King* scooped 11 Oscars

- *Top Gear* named the Nissan 350Z its Car of the Year

27 During its four years in production – 1969 to 1973 – the Datsun 240Z was the world's top selling sports car of the time. True or false?

28 Which Nissan model was arguably Japan's greatest performance car until it ceased production in 2002?

29 Honda was originally a motorcycle maker. In which decade did they branch out into car production?
a) 1940s
b) 1950s
c) 1960s

30 When Honda returned to F1 in 2000 they supplied engines for which team?

31 In the 1960s which manufacturer had acquired the rights to produce engines based on an idea Felix Wankel had developed in the early 20th century, which was ultimately used to make their RX-7 rotary powered sports car in 1978?

32 Which of the following is not a limited edition Mazda MX-5?
a) Merlot
b) Monaco
c) Madeira

33 Which Japanese manufacturer developed the VTEC engine?
a) Toyota
b) Nissan
c) Honda

34 How is Mazda's classic, known in some countries as the Eunos or Miata, better known in the UK?

35 The Mitsubishi Evo was developed as a car for what particular type of event?

36 Sales of the Mazda RX-7 declined in the 1990s as it went so fast there was nowhere in the UK to drive it (legally!). True or false?

37 Which manufacturer revealed its MX-5 open top sports car in 1989?

38 What was the name of the Isuzu 4x4 launched in Japan in 1998?

39 Which Japanese car was considered to be the first Japanese supercar?

40 Datsun undeniably had some more unusual names for its models sold in the west. True or false, was one of them the Datsun Percy?

41 Name the year

- The Ryder Cup was postponed because of the September 11 attacks
- First and fourth in the drivers' championship were called Schumacher
- The Lexus IS 200 competed in the British Touring Car Championship for the first time

42 Toyota was founded by Toyoda, but it was felt that Toyota was easier to pronounce in English. True or false?

43 Which Suzuki shares its name with a style of coffee?

44 Who developed the Integra Type R which was sold as the Acura in the USA?

45 Who am I?

- I was born in Finland
- I won the Monte Carlo Rally in 2002
- I won four consecutive World Rally Drivers' Championship titles driving a Mitsubishi Evo

The Answers

1 Suzuki
2 c) Marilyn
3 Accord
4 Datsun
5 a) Electronically operated removable roof
6 True
7 1970
8 Cherry
9 Nissan
10 b) 7.9
11 Toyota
12 Nissan 200SX
13 1997
14 Celico
15 c) The whizzkid
16 True
17 Silk
18 Australian
19 True (They never came to fruition)
20 Sakichi Toyoda (Founder of the Toyota company)
21 Honda
22 Hungarian
23 Mexico
24 Datsun 240Z

25 Sunny GTI-R
26 2004
27 True
28 Skyline GTR
29 c) 1960s
30 British American Racing (BAR)
31 Mazda
32 c) Madeira
33 c) Honda
34 MX-5
35 Rallying circuits
36 False (New legislation came into force concerning emissions)
37 Mazda
38 Vehicross
39 Honda NSX
40 False (There was the Datsun Cedric!)
41 2001
42 True
43 Cappuccino
44 Honda
45 Tommi Makinen

18 A Bit about Bikes

There are myriad claims to the 'first' motorcycle, but it was, perhaps inevitably, the Germans who got proper production off the ground. Shadowing its four wheel counterpart, the bike rapidly abandoned its practical 19th-century origins in the face of ever increasing speed and power. Whether racing, touring, or just scaring yourself witless on a sunny Sunday morning, the motorcycle offered a purity of purpose that has never abated.

1 Who is credited with building the first motorcycle in 1885?
   a) Daimler
   b) Benz
   c) Rolls

2 When a 20mph speed limit was imposed on British roads, motorcycle racing began on which Isle? The Isle of Wight or the Isle of Man?

3 German bicycle manufacturer Adler also made which important machines at the beginning of the 20th century? Typewriters or vacuum cleaners?

4 Which popular accessory did William Lyons and William Walmsley provide for motorcycles in the 1920s?

5 Was the first official motorcycle race held in 1896 for bicycles or tricycles?

6 In which seaside resort was Jaguar set up as a motorcycle sidecar company? Brighton or Blackpool?

7 Who am I?
- I was born in London in 1950 and rode my first bike, built by my father, when I was five
- Between 1975 and 1982 I won more international 500cc and 750cc Grand Prix titles than any other rider
- I won 23 GPs and a further 29 podium places before retiring in 1984 after a series of spectacular crashes

8 Which Japanese company, now also famous for its cars, was the world's biggest manufacturer of motorcycles in the 1950s, even though it had only delivered its first motorcycle in 1948?

9 In which city was motorcycling's first international federation founded?

a) Berlin
b) London
c) Paris

10 Who was the first Japanese winner of the Japanese GP?

11 Which manufacturer did Barry Sheene ride for when he was world champion?

12 The Roxette was established in which UK city, famous for its motor engineering companies? Coventry or Luton?

13 Which motorcycles have five model families – Touring, Softail, Dyna, Sportster and Vrod?

14 AJS, who took the manufacturer's title in the inaugural 500cc World Championship, were sold to which company during the 1930s?

15 One of the most famous motorcycling companies of all time would have been known as William Arthur if its founders had used their first names instead of their surnames as a company name. Who were they?

16 In 1966 which manufacturer became the first to win the manufacturer's title in all five classes (50cc, 125cc, 250cc, 350cc and 500cc)?

17 Which world famous manufacturer won the first Isle of Man TT race in 1907?

18 Who was the first rider to win GPs at 50cc and 500cc?

19 In the Isle of Man TT Race, what does TT stand for?

20 Who am I?
- My father Graziano was a former Italian champion
- I won the Moto GP championship in 2002
- I have always raced with the number 46

21 In 1928 Speedway was introduced to the UK from which country?
a) Australia
b) Germany
c) USA

22 What was motocross and supercross previously called, especially in the aftermath of WWII?

23 Yamaha is now a world famous producer of motorcycles but Torakusu Yamaha, the company's founder was a producer of what?

24 Who made the first production racing bike?

25 The first things the Suzuki factory made were clothes. True or false?

26 Name the year
- The football World Cup took place in South Africa and David Cameron became Prime Minister
- A luxury car worth £1.2 million was seen clamped outside London store Harrods
- Spaniard Jorge Lorenzo took the World Moto GP title

27 In which country did the 2013 MotoGP season begin?

28 Which circuit near Lisbon was first used for motocross in 2000?

29 Who was the first motorcycle sportsman outside road racing to be awarded the MBE in 1970?

30 Which Blackburn born former World Champion formed the Foggy Petronas Superbike team when he retired?

31 Which motorcycling legend, nicknamed Mike the Bike, won the George Medal for rescuing Clay Regazzoni from a blazing Ferrari in 1973?

32 Why did Giacomo Agostini refuse to race in the Isle of Man after 1972?

33 In ice speedway what do the bikes have inserted into their tyres to grip the ice?
a) Blades
b) Spikes
c) Chains

34 In which country is the Autodromo Nelson Piquet?

35 What is the AMA?

36 When British champion Dave Bickers retired he set up Bickers Action. What did the company do?
a) Train motocross champions
b) Develop motorcycles
c) Organise stunt performers for films

37 Which New Zealander was the first speedway rider to be awarded the MBE?

38 Who retired from motorcycling in 1981 but went on to F1 with Ayrton Senna as his team mate?

39 Which track has McLeans, Coppice and the Melbourne Hairpin among its corners?

40 Geoff Duke was the first motorcyclist to wear what?
a) A helmet
b) Goggles
c) One piece leathers

41 Name the year
- The first World Superbike race took place at Silverstone
- Defending champions France were knocked out in the first round of the World Cup by Senegal
- MotoGP class replaced 500cc class

42 Which legislation was passed in 1904 which allowed motor racing on the Isle of Man?

43 Which circuit in Holland first hosted the World Championship in 1949 and is the only venue to have done so for the rest of the 20th century?

44 Including stabilisers, how many wheels did the first Daimler Maybach motorcycle have?

45 Who did Valentino Rossi race for in the opening MotoGP test of 2013?

The Answers

1 a) Daimler
2 Isle of Man
3 Typewriters
4 Sidecars
5 Tricycles
6 Blackpool
7 Barry Sheene
8 Honda
9 c) Paris
10 Norick Abe
11 Suzuki
12 Coventry
13 Harley Davidson
14 Matchless
15 Harley Davidson
16 Honda
17 Norton
18 Barry Sheene
19 Tourist Trophy
20 Valentino Rossi
21 a) Australia
22 Scrambling
23 Musical instruments
24 Norton

25 True
26 2010
27 Qatar
28 Estoril
29 Jeff Smith
30 Carl Fogarty
31 Mike Hailwood
32 His friend Gilberto Parlotti was killed there
33 b) Spikes
34 Brazil
35 American Motorcyclist Association
36 c) Organise stunt performers for films
37 Barry Briggs
38 Johnny Cecotto
39 Donington Park
40 c) One piece leathers
41 2002
42 Public roads could be closed to allow the race to go ahead
43 Assen
44 Four
45 Yamaha

19 Shed Built Shenanigans

Britain's truly unique contribution to the history of the car is an occasionally brilliant, usually embarrassing heap of highly flammable guff knocked together in backwater sheds or sold with a straight-ish face by cheerful chaps with a desperate look in their eyes.

Ginetta, Davrian, Turner, TVR, Elva; kit cars for the cash-strapped enthusiast, they were only ever as good as the man who built them, often in a merry haze after a boozy Sunday lunch.

1 The sports car the Briggs & Stratton Flyer was made by a company which usually manufactured something more usually found in your garden shed. What was it?

2 A vacuum cleaner maker was given the contract to produce the Sinclair C5. True or false?

3 Which country, hardly renowned for its lengthy coastline, manufactured the first mass produced amphibious car?
   a) Germany
   b) Switzerland
   c) Belgium

4 Which quirky Nissan has a name which sounds like the French word for snail?

5 In 2011 the *Top Gear* team decided to build a train out of a car. Which model car was JC's suggestion?
   a) Jaguar XJS
   b) Suzuki Liana
   c) Porsche 924

6 Which Austin had the same designer as the Triumph TR7?
   a) Mini
   b) Princess
   c) Allegro

7 Who am I?
- I described the TVR Sagaris as looking like 'it has been designed by a lunatic and hit by an axe'
- I appear on a TV show which is one of the BBC's biggest exports
- My initials are JC

8 In the movie *Back to the Future* the DeLorean DMC-12 was supposedly powered by what?

9 In the amphibious cars challenge of 2006 Richard decided to merge his camper van with what?

a) A rowing boat
b) A jetski
c) A canal boat

10 The 1901 Stanley Runabout ran on steam but how long did it take to generate enough steam to get it going?

a) 10 minutes
b) 20 minutes
c) 40 minutes

11 One of the first Fiats, the S76 had an engine which took up most of the 9 foot length of the car and later powered an airship.True or false?

12 What were the mechanics of the Lotus Mark VI, available only in kit form?

a) Ford Anglia
b) Ford Popular
c) Ford Prefect

13 The Ginetta G50 has a very sporty exterior and is powered by what?

14 The Hammerhead-iEagle Thrust was created in an attempt to outdo which electric car?

a) G-Wiz
b) Prius
c) Leaf

15 How much extra did a factory finished Lotus ElanSprint cost as opposed to the same car in kit form?

a) 25%
b) 50%
c) 100%

16 One of the first amphibious cars offered for sale to the public was made by a company called Troll Plastik. True or false?

17 Which was the only Welsh car maker of the 1950s?

18 Is it a car? Is it a plane? The Hélicron No 1 was discovered in a French shed where it had been for 60 years. Bearing in mind its hybrid nature what obstructed the view from the front windscreen?

19 Although designed to rival the Lamborghini Miura the ADD Nova was based on which more humble ancestor?

20 Who am I?

- I wrote a book about *Magnificent Machines: How Men in Sheds Have Changed Our Lives*
- I suggested that the Land Rover Defender would benefit from being 'barn aged'
- I have presented *Man Lab* and *Top Gear*

21 How many headlamps did the Aston Martin Bulldog have?

22 The Daimler Dart had to change its name to SP250 after a challenge from Chrysler. What did the SP250's owners dislike about early models?

a) The foldable back seat would fold without warning
b) The doors would fly open when going too quickly round corners

c) You had to take out the back seat to get to the boot

23 What did Jeremy stuff the Hilux with in an attempt to keep it afloat in the amphibious car challenge?
  a) Balloons
  b) Bubble wrap
  c) Foam

24 Which was the last Lotus to be offered in kit form?

25 The Gilbern GT had a chassis made from what?

26 What was written on the plastic Lego pillows in James May's Lego house?
  a) Don't Snore
  b) Sweet Dreams
  c) Night Night

27 The 1960s Le Mans contender the Unipower GT had an engine and gearbox from which car?

28 In the MG TC Midget, was the speedometer located in front of the driver or his/her front seat passenger?

29 Lotus supplied most of its cars in kit form until which decade?
  a) 1950s
  b) 1960s
  c) 1970s

30 The Gilbern GT was built in an outbuilding behind what kind of retail outlet?
  a) Car showroom
  b) Furniture store
  c) Butcher's shop

31 The Marcos 1800 had a chassis of which a significant amount was made of what?
   a) Plastic
   b) Wood
   c) Polystyrene

32 Which car did the *Top Gear* team start with to create a convertible people carrier?
   a) Suzuki Vitara
   b) Renault Espace
   c) Toyota Highlander

33 The TVR 350i was earlier known as what?
   a) Tracy
   b) Tasmin
   c) Tara

34 In the amphibious car challenges who was the only one of three presenters to use the same car twice?

35 After Lotus ceased production of the Seven, who took it over with kit form and fully assembled cars?

36 The Inter 175 Berline's front wheels could be folded in so it could pass through a doorway. True or false?

37 Why was no record taken of the power of the TVR Cerbera in action?

38 In 2007 Jeremy's unlikely starting point for a stretch limo was which car?

39 The Leyat Helica of 1919 had no clutch or transmission and was powered by what?

40 The Formula Hammer was a sort of Airfix car kit. True or false?

41 What did the TVR Sagaris have on the dashboard to act as a door handle?
- a) Button
- b) Lever
- c) Corkscrew

42 What was the Triumph TR7's codename while under production?
- a) Bullet
- b) Rocket
- c) Arrow

43 What did James May use to enable his caravan to take to the skies?
- a) Hot air balloon
- b) Hang glider
- c) Airship

44 The chassis for the ultra wedge shaped Ghia was taken from which less spectacular Ford?
- a) Capri
- b) Escort
- c) Cortina

45 In the fabric of the Lotus Elite, GRP was glass reinforced what?
- a) Polystyrene
- b) Paper
- c) Plastic

The Answers

1 Lawnmowers
2 True (It was Hoover)
3 a) Germany
4 S Cargo
5 a) Jaguar XJS
6 b) Princess
7 Jeremy Clarkson – who else?
8 Plutonium
9 c) A canal boat
10 c) 40 minutes
11 True
12 c) Ford Prefect
13 Electricity
14 a) G-Wiz
15 b) 50%
16 True (Troll Plastik & Bilindustri to give it its full name)
17 Gilbern
18 Huge propeller
19 VW Beetle
20 James May
21 Five
22 b) The doors would fly open when going too quickly round corners
23 c) Foam

24 Europa
25 Glass fibre
26 b) Sweet Dreams
27 Mini
28 His/her front seat passenger
29 c) 1970s
30 c) Butcher's shop
31 b) Wood
32 b) Renault Espace
33 b) Tasmin
34 James May
35 Caterham
36 True
37 The device which measured this was destroyed at its first attempt!
38 Fiat Panda
39 Propeller
40 True
41 a) Bullon
42 a) Bullet
43 c) Airship
44 b) Escort
45 c) Plastic

20 Formula 1 Part 2

F1 in the 1970s was dominated by huge characters and their huge hair. Crash helmets were almost surplus to requirements for the likes of James Hunt and Jackie Stewart, especially when bolstered by the side impact protection of gigantic sideburns.

Beyond the fashions, however, there was some serious racing to be done. If they could only find the time between chain smoking and sleeping with Miss World contestants.

1 Jackie Stewart was World Champion runner up in 1972. Who was runner up to Jackie Stewart the following year?

2 Who was the last Ferrari World Champion of the 20th century (in 1979)?

3 Who became the youngest World Champion when he won the title in 1972 at the age of 25 years 273 days?

4 How many Grand Prix victories did James Hunt have?
   a) Eight
   b) Ten
   c) Twelve

5 When Jody Scheckter won the Argentine Grand Prix in 1977 what was he driving?
   a) Wolf
   b) Jaguar
   c) Tiger

6 'There's only two things you can't criticise a man for. One is his prowess in bed and the other is his driving.' Which F1 driver said this?
   a) Nelson Piquet
   b) James Hunt
   c) Jackie Stewart

7 Who am I?
- I was born in Vienna in 1949
- I had 25 F1 victories in the 1970s
- I founded an airline when I quit motor racing

8 Who was the first posthumous F1 World Champion, having had a winning lead when he was killed in practice in 1970?

9 Which driver was World Champion in Tyrell's first full season as a constructor?

10 Which Brazilian was the youngest Driver's Champion in 1972?
   a) Ayrton Senna
   b) Nelson Piquet
   c) Emerson Fittipaldi

11 Which was the first constructor to score over 100 points in a racing season? (It was 1979.)

12 Which 1979 World Champion went on to become the world Superstars champion after his retirement from F1?

13 Name the year
   - Williams entered Formula 1 for the first time under the name ISO
   - The Watergate Scandal broke in the USA
   - Paul Newman and Robert Redford appeared in *The Sting*

14 How old was James Hunt when he first became World Champion?

15 The Canadian circuit is named after which driver who made his first Grand Prix start in his home country in 1977 and had a total of six Grand Prix wins?

16 By which first name is 1974 runner up Gianclaudio Regazzoni better known?

17 Which World Champion drove for Hesketh in 1973–1975 and

McLaren in 1976–1979?

18 The Österreichring had its inaugural race in the 1970s, but in which country is this circuit?

19 In its first full year in F1 Ken Tyrrell's team won World Champion team and World Champion driver. Who was the driver?

20 Who am I?
- I was born in South Shields in 1942
- I founded my own team in 1977 and they had their first win in Argentina the following year
- Despite suffering very serious injuries in a car crash, my team is a force to be reckoned with in F1

21 Which manufacturer was the first to have a Grand Prix win in a turbo charged car?
  a) Renault
  b) Tyrrell
  c) Brabham

22 Who worked with Maurice Philippe to produce the Lotus 72 in 1970?

23 A safety measure introduced in 1971 said that a driver must be rescued from the cockpit in how many seconds?
  a) Five
  b) Seven
  c) Nine

24 1974 saw Niki Lauda driving for which constructor?

25 Niki Lauda was once forced to pull out of a race, losing the world championship in the process, because of rain. True or false?

26 Name the year

- Jackie Stewart won his third and final World Championship
- In December Prime Minister Edward Heath announced a three day week
- Sunderland won the FA Cup beating favourites Leeds Utd

27 Williams had their first F1 win at the Brazilian Grand Prix. True or false?

28 At which circuit did Niki Lauda suffer an horrific crash in 1976?

29 In the 1970s what became mandatory?

a) Helmets
b) Overalls
c) Outside mirrors

30 How many wins did James Hunt have in 1976, the same figure as fellow Brits Jackie Stewart had in a season in the previous decade and Nigel Mansell in the following one?

31 Which driver gave Williams their first F1 win?

32 In 1972 what colour rear lights were introduced?

a) Red
b) Amber
c) White

33 Lauda, Reutemann and Andretti wore overalls made from material used by NASA. True or false?

34 Who did Andretti and Peterson drive for in 1978?

35 Who did James Hunt drive for in the 1976 season when he battled against Lauda?

36 When Lauda left Ferrari in 1977 which Canadian took his place?

37 1975 saw the first F1 win for a Welsh driver. What was his name?

38 What did Ken Tyrrell call his first car? Was it the 001 or the AA1?

39 Which driver had his first F1 win at the Austrian Grand Prix in 1976 and became director of the performance driving school at Silverstone after his retirement from racing?

40 Which Briton was on the top of the podium 10 times in the 1970s?

41 In which country did James Hunt clinch the 1976 Championship after Lauda's devastating crash earlier in the season?

42 Jody Scheckter was born in East London. True or false?

43 How many times was James Hunt World Champion in the 1970s?

44 The Lotus 72 and Lotus 79 sported which colours?

45 Who am I?

- My father was a Jaguar dealer and I failed to qualify for the 1960 Olympics for trap shooting
- When I retired from motor racing in the early 1970s I was the sport's biggest money earner
- I was awarded the OBE in 1972 and was BBC Sports Personality of the year in 1973

The Answers

1 Emerson Fittipaldi
2 Jody Sheckter
3 Emerson Fittipaldi
4 b) Ten
5 a) Wolf
6 a) Jackie Stewart
7 Niki Lauda
8 Jochen Rindt
9 Jackie Stewart
10 c) Emerson Fittipaldi
11 Ferrari
12 Jody Scheckter
13 1973
14 29
15 Gilles Villeneuve
16 Clay
17 James Hunt
18 Austria
19 Jackie Stewart
20 Frank Williams
21 a) Renault
22 Colin Chapman
23 a) Five
24 Ferrari

25 True
26 1973
27 False (It was the British Grand Prix)
28 Nurburgring, Germany
29 c) Outside mirrors
30 Six
31 Clay Regazzoni
32 a) Red
33 True
34 Lotus
35 McLaren
36 Gilles Villeneuve
37 Tom Pryce
38 001
39 John Watson
40 James Hunt
41 Japan
42 True – but East London, South Africa!
43 Once
44 Black and gold
45 Jackie Stewart

21 Land Speed Lunacy

Ever since the first wheel turned in anger, Man has been compelled to go fast. And the only way to truly determine 'fast' is to be faster than everyone else. This is why you are always tailgated on the motorway by middle-aged men in white Audis, and why the land speed record has been contested since the late 19th century when cars were made of wood. Nowadays the carts are more like wingless jet fighters. It's all got a bit silly but we simply can't help it.

1 In 1898 Gaston de Chasseloup-Laubat was the first holder of a land speed record at which speed?

a) Just under 40mph
b) Just under 50mph
c) Just under 60mph

2 What was the name of Art Arfons record-breaking machine of the 1960s?

a) Blue Monster
b) Green Monster
c) Black Monster

3 The first ten holders of the Land Speed Record all broke the record in which country?

a) France
b) USA
c) UK

4 Who was the first man to break the 300mph barrier on land?

a) Malcolm Campbell
b) Andy Green
c) Richard Noble

5 Which engine was used to make this 300mph record breaking speed?

a) Rolls Royce
b) Ferrari
c) Porsche

6 Which Briton broke the world land speed record in the US in 1983?

7 Who am I?
- I was a famous British racing driver of the 1950s and 1960s
- I signed for Mercedes in 1955
- I made a land speed record attempt at Bonneville Salt Flats in May 1957

8 Henry Ford was one of the first US holders of the land speed record. True or false?

9 The first six holders of the land speed record came from which country?

10 In 1996 Craig Breedlove attempted the land speed record in which car?
a) Soul of America
b) Heart of America
c) Spirit of America

11 Which land speed record holder was just the 7th person to appear on the classic TV programme *This Is Your Life*?

12 If you were travelling at 230mph on the 27 Nozomi, you would be travelling by train where?

13 From 1929 to the early 1960s world land speed records were held by which country?

14 Who was the first person to break the sound barrier on land?

15 Kaye Don made an attempt on the land speed record at Daytona in March 1930 in what?
a) Silver Shot
b) Silver Bullet
c) Silver Rocket

16 Which director of ThrustSCC held the land speed record from 1983 to 1997?

17 In 1924 Malcolm Campbell reached 146.16mph to break the land speed record. Where did he achieve this feat?
   a) Australia
   b) USA
   c) Wales

18 In 1922 Sig Haugdahl broke the standing mile record at Pablo Beach Florida in a speed of 22.6 seconds? How big was his car at its widest point?
   a) 20 inches
   b) 24 inches
   c) 30 inches

19 Mr Woppit fulfilled which role in Malcolm Campbell's speed record making team?
   a) His mascot
   b) His mechanic
   c) His agent

20 Which muscle car broke almost 300 US land speed records at Bonneville Salt Flats, US?

21 In 2009 the British Steam Car hit a record speed of 148mph in which desert?
   a) Sahara
   b) Kalahari
   c) Mojave

22 Which engine powered Captain George Eyston's 73 litre Thunderbolt which set a land speed record of 357.5mph in 1938 at the Bonneville Salt Flats?

23 Which SSC car was destined to replace the superfast Aero?

24 Who had a superfast car and a superfast boat called Bluebird?

25 Thrust driver Andy Green captained the RAF's toboggan team on the Cresta Run. True or false?

26 Name the year
- Paul McCartney announced he was leaving The Beatles and recorded his first solo album
- The movie *M*A*S*H* was a smash hit
- Gary Gabelich and Blue Flame broke the land speed record which stood until 1984

27 In which London department store was the Golden Arrow displayed in 1929?
 a) Simpson's of Piccadilly
 b) Harrods
 c) Selfridges

28 The Silver Fox and the Silver Link were both high speed what?

29 Henry Seagrave set a land speed record of 203.79mph in 1927 in a Sunbeam. Which English town's name was therefore on the side?
 a) Woking
 b) Wolverhampton
 c) Warrington

30 In 1964 Donald Campbell set a record of 403.1mph at Lake Eyre. Where is Lake Eyre?
 a) USA
 b) Australia
 c) South Africa

31 Which driver set a record of 394.2mph in his Railton Mobil Special at Bonneville in 1947?

32 Who was the manufacturer when the land speed record was broken in the USA for the first time?

33 Who sponsored the Rocket which carried out speed trials at Edwards Air Force Base, California, in 1979, reaching mind blowing speeds that weren't officially recognised?

34 Who were the first father and son to hold the land speed record?

35 In 2005 Mike Newman set a land speed record of 178.5mph. In what way was this feat most unusual?

36 In 2012 project director Richard Noble announced a rocket and jet powered vehicle would be making an attempt on the world land speed record. What is the project called?
   a) Greyhound
   b) Bloodhound
   c) Foxhound

37 The first train in the world to exceed 100mph was in which country?
   a) USA
   b) Russia
   c) France

38 Which two flags were on the the front of land speed record holder ThrustSSC?

39 In which US state are the Bonneville Salt Flats used for motorsports since 1912 a favourite location for setting land speed records?

40 Malcolm Campbell called his car Bluebird as it was a symbol of good luck on land and in the air. True or false?

41 Which UK seaside resort's Motor Club held speed trials on their sands although a sign announced a fine of £5 if you drove at over 10mph the rest of the year?

a) Brighton
b) Blackpool
c) Southport

42 What was the name of Andy Green's record breaking vehicle in 1997?

a) Power
b) Force
c) Thrust

43 How many years elapsed between the breaking of the sound barrier in the air and the breaking of the sound barrier on land?

a) 20 years
b) 35 years
c) 50 years

44 Is the French TGV a high speed car or a high speed train?

45 British Steam Car driver Don Wales is what relation to land speed legend Sir Malcolm Campbell?

The Answers

1 a) Just under 40mph
2 b) Green Monster
3 a) France
4 a) Malcolm Campbell
5 a) Rolls Royce
6 Richard Noble
7 Stirling Moss
8 True (In 1904 in the Ford Arrow)
9 France
10 c) Spirit of America
11 Donald Campbell
12 Japan
13 Great Britain
14 RAF pilot Andy Green
15 b) Silver Bullet
16 Richard Noble
17 c) Wales
18 a) 20 inches
19 a) His mascot (a teddy bear)
20 Mustang Mach 1
21 c) Mojave
22 Rolls Royce
23 Tuatara
24 Malcolm Campbell

25 True
26 1970
27 c) Selfridges
28 Locomotives
29 b) Wolverhampton
30 b) Australia
31 John Cobb
32 Henry Ford
33 Budweiser
34 Malcolm and Donald Campbell
35 He couldn't see
36 b) Bloodhound
37 a) USA
38 Union Flag & Stars and Stripes (UK & US)
39 Utah
40 False (It was named after a play where the bluebird was a symbol of the unattainable)
41 c) Southport
42 c) Thrust
43 c) 50 years
44 A high speed train
45 Grandson

➲

22 Cars on the Box

The best way to bestow iconic status on a car is to get it on the telly. There are some spectacularly ropey motors that have won the hearts of generations when driven by a grizzly 1790s cop. Decades of dubious British engineering were cleansed from the memories of a nation by Bodie and Doyle and their assortment of dodgy Fords. Product placement was in its infancy, but it never looked back.

1 The Datsun 280ZX appeared on TV screens later in the year after its 1982 launch in which show?
   a) *Batman*
   b) *Knight Rider*
   c) *Starsky & Hutch*

2 Which police duo drove a red 1974 Gran Torino with a white stripe on the side?

3 In *The Avengers* what was Steed's car of choice?

4 The Lincoln Futura with its transparent cockpit cover was adapted to become which famous TV vehicle?

5 What type of car was Herbie?
   a) Mini
   b) Bubble Car
   c) VW Beetle

6 Which US city features on the side of Trotters Independent Trading vehicle in the series featuring Del Boy and Rodney?

7 Who am I?
- My car's registration number was 248 RPA
- I appeared with it in all 33 episodes of a TV series between 1987 and 2000
- It was a burgundy Jaguar Mark II

8 What was the registration plate of the six wheeled, flying pink car from *Thunderbirds*?

9 In *Knight Rider* what was the name of David Hasselhoff's incredible computerised black car?

10 Lt Columbo, famous for his beaten old raincoat, drove which beaten-up old car?
   a) Peugeot
   b) Ford
   c) Fiat

11 Which company used Tom & Jerry to advertise one of its cars in 2003?

12 Which variation of the Mini had a name which is Australian slang for 'donkey' and was frequently found in the TV series *The Prisoner*?

13 In 2010 two enterprising manufacturers won enough to invest in the remanufacture of the Peel 50 after appearing on which show?
   a) *The Apprentice*
   b) *Dragon's Den*
   c) *Pointless*

14 The Ferrari Testarossa featured in which 1980s cop series which starred Don Johnson?

15 What colour was the original TV Batmobile?

16 What was the name of the 1969 Dodge Charger driven disastrously in *The Dukes of Hazzard*?
   a) General Lee
   b) General Custer
   c) General Grant

17 In which series did investigator James Garner drive a Gold Pontiac Firebird when he wasn't living in his trailer on he beach?

18 Which model Ford was one of the stars of *Life on Mars*?
   a) Mondeo
   b) Cortina
   c) Anglia

19 Which wacky TV series of the 1960s and '70s had a sketch called 'Mr & Mrs Brian Norris's Ford Popular', in honour of the cheapest British car on the market?

20 Who am I?
- I played Terry McCann in *Minder*
- I starred in the TV series *New Tricks* with James Bolam and Alun Armstrong
- I famously starred as George Carter in *The Sweeney* with John Thaw in a fast moving Rover P6 200

21 In *The Prisoner*, Patrick McGoohan as Secret Agent No Six famously drove which car with a corresponding number?

22 How is the GMC Mandura better known to 1980s telly fans?

23 Rowan (Mr Bean) Atkinson advertised which Japanese car on TV?
   a) Datsun
   b) Toyota
   c) Nissan

24 In which series did DCI Gene Hunt hit the road in his Audi Quattro?

25 A 1936 Stutz Bearcat was owned by Mr Burns in which TV show? Was it *The Simpsons* or *Friends*?

26 In *Starsky & Hutch* who actually drove the car? Starsky or Hutch?

27 ITV broadcast a sitcom situated in a car park called *Pay and Display*. True or false?

28 Which 1960s police series was the first to show the gritty side of life of police officers in their patrol vehicles?

29 The German designed amphibious car, the Amphiranger, appeared in early episodes of which series?
- a) *Baywatch*
- b) *Miami Vice*
- c) *Benidorm*

30 Which TV series about an antique dealer featured the Mercury Cougar?
- a) *Flog It*
- b) *Dickinson's Real Deal*
- c) *Lovejoy*

31 Which series with Tom Selleck had the Private Investigator at the wheel of a Ferrari 308?

32 Which series has the opening credits which show a car coming over the brow of a hill overloaded with collectables including a grandfather clock?
- a) *Cash in the Attic*
- b) *Bargain Hunt*
- c) *Antiques Roadshow*

33 A Pontiac GTO was used in a TV show featuring a 1960s pop band. What name was the vehicle known as?
- a) Beatlemobile
- b) Monkeemobile
- c) Shadowmobile

34 In the 1996 Christmas Special of *Only Fools and Horses* the Reliant Robin (inevitably) breaks down when Del and Rodney are on their way to a fancy dress party dressed as who?

35 In which TV show do two antiques experts drive around the country in a sports car buying antiques and competing with each other as to who makes most at auction?

36 Larry Hagman and the character he made famous were both given Cadillac Allante luxury cars when he starred in which soap?

37 Diana Rigg played Emma Peel In *The Avengers*. Which car did she drive?

38 Which classic comedy series featured a 1935 Ford van with J Jones displayed on the front?

39 Which car does Inspector Morse drive in Colin Dexter's books, which was changed in the TV series at the suggestion of John Thaw himself?

40 *The Professionals* made an icon out of which British muscle car?

41 Name the year

- Computers were first linked as a network via Ethernet
- There was a threat of petrol rationing due to the Middle East oil crisis
- In *Life on Mars*, Sam Tyler is sent back here after being run over by a Vauxhall Cavalier

42 Before driving Bond cars Roger Moore played *The Saint* behind the wheel of which Swedish classic? Was it a Volvo or a Saab?

43 Which actor, famous for driving a Ford Mustang on the big screen, was used in ads by Ford on TV in the 1990s and at the start of the 21st century despite having died in the 1980s?

44 The Triumph TR7 featured in *The New Avengers* with Patrick Macnee as Steed and which actress as his sidekick Purdey?

45 Who am I?

- I am Jennifer Aniston's godfather
- I played a US detective with a liking for lollipops
- I appeared alongside a Cadillac Calais in my most famous TV series

The Answers

1 b) *Knight Rider*
2 Starsky & Hutch
3 Bentley
4 The Batmobile
5 c) VW Beetle
6 New York
7 Inspector Morse
8 FAB 1
9 KITT (Knight Industries Two Thousand)
10 a) Peugeot
11 Ford
12 The Moke
13 b) *Dragon's Den*
14 *Miami Vice*
15 Black with red trim
16 a) General Lee
17 *The Rockford Files*
18 b) Cortina
19 *Monty Python's Flying Circus*
20 Dennis Waterman
21 Lotus Seven
22 The *A-Team* van
23 c) Nissan
24 *Ashes to Ashes*

25 *The Simpsons*
26 Starsky
27 True (It starred James Bolam)
28 *Z Cars*
29 a) *Baywatch*
30 c) *Lovejoy*
31 *Magnum PI*
32 c) *Antiques Roadshow*
33 b) Monkeemobile
34 Batman and Robin
35 *Antiques Road Trip*
36 *Dallas*
37 Lotus Elan
38 *Dad's Army* (It was the butcher's van of Corporal Jones)
39 Morse drives a Lancia
40 The Ford Capri
41 1973
42 Volvo
43 Steve McQueen
44 Joanna Lumley
45 Telly Savalas aka Kojak

23 Inventions: Genius v Madness

Designing cars takes Mankind to the cutting edge of invention. But for every moment of divine inspiration there is a corresponding incident of stark raving lunacy. Whether on three, four or, ahem, six wheels the car is a minefield of things that seemed like a good idea at the time but very definitely weren't. Yes, Mr Covini, that means you.

1 Which manufacturer continued to use break cables unlike his rivals who moved to hydraulic brakes, and when asked about it said, 'I make my cars to go not stop.'

a) Enzo Ferrari
b) W.O. Bentley
c) Ettore Bugatti

2 Perry Watkins claimed to have made the world's smallest roadworthy car. It was taxed and legal to drive. Is it true or false that he made it out of a *Postman Pat* children's ride?

3 Which car maker made the first car in the world to have fibre optic headlamps?

a) Ferrari
b) Honda
c) Ford

4 Malaysia's ground breaking car the Proton Saga was named after what?

a) A business which helps the elderly
b) A tree
c) The surname of the Malaysian Prime Minister at the time

5 What was the name of the world's first purpose race circuit near Weybridge, Surrey, which opened in 1909 and closed in 1939?

6 Australia's first supercar was the Giocattolo, which is the Italian word for what?

a) Power
b) Toy
c) Cat

7 The Citroen 5CV, which was marketed as suitable for women, was thus advertised because it came in a variety of colours. True or false?

8 The first motorway between two cities opened in 1923 in which country?

9 The ill fated EB 110 came from the Bugatti stable. EB stood for Ettore Bugatti, but what did the 110 signify?

a) 110th Bugatti model
b) 110 years since Bugatti's birth
c) Only 110 were built

10 How many models of the innovative smart car had been sold in its first decade?

a) 300,000
b) 500,000
c) 1 million

11 Which was the first country to have seatbelts?

a) Sweden
b) Switzerland
c) Czechoslovakia

12 The prototype of the Phantom Corsair of 1938 was built to a design by Rust Heinz of the Heinz ketchup family. True or false?

13 Name the year

- Bobby Kennedy and Martin Luther King were killed in the USA
- Dustin Hoffman starred in the movie *The Graduate*
- Allen Breed received a patent for his sensor and safety system – the airbag

14 Red Diesel is so called because Herr Diesel's first name was Rudolf. True or false?

15 Which was the first French car to sell more than a million? Is it the Renault 4CV or the Citroen 2CV?

16 In 1925, in a bid to publicise the marque, Citroen began a nine year sponsorshop of which landmark?
- a) Arc de Triomphe
- b) Louvre museum
- c) Eiffel Tower

17 In which country did Skoda cars originate?

18 The Maestro offered which talking accessory to alert the driver to problems?
- a) The talking steering wheel
- b) The talking dashboard
- c) The talking glove compartment

19 If you bought an early Ford Capri you had to pay extra for seatbelts. True or false?

20 Which 1990s Renault performance car could travel on land and water and shared its name with an American mammal with a bushy tail?
- a) Raccoon
- b) Skunk
- c) Squirrel

21 The HTT Plethore was the first supercar from which Commonwealth country?

22 How many Aston Martin One-77s did the company announce it was going to make in 2008?

a) 1
b) 77
c) 177

23 The Tramontana R 2009 was the first supercar from which country?

a) Portugal
b) Spain
c) Bolivia

24 Which was the first country in the world to have number plates?

a) USA
b) France
c) UK

25 Citroen's Berlingo modified as a coupe de plage was designed to be used where?

a) On the beach
b) On water
c) On mountain roads

26 The Honda WOW replaced the glove box with what?

a) A wine rack
b) A freezer compartment
c) A dog crate

27 The C5 had five wheels. True or false?

28 What was the UK's first number plate?

a) A1
b) M1
c) M25

29 Which Austin Healey was known as Frogeye as Healey had stuck headlamps on top of the bonnet?

a) Sprite
b) 3000
c) Sebring

30 How many wheels did the 1986 Volkswagen Scooter have?

31 Which US manufacturer made the Town & Country Blackjack, an MPV with its very own casino?

a) Ford
b) Chrysler
c) Jeep

32 The Ford Falcon was designed in and for which country?

33 In 1935 Jean Reville's car claimed to be smallest racing car in the world. What was its nickname?

a) The Flea
b) The Midge
c) The Gnat

34 Where did the Fiat factory unusually have its test track?

35 Which make of car was the first with cruise control?

a) Ford
b) Rolls Royce
c) Chrysler

36 In Britain the first motorway bypassed which northern town?

a) Preston
b) Blackburn
c) Bolton

37 Which company first used the three point lap and diagonal seatbelt in their cars? Clue: The belt was invented by Swedish inventor Nils Bohlin.

38 Who was the first mass producing car maker outside the US?
a) Citroen
b) Volkswagen
c) Austin

39 In 2002, what was the mpg of the Dodge Ram?
a) 9mpg
b) 19mpg
c) 29mpg

40 The Auburn Motor Company was so called because the brothers who founded it all had auburn hair. True or false?

41 Name the year
- The first postwar London Motor Show took place at Earl's Court
- The railways were nationalised from midnight on 1 January
- Macdonald's opened its first drive though restaurant

42 The Laraki Fulgura was which famous first?
a) The first South American supercar
b) The first Arab supercar
c) The first sub Saharan Africa supercar

43 Who was the first car manufacturer to equip its vehicles with pneumatic tyres?
a) Volkswagen
b) Rolls Royce
c) Peugeot

44 The Wartburg Knight originated in which East European country?

45 Who am I?

- My first production car was the Type 13 in 1910
- I described the Bentley 4.5 litre as the fastest lorry in the world
- My name lives on in the name of the supercar the Veyron

The Answers

1 c) Ettore Bugatti
2 True (It sounds like a good *Top Gear* challenge!)
3 c) Ford
4 b) A tree
5 Brooklands
6 b) Toy
7 False (It had an electric starter rather than a hand crank)
8 Italy – between Milano and Varese
9 b) 110 years since Bugatti's birth
10 c) 1 million
11 c) Czechoslovakia
12 True
13 1968
14 False (Red diesel contains a dye to distinguish it from standard diesel)
15 Renault 4CV
16 c) Eiffel Tower
17 Czechoslovakia
18 b) The talking dashboard
19 True
20 a) Raccoon
21 Canada
22 b) 77
23 b) Spain

24 b) France
25 a) On the beach
26 c) A dog crate
27 False (It had three)
28 a) A1
29 a) Sprite
30 Three
31 b) Chrysler
32 Australia
33 c) The Gnat
34 On the roof
35 c) Chrysler
36 a) Preston
37 Volvo
38 a) Citroen
39 a) 9mpg
40 False (They founded it in Auburn, Indiana)
41 1948
42 b) The first Arab supercar
43 c) Peugeot
44 East Germany
45 Ettore Bugatti

24 Rallying Call

Rallying separates the men from the boys, drivers and spectators alike. While your F1 team boss sits in his air conditioned motorhome having Indian head massages and coffee enemas, the rallying equivalent is standing a foot deep in snow, his head numb with cold, drinking Nescafe from a Styrofoam cup. The fans look on, green with envy, while the drivers, hitting 100mph on ice in a blizzard, try not to run them over.

1 Which manufacturer won the first World Rally Championships in 1977?
   a) Renault
   b) Porsche
   c) Lancia

2 Former Bentley Boy Eddie Hall drove for which team in the 1934 Mille Miglia?

3 The Essex 6 Hours held in 1927 was held in Essex. True or false?

4 The only closed-road rally in the UK is named in honour of which motor racing legend?

5 In which rally is the Col de Turini used as a special stage?

6 World Rally Champion Juha Konkkunen broke the world ice driving speed record off which country?

7 Who am I?
- I was born in France in February 1974
- I won the Monte Carlo Rally in 2013
- I bowed out of the World Championship in 2013

8 The cars' race number in the Mille Miglia was the order in which they started the race. True or false?

9 Which Austin Healey Sprite was renamed after a Florida endurance test where it came first, second and third?

10 Which Hillman won the British Saloon Car Championship three years running?
   a) Imp

b) Hunter
c) Minx

11 To celebrate the success of the London to Mexico World Cup Rally, Ford produced which Ford Escort?
a) The London
b) The Mexico
c) The Rally

12 Which 1970s Simca was called Le Mille?

13 Name the year
- Britain's winter of discontent was followed by Margaret Thatcher's election as Prime Minister
- Revolution in Iran saw rising oil prices in the UK
- The Paris Dakar Rally began

14 Which British car saw off its more wealthy rivals to clinch the World Rally Championships in 1981?

15 To keep mechanics warm, Norwegian rally organisers constructed a service park in a building designed to look like what?
a) A giant rally car
b) The Norwegian flag
c) An upside down Viking ship

16 Widely seen on the 1980s rally scene, the tipple advertised on the bodywork of the Lancia 037 was a favourite of 007. What was it?

17 Which rally is deemed the 'toughest race on Earth'?

18 Kamaz trucks are already in double figures for Dakar Rally wins,

but where are these super trucks made?

19 In 1988 a Peugeot was stolen during the Paris Dakar Rally and held to ransom. True or false?

20 By the end of 2012 how many World Rally Championships had Sebastian Loeb won?
  a) 5
  b) 9
  c) 13

21 Which team were the first to win the Dakar rally, three times in succession, with a diesel engined car?

22 Which animal did VW's Race Touareg have on the side – all in the name of sponsorship?

23 Which Prime Minister's son was lost for six days during the Paris Dakar Rally?
  a) Harold Wilson's
  b) Margaret Thatcher's
  c) John Major's

24 How long was the Mille Miglia? 1,000 miles or 1,000 kilometres?

25 World Rally Championship star the Lancia Delta Integrale was only made with a left hand drive. True or false?

26 Name the year
- US President Nixon took responsibility for the Watergate scandal
- Slade had their first Xmas No 1 with 'Merry Xmas Everybody'
- The first World Rally Championship took place

27 The world's first long distance rally ended in Paris, but in which country did it begin?
   a) China
   b) Russia
   c) Turkey

28 The 1939 Mille Miglia was held in Libya. True or false?

29 Bowler's 2007 offroad star was a success at the Dakar rally. What was it called?
   a) Wildcat
   b) Bobcat
   c) Topcat

30 The Safari Rally was originally held in Kenya, Tanzania and which other country?
   a) Zambia
   b) Ghana
   c) Uganda

31 Rally driver Colin McRae perished in what kind of crash?
   a) Car
   b) Motorcycle
   c) Helicopter

32 Which team won the 2013 Acropolis Rally, one of the toughest on the rallying calendar? Was it VW or Citroen?

33 Which rally driver was dubbed 'The Iceman'?

34 The 2013 Dakar rally began in which South American city?
   a) Lima
   b) Rio de Janeiro
   c) La Paz

35 Which came first the Monte Carlo Rally or the RAC International Rally of Great Britain?

36 Which Porsche replaced the 911 4x4 in the Paris Dakar after the 911 won the rally at its first attempt?

37 Why was the Monte Carlo rally cancelled in 1974?
- a) Crash during training
- b) High oil prices
- c) Severe weather

38 In 2006 Sebastien Loeb missed four races as he had fallen off a mountain bike. True or false?

39 How long was the Paris Dakar Rally?
- a) 3,000 miles
- b) 5,000 miles
- c) 7,000 miles

40 Former rally ace Kimi Raikkonen entered a powerboat race dressed in a penguin onesie. True or false?

41 Name the year
- Oasis released 'Wonderwall'
- Eric Cantona practised his kung fu moves at Selhurst Park
- Britain had its first World Rally Champion

42 Rally driver Ken Block hails from which country?

43 How many times did the VW Race Touareg win the Dakar Rally back to back?

44 Driver Khalid Al Oassimi hails from which country?

45 Who am I?

- I was England's first World Rally Champion
- I was the first Briton to win the home rally in three successive years
- I won in 2001 in a Subaru Impreza

The Answers

1 c) Lancia
2 MG
3 False (It was held at Brooklands, Surrey)
4 Jim Clark
5 Monte Carlo Rally
6 Finland
7 Sebastian Loeb
8 False (It was the time they started, e.g. a 6.30 start gives the race number 630)
9 Sebring
10 a) Imp
11 b) The Mexico
12 Simca 100 Rallye 2
13 1979
14 Talbot Sunbeam Lotus
15 c) An upside down Viking ship
16 Martini (It didn't specify if it was a dry Martini or not)
17 Paris Dakar
18 Russia
19 True
20 b) 9
21 VW
22 (Red) bull
23 b) Margaret Thatcher's

24 1,000 miles
25 True
26 1973
27 a) China
28 True
29 a) Wildcat
30 c) Uganda
31 c) Helicopter
32 VW
33 Kimi Raikkonen
34 a) Lima
35 The Monte Carlo Rally
36 Porsche 959
37 b) High oil prices
38 True
39 b) 5,000 miles
40 False (He did once enter dressed in a gorilla suit)
41 1995
42 USA
43 Three
44 United Arab Emirates
45 Richard Burns

25 Reverse Gear: Mishaps and Misfortunes

Over a century of driving has produced some remarkable tales of derring-do and a comparable number of derring-don't-even-think-about-it. From the heroic to the moronic and everywhere in between, Man's relationship with the car is one of astonishing highs and humiliating lows. Sometimes that horse still looks like a better option.

1 In April 1937 driver Dennis Scribbons drove round the Crystal Palace track in the Coronation Trophy holding what in place in his left hand?
   a) Door
   b) Windscreen
   c) Exhaust pipe

2 In *Top Gear*'s amphibious car challenge what happened to Richard's Volkswagen camper van?
   a) Caught fire
   b) Just fell apart
   c) Sank

3 A naming mishap, SS Cars did not seem like a good name to have after WWII. What did the company change its name to?

4 In 2005 the AA said their patrolmen had delivered 18 'surprises' in that year. What were they?
   a) Coffins
   b) Babies
   c) Stranded wedding couples

5 Until the mid 1980s diplomats were immune from parking fines. At the beginning of the 1990s which country had most parking fines outstanding?
   a) USA
   b) Saudi Arabia
   c) Greece

6 Which was the worst year for road fatalities in the UK? 1941 or 1971?

7 Why did early examples of the 2010 Ferrari Italia catch fire in their

rear wheel arches?

8 Many people fell foul of the pesky parking meter. Britain's first were outside which country's embassy?
- a) USA
- b) USSR
- c) China

9 In the US a car is stolen how frequently?
- a) Every minute
- b) Every 25 seconds
- c) Every 5 seconds

10 Italian Claudio Langes had 14 attempts at F1 qualification in 1990? How many times did he fail?

11 Which car became a less than successful space shuttle for James and Richard?

12 Which Duchess sold her car complete with a number of private royal addresses still programmed into the sat nav?

13 In 1924 at the Targa Florio held in Sicily, why were Mercedes cars painted red for the only time?

14 Italian driver Tazio Nuvolari worryingly said that 'Brakes are no good.' What reason did he give?

15 In 1967 which country stopped all its traffic, which was driving on the left, at 1am and restarted it at 6am with all traffic now travelling on the right?

16 The Waterman Arrowbile flew at 110mph and drove on the road at 55mph. True or false?

17 The Austin 3 litre started out as a collaboration with Rolls Royce, who pulled out of the deal. It ended up with which nickname?

a) Land Lubber
b) Land Lobster
c) Land Loser

18 What was the main drawback with the Fiat 124?

a) Greedy in terms of fuel consumption
b) Uncomfortable seats
c) Rust

19 Why was Stirling Moss disqualified from the French GP in 1959?

20 Who am I?

- I was born in Argentina in 1911
- I drove for Alfa Romeo, Maserati and Mercedes
- I broke my neck in a crash in 1951 and had my neck in plaster but continued racing

21 The Nissan Figaro, built to celebrate 50 years of Nissan, was so popular you had to what to put in a bid to buy one?

22 The Porsche Spyder was so low that Hans Herrman drove under what during the Mille Miglia of 1954?

a) The gates of a closed level crossing
b) A bus
c) Low bridge

23 In June 1939 which world leader made the kind gesture of sending a wreath for driver Dick Seaman, killed in the Belgian GP in heavy rain?

24 In 1952 how did Consalvo Sanesi get his car over the finishing line in the French GP?

25 If you win the Mountain Speedway in Pennsylvania you are rewarded by having your car destroyed. True or false?

26 The Swedish Winter Grand Prix in February 1947 was run on what surface?

a) Tarmac
b) Clay
c) Ice

27 In February 2013 the *Daily Mirror* featured a photograph of a car in Sevenoaks, Kent, that had crashed into what?

28 In which country is the world's most dangerous road, Le Camino del Muerte?

a) Mexico
b) Brazil
c) Bolivia

29 His family firm made wrought iron gates, but in the 1950s Brian Lister branched out and made a bizarrely named sports car. What was it called?

a) The Wobbly
b) The Knobbly
c) The Jubbly

30 What was unusual about the BMW Isetta bubble car's only door?

31 In an action that Jeremy Clarkson would applaud, what happened to the established speed limit in the UK in 1930?

a) It was restricted to Saturday and Sunday only
b) It was doubled
c) It was abolished

32 The 1970s massive Fairchild Hiller NY State Safety Sedan, developed to maximise passenger safety, guaranteed passenger protection up to what speed?

a) 15mph
b) 30mph
c) 50mph

33 In the USA the Little John can help you avoid a most unfortunate mishap. What is it?

a) Satnav
b) Portable loo
c) A pistol to see off road rage drivers

34 Which of the following is the dirtiest and therefore unhealthiest part of the car?

a) Steering wheel
b) Seatbelt
c) Screenwash

35 What was the name of the craft in which Donald Campbell tragically tried to break the water speed record on Coniston Water in 1964?

a) Green Monster
b) Bluebird
c) Thrust

36 How is the motorist's anti-Christ 'the Denver boot' better known?

37 Which city, also the name of a musical, was the first home of another motoring misery, the parking meter? Was it Oklahoma or Chicago?

38 Brazil developed cars which could run on fuel made from coffee. True or false?

39 Why were Britain's first traffic lights removed only a year after they were put up?

40 The first road deaths attributed to cars were in the 19th or 20th centuries?

41 Herr Horch couldn't use his own name for his motor company under a severance arrangement with his previous company, so what name did he give the new business?
a) Volkswagen
b) Porsche
c) Audi

42 What was the profession of the first person in Britain to be charged with drink driving?
a) MP
b) Police officer
c) Taxi driver

43 In which of the following countries would you drive on the right – to avoid a collision with oncoming traffic that is?
a) Sweden
b) Singapore
c) South Africa

44 The AA has how many call outs a day because of flat batteries? Is it around 15 or around 1,500?

45 When Jeremy was assembling the Caterham, what did he put in the wrong way round?
a) The engine
b) The exhaust
c) A seat

The Answers

1 c) Exhaust pipe
2 c) Sank
3 Jaguar
4 b) Babies
5 b) Saudi Arabia
6 1971
7 The glue melted at high temperatures
8 a) USA
9 b) Every 25 seconds
10 14
11 Reliant Robin
12 Sarah Ferguson, Duchess of York
13 Sicilians rolled boulders in front of non red cars (presumably Ferraris were all red)
14 He said they only make you go slower!!
15 Sweden
16 True (Only five were ever built)
17 b) Land Lobster
18 c) Rust
19 He received help to push start the car
20 Juan Manuel Fangio
21 Buy a lottery ticket
22 a) Under the gates of a closed level crossing
23 Adolf Hitler. Later that year his actions precipitated WWII.

24 He pushed it!
25 True
26 c) Ice (It was staged on frozen lake Vallentuna)
27 Optician's (Yes, the driver had gone to Specsavers)
28 c) Bolivia
29 b) The Knobbly
30 It was the entire front of the car.
31 c) It was abolished (It was to be reinstated!)
32 a) 15mph – it never really caught on!
33 b) Portable loo
34 a) Steering wheel
35 b) Bluebird (The remains of the craft were finally recovered in 2000)
36 Wheel clamp
37 Oklahoma
38 False (They did have cars which could run on fuel made from sugar!)
39 They exploded in the hands of the operator
40 19th (1896)
41 c) Audi (It's a Latin adaptation of Horch meaning hark or listen in German)
42 c) Taxi driver
43 a) Sweden
44 Around 1,500
45 c) A seat

➲

26 Top Gear
Telly

For over ten years now, three increasingly fat and decrepit middle-aged men have been wasting your Sunday evenings doing ridiculous things for their own amusement that the BBC has seen fit to film in the name of entertainment. Here's your chance to work out how many hours you have lost to this bizarre global ritual.

1 Which early *Top Gear* presenter's races have included Le Mans, F1 and British Rallycross?

2 How long is the *Top Gear* circuit?
- a) 1 mile
- b) 1.75 miles
- c) 2 miles

3 Who was the first 'Sir' to guest on the new *Top Gear* – he made an impression in the first series of the new format?
- a) Sir Derek Jacobi
- b) Sir Ian McKellen
- c) Sir Michael Gambon

4 Prior to 2002, *Top Gear* reviewed what aspect of driving which the post 2002 series don't? Was it two wheeled vehicles or caravans?

5 Crooner Corner is part of the *Top Gear* circuit. Is it named after James May's liking of the music of crooner Frank Sinatra or the fact that it's The Stig's favourite kind of music?

6 In a Comic Relief special the *Top Gear* band was joined by Justin Hawkins, who was the frontman for which group?
- a) The Darkness
- b) The Killers
- c) The Who

7 Who am I?
- I collected *Top Gear*'s third award for Best Factual Programme at the 2008 British National Television Awards
- I have an American Cousin, an African Cousin and a Communist Cousin

- When I was first asked to be on *Top Gear* I was going to be called The Gimp

8 James May read engineering at University. True or false?

9 Who drove a Ford SportKa in a challenge with a racing pigeon?
   a) James
   b) Jeremy
   c) Richard

10 *Top Gear Turbo* is the *Top Gear* magazine for the over 55s. True or false?

11 Following his serious car crash in 2006 which food did the Hamster say he liked whereas before the crash he didn't? Was it beetroot or celery?

12 Which actor was the first Doctor Who to appear on *Top Gear* with Clarkson, Hammond and May at the helm?

13 Name the year
- Brazil won the football World Cup in Japan
- Coldplay had a hit with 'In My Place'
- Richard Hammond joined *Top Gear*

14 In series 5 James May and Richard Hammond played a vicious game of conkers which involved using which vehicles much hated by *Top Gear* presenters?

15 Which English county can proudly say that it witnessed James and the Stunt Man establish a record for jumping backwards.

16 The first *Top Gear* shows were broadcast from Salford, Manchester. True or false?

17 Which was the first country to have *Top Gear* specially made for its own market?

a) Australia
b) Canada
c) South Africa

18 Who or what are Chicago and Hammerhead?

a) Corners on the *Top Gear* circuit
b) The first Ford models
c) The names of James May's dogs

19 Who was the first female guest on the new *Top Gear*?

20 Who am I?

- I was an early presenter of *Top Gear*
- When I appeared on Radio 4's *Desert Island Discs* I chose a motorway service station as the luxury I would want to take to the desert island
- I have presented *Deal or No Deal* on Channel 4

21 Which *Top Gear* project was called Inside the *Top Gear* office Vampire the Need for Speed?

a) The Bugatti Veyron Challenge
b) Richard Hammond's attempt to exceed 300mph
c) The Stig's driving of the Ferrari FXX track car

22 Which presenter left *Top Gear* in 1999?

23 James May once described *Top Gear* as 'a sort of cross between *That's Life* and –' which other programme?

a) *Casualty*
b) *Last of the Summer Wine*
c) *Outnumbered*

24 Who appeared in every *Top Gear* programme for a decade from 1991?

25 Supercar fan Jay Kay had a faster lap time than supermodel Jodie Kidd as the Star in a Reasonably Priced Car. True or false?

26 In the closing credits of which Sport Relief Special, based on a popular makeover programme of the time, did the team assume the names Alan Clarkson, Charlie May and Handy Hammond?

27 James May owns a Morgan Aero 8. True or false?

28 Which manufacturer made the Invincible after its pick-up was seen to be indestructible despite endless abuse on the show?

29 Where is the *Top Gear* track? Is it Trafford Park, Dunsfold Park or Holland Park?

30 On which channel was *Top Gear* first broadcast, BBC One or BBC Two?

31 How was the Suzuki Aerio better known in Europe and on *Top Gear*?

32 Name the year
- The Grand National ended in chaos
- Mr Blobby had a No 1 hit
- *Top Gear Magazine* was launched

33 What happened to the Reasonably Priced Car when star Lionel Richie drove it?
a) The suspension broke
b) A wheel fell off
c) The clutch failed

34 In which country did James May morph into Captain Fast when he clocked up 235mph?

35 According to Jeremy, the aim of attaching a V8 engine to a rocking chair was so that an elderly person could be helped to reach the remote control and not have to watch which presenter?

36 It's fair to say that caravans don't always get a particularly good press on *Top Gear*, but which of the presenters wrote the book *A Short History of Caravans in the UK*?

37 Out in Florida, James met up with car enthusiast Brian Johnson who is the frontman of which rock band?

38 How many caravans did the Volvo 240 manage to jump over in its heroic leap? Was it two, four or six?

39 Who said, 'The acceleration is so brutal I feel like my eyes have been moved around the side of my head like a pigeon's'?

40 Which female singer/songwriter who recorded 'Slow It Down' did exactly the opposite when she set a new best lap time for a female driver in a Reasonably Priced Car in 2013?

41 Name the year

- The world's first test tube baby was born
- UK No 1 hits included Rod Stewart's 'Do Ya Think I'm Sexy' and the Bee Gees' 'Night Fever'
- *Top Gear* became a nationwide TV series

42 OK, Jeremy isn't a fan of caravans, but it was a genuine accident when he set fire to one while cooking. What dish was our celebrity chef creating at the time?

43 James and Richard tested a car for pensioners in which English county?

44 In which series of *Top Gear* did Richard return following the 2006 crash? Was it series six, series nine or series 12?

45 Name the year
- Prince Charles married Lady Diana Spencer
- John McEnroe won the Wimbledon Singles title for the first time
- Prestigious *Tomorrow's World* presenter William Woollard joined the *Top Gear* team

The Answers

1 Tiff Needell
2 b) 1.75 miles
3 c) Sir Michael Gambon
4 Two wheeled vehicles
5 It's The Stig's favourite kind of music
6 a) The Darkness
7 The Stig
8 False (He read music)
9 a) James
10 False, it's the *Top Gear* magazine for children
11 Celery
12 Christopher Eccleston
13 2002
14 Caravans
15 Suffolk
16 False (They were broadcast from Edgbaston, Birmingham)
17 a) Australia
18 a) Corners on the *Top Gear* circuit
19 Tara Palmer-Tomkinson
20 Noel Edmonds
21 b) Richard Hammond's attempt to exceed 300mph
22 Jeremy Clarkson – but he did return!!!
23 b) *Last of the Summer Wine*
24 Quentin Willson

25 False (Jodie was faster)
26 *Top Gear Ground Force*
27 False (The Hamster is on the list of past and present Aero 8 owners)
28 Toyota (Hilux)
29 Dunsfold Park
30 BBC Two
31 Liana – the reasonably priced car no less
32 1993
33 b) A wheel fell off
34 Germany
35 Adrian Chiles
36 Richard Hammond
37 AC/DC
38 Two
39 James May
40 Amy Macdonald
41 1978
42 He was cooking some chips
43 Dorset
44 Series nine
45 1981

➲

27 Yuppie Heaven

If you are lucky enough to be too young to understand what Yuppies are, imagine someone you really don't like, with lots more money than you, overtaking you in a car you can't afford on a residential street while shouting loudly into their mobile phone. These were the pioneers of consumption. The very reason we are all in the financial cesspit now. But they did have some jolly nice cars.

1 Which Lamborghini was restyled in honour of the maker's silver jubilee?
   a) Countach
   b) Diablo
   c) Espada

2 The gear knob on the VW Golf GTI was a golf ball. True or false?

3 The Porsche 911 or the 944 – which new model would the 1980s yuppie have to fork out more cash to buy?

4 Which was the wider Ferrari, the Testarossa or the F40?

5 Car phones became popular in the 1980s but in which decade were they first available?
   a) 1940s
   b) 1950s
   c) 1960s

6 Which Porsche convertible made its debut at the Geneva Auto Show in 1982?

7 Name the year
- The Porsche 959 was the fastest production car of the year
- Nigel Mansell won the British Grand Prix
- Ford bought luxury car group Aston Martin

8 How many Porsche 911 Turbos were made in 1975?
   a) Just under 300
   b) Just under 500
   c) Just under 600

9 What did Maserati include with its BiTurbo, an item more usually associated with aircraft?
   a) Black box
   b) Ejector seat
   c) Tail fins

10 Which was the first high performance car with four wheel drive – a big clue is in its name?

11 The Ferrari F40 could accelerate from 40 to 70mph in how many seconds?
   a) Two
   b) Four
   c) Six

12 Which make of car removed the Jaguar XJ220 from its position as the fastest road car in the world?

13 The Toyota MR2 had a top speed of 120mph. What did MR stand for?

14 What make of engine was hidden within the TVR 350i?

15 The BMW Z1 was originally made as a test car for which components?
   a) Brakes
   b) Suspension
   c) Transmission

16 The Ferrari GTB Turbo and GTS Turbo were developed for the US market. True or false?

17 The Type 930 was more usually known by which name?

18 The first 100 of the Jaguar XJR-S sold were named in honour of Jaguar's 1988 win where?

19 Which make of engine powered the Caterham Seven?

20 Who am I?
- I was born in Pinner
- I owned a Jaguar XJ220
- My hit records during the 1980s include 'Nikita' and 'I'm Still Standing'

21 Porsche is inextricably linked with Germany, Ferrari with Italy. Where was the Marcos Mantula made?

22 How many air intakes did the F40 have at the front of the car?

23 Which 4x4 was a soft roader success for Suzuki?

24 Which Mazda was also called the Miata?

25 VW used German designers to create the original VW Golf. True or false?

26 Name the year
- Sally Ride was the first woman to take a ride in space
- The first wheel clamps were seen in two London boroughs
- Ford launched its Escort XR3I

27 The VW Golf Rallye G60 was four wheel drive. True or false?

28 What distinguished the Ferrari GTS from the less successful GTB?

29 The Lamborghini Countach in common with all Lamborghinis had a bull as its emblem. What was the significance of the bull?
   a) Ferrucio Lamborghini's passion for bullfighting
   b) His family owned a cattle farm
   c) He was born under the sign of Taurus the Bull

30 The Ferrari F40 was only sold in either red or white. True or false?

31 Which 4x4 beloved of yuppies was on show in the Louvre in Paris as an example of an outstanding piece of modern sculpture?

32 The Porsche 944 Turbo S could accelerate to 60mph in how many seconds?

33 Which *Top Gear* presenter regarded the VW Corrado as a potential classic?

34 Which was the first front wheel drive sports car which Lotus ever built?

35 The Mercedes 560 SEC was part of the W126 series. What did W126 refer to?

36 The Lotus Turbo Esprit had previously been called what?
   a) The Lotus Norfolk
   b) The Lotus Essex
   c) The Lotus Kent

37 Lancia were obliged to build 5,000 Delta Integrales to comply with rally rules. It was so successful that how many were eventually made?
   a) 20,000
   b) 30,000
   c) 40,000

38 The Ford Sierra XR4i was a joint venture between Great Britain and which other country?

39 What did the 8 stand for in the Ferrari 328?

40 Which manufacturer launched the Graduate Spider in yuppie homage to the Sixties movie classic *The Graduate*?

41 Name the year

- Europe won the Ryder Cup for the first time on 28 years
- The Live Aid concert took place
- A turbocharger took the Porsche 944's performance to a new level

42 Did the original VW Golf GTI have three doors or five doors?

43 The Porsche 911 Turbo had a spoiler with which nickname?

a) Shark tail
b) Whale tail
c) Fish tail

44 Which 1980s Ford Fiesta was launched to rival the Mark 1 Golf GTI?

45 How did Saab update their 900 model in 1986?

The Answers

1 a) Countach
2 True
3 911
4 Testarossa
5 a) 1940s
6 911 Cabriolet
7 1987
8 a) Just under 300
9 a) Black box
10 Audi Quattro
11 a) Two
12 McLaren
13 Mid engined recreational
14 Rover
15 b) Suspension
16 False (They were developed for Italian car lovers)
17 911
18 Le Mans
19 Ford
20 Elton John
21 UK
22 Three
23 Vitara
24 MX-5 Mark1

25 False (It was designed in Italy)
26 1983
27 True
28 A removable roof
29 c) He was born under the sign of Taurus the Bull
30 False (They were all red)
31 Range Rover
32 A mere 5.5!
33 Richard Hammond
34 Elan M100
35 Chassis
36 b) The Lotus Essex
37 c) 40,000
38 Germany
39 8 cylinders
40 Alfa Romeo
41 1985
42 Three doors
43 b) Whale tail
44 XR2
45 Introduced a convertible

28 Blues and Twos

Although you're unlikely to admire the police car that's sitting behind you on the hard shoulder while its driver issues you a ticket, there is something special about the wheels of law enforcement through the ages that brims some atrocious bangers with improbable significance. Pop a flashing light on something and the adage sticks: you can't polish a turd, but you can roll it in glitter.

1 Which car started life as a 1950s Morris Oxford and became a stalwart of the Indian police force?

a) Hindustan Ambassador
b) Hindustan Diplomat
c) Hindustan Commissioner

2 Italian police in the 1980s used the smallest 4x4 in the world at the time. What was it?

3 Which Man Utd football star was driven from the city's magistrates court in the back of a police Mini in 1973 after a drunken incident?

4 Which car did the Hamster buy to turn into a police car in a famous *Top Gear* Challenge?

5 In which country did the Dodge Charger replace the Chevrolet Camaro in many of its forces?

6 What type of Subaru was used by local police forces for high speed rural pursuits?

7 Who am I?

- I have been President of Russia
- I was an officer in the KGB
- I own a Gaz M-21 Volga, a classic Russian police vehicle

8 What did Wolseley Motor Traffic Patrol Cars have on their roofs to make their presence felt? Was it Tannoy loudhailers or Pye radio transmitters?

9 In which country has the Porsche 911 been a police car?

a) Austria

b) Italy
c) USA

10 Which police force bought the Citroen 2CV Sahara?
a) Algeria
b) France
c) Spain

11 How much were the *Top Gear* trio first given to create their own police car?
a) £500
b) £1,000
c) £3,000

12 Which reliable saloon became the standard police car of the 1940s? Was it the Wolseley 6/80 or Humber Pullman?

13 Sixty Peugeot turbo charged four wheel drive MI16s were made for the French police force under what name?

14 The Porsche Boxster is the police car of choice for highway patrol CHiPs. CHiPs is from which US state?
a) Colorado
b) California
c) Carolina

15 Which Brothers had a police car with magic powers 'on a mission from God'?

16 The P5 appealed to the British police force in the late 1960s. Who made it?

17 Who made the legendary 442, a popular highway patrol car in mid 1960s America?

a) Ford
b) Oldsmobile
c) Plymouth

18 What colour are the markings on the German police's Porsche Carrera S?

19 The Dutch police have used a two seater Opel Speedster as a police car of choice. True or false?

20 In their Lamborghini Gallardo LP560-4 the Italian police can hit speeds of…?
a) 150mph
b) 180mph
c) 200+mph

21 In the mid 1960s two female traffic police officers were famously allocated an MGB GT patrol car. Where were they based?
a) Cornwall
b) Sussex
c) Norfolk

22 Which Alfa Romeo chased villains in the movie *The Italian Job* and was the car of choice by Italian police of the time?
a) Berlina
b) Stradale
c) Zagato

23 City of London police travel on Wispers. What are they?

24 In April 2013 which country unveiled the Lamborghini Aventador with a price tag of £360,000 as its latest police car?

25 The Segway Patroller used by police in countries such as the US and China has how many wheels?

26 Which British manufacturer produced a police version of its XF saloon in 2009?

27 In which city, once famous for its gangsters, was the Dodge Monaco used by its police force in the 1970s?

28 The Grentz Trabant was used by border police in which country?

29 Which police force used the Saab 900 Turbos?

30 If you had committed a motoring misdemeanour in Dubai, what would be the two colours of the police vehicles that were after you?

31 Which 'green' car was delivered to the Portuguese police force?
 a) Nissan Leaf
 b) Toyota Prius
 c) Renault Twizy

32 The Chrysler Valiant Charger was bought by which police force in the early 1970s, customised with pink and blue stripes?
 a) Australia
 b) South Africa
 c) USA

33 In which country might you see a Mini Cooper with 'polizei' on the front?

34 The American Dodge Magnum can be seen on the streets of which state? Clue: It's Motown on the stereo.

35 What is the nickname of the Mercedes CLS Brabus built for the German police force? Clue: It has a top speed of 225mph.

36 Italy uses the Smart to police its city streets. True or false?

37 Which Ford that appeared on TV's *Heartbeat* was widely used in Britain in the 1960s and had a blue and white livery?
a) Popular
b) Anglia
c) Consul

38 The Porsche 911 is widely used by the fuzz in Germany and which of its near neighbours?
a) France
b) Luxembourg
c) Austria

39 Which police cars first seen in the 1960s were so called because of their black and white stripes?

40 In 2010 which Korean manufacturer became a 'preferred supplier' to the UK police force?
a) Hyundai
b) Daewoo
c) Kia

41 Which police force unveiled the 168mph Lexus IS-F in 2009?
a) Merseyside
b) Tayside
c) Humberside

42 What colour was the Ferrari 250GTE commissioned by Italian police in 1962?
a) Black

b) Red
c) White

43 Dodge by name and Dodge by nature, the 2006 Dodge Charger is a police favourite in which country?

44 British police officers drove a Ferrari 612 Scaglietti in the Noughties. True or false?

45 The Dutch police supercar the C8 Spyder has a 4.2L V8 engine made by whom?
a) BMW
b) Porsche
c) Audi

The Answers

1 a) Hindustan Ambassador
2 Fiat Panda 4x4
3 George Best
4 Suzuki Vitara
5 USA
6 Impreza Turbo
7 Vladimir Putin
8 Tannoy loudhailers but some had Pye radio transmitters in the boot
9 a) Austria
10 c) Spain
11 b) £1,000
12 Wolseley
13 T16
14 b) California
15 Blues Brothers
16 Rover
17 b) Oldsmobile (Made by General Motors)
18 Green
19 True
20 c) 200+mph
21 b) Sussex
22 a) Berlina
23 Electric bikes

24 Dubai
25 Two
26 Jaguar
27 Chicago
28 East Germany
29 Sweden
30 Green and white
31 a) Nissan Leaf
32 a) Australia
33 Germany (Particularly in Bavaria)
34 Michigan
35 Rocket
36 True (It's blue to match its blue flashing lights)
37 b) Anglia
38 c) Austria
39 Panda cars
40 Hyundai
41 c) Humberside
42 a) Black
43 USA
44 True, but only to promote road safety
45 c) Audi

➲

29 Formula 1 Part 3

This was the start of the modern era of F1, with technology beginning to address safety at the same time as it addressed things like turbochargers that put over 1,000bhp through a manual gearbox. A conflicted period of huge technological advances in various directions, this was to be the moment when the Grim Reaper had his paddock pass revoked, but not before he'd robbed us of Ayrton Senna.

1 About which Grand Prix did Jacques Villeneuve comment in 1996, 'All I could see was a torrent of water, like the wake from a boat, and for the rest of the afternoon many people went sailing'?

a) Spanish
b) British
c) Belgian

2 In 1994 the first Austrian since Niki Lauda won the German Grand Prix. Who was he?

3 Which French driver was nicknamed 'the Professor' because of his calm approach to his sport?

4 Whose pioneering carbon fibre car was sliced in two at the 1981 Italian Grand Prix after a high speed 140mph crash?

5 Which Irish driver made his F1 debut for Jordan in 1993?

6 How many times was Renault World Champion F1 constructor between 1992 and 1997?

a) Two
b) Four
c) Six

7 Who am I?

- I made my debut for Tyrrell in the 1984 Brazilian Grand Prix
- I drove for Ligier, McLaren and Jordan among others
- I won Le Mans in 1990 and became a TV sports commentator after my retirement

8 With which manufacturer had Michael Schumacher won two titles in 1994 and 1995, before he moved to Ferrari?

9 All Nelson Piquet's World Championships were in which decade?

10 Which driver won the Jordan team its first pole position?

11 Who made his debut at the 1994 Spanish Grand Prix after the tragic death of Ayrton Senna?

12 In 1991, in Belgium, Michael Schumacher had his first F1 start, for which team?

13 Name the year
- The euro was officially launched
- David Beckham married Spice Girl Victoria Adams
- Damon Hill had his final Grand Prix win

14 Who moved aside to let Mika Hakkinen through in the 1998 Australian Grand Prix?

15 When he won the World Championship in 1992 Nigel Mansell was driving for which team?

16 Which Briton did Alain Prost overtake to hold the record number of Grand Prix wins?

17 Who lost his place with the Williams team the year he became World Champion?

18 Out of 31 GP wins, Nigel Mansell had 28 for Williams and three for which manufacturer?

19 Christian Fittipaldi is the son of driver Emerson Fittipaldi. True or false?

20 Who am I?

- My father Gilles had six Grand Prix wins
- I was IndyCar CART Rookie of the Year in 1994
- I was World Champion in 1997 driving for Willliams

21 The McLaren-Mercedes team provided wins for which driver in 1998 and 1999?

22 Who was the first driver to register 50 Grand Prix victories?

23 Who partnered Michael Schumacher at Ferrari in 1997?

24 Which son of a racing legend made his F1 debut with Williams in 1992 and retired after the Italian Grand Prix seven years later?

25 Name the year

- Windsor Castle was badly damaged by fire
- Bill Clinton became US President
- Nigel Mansell was World Champion driving a Williams

26 Ayrton Senna lost his life in 1994. Which other driver also was killed in the same tragic season for F1?

27 How old was Damon Hill when he finally became World Champion?

28 Who won the Australian Grand Prix in 1994 when the two main rivals for the race, Hill and Schumacher, collided?

29 In 1996 who said, 'Schumacher is the fastest man on the track. He's going quicker than anyone else'?

30 In which country was the first Pacific Grand Prix held in 1994, which was won by Michael Schumacher?

31 In 1986 who beat Ayrton Senna by 38 seconds at the Hungaroring, the first F1 race to have been held there?

32 The Las Vegas Grand Prix was held at Caesar's Palace in 1981 and 1982. True or false?

33 Where did Nigel Mansell realise in 1992 that he had enough points to secure the World Championship?

34 Where did Oliver Panis have his first Grand Prix win, in 1996?

35 Which British team did Ayrton Senna drive for between 1985 and 1987?

36 In Derek Warwick's debut season he scored no championship points. True or false?

37 In 1996 who did Frank Williams recruit from Indy Car?

38 In 1999 Johnny Herbert moved to which team? Clue: Think Scottish F1 driver!

39 Which driver replaced Damon Hill at Williams in 1997?
a) Heinz Harald Frentzen
b) David Coulthard
c) Mika Hakkinen

40 In 1997 what did Florian Lauda donate to his brother Niki?

41 Name the year
- Bruce Willis starred in the first *Die Hard* movie
- Ayrton Senna won his first driver's championship
- Enzo Ferrari died, as did Mini designer Alex Issigonis

42 Which Essex born driver made his F1 debut in the 1989 Brazilian Grand Prix with Tyrrell and won Le Mans in 1991?

43 Alain Prost's first three World Championships were with which team?

44 Ralf Schumacher's driving career began at the age of three when he drove what?

45 Who am I?

- I began racing in the 1970s when I was still an aerospace engineer
- My first F1 win was the 1985 European Grand Prix at Brands Hatch
- I was the next British F1 champion after James Hunt

The Answers

1 a) Spanish
2 Gerhard Berger
3 Alain Prost
4 John Watson
5 Eddie Irvine
6 c) Six
7 Martin Brundle
8 Benetton
9 1980s
10 Rubens Barrichello
11 David Coulthard
12 Jordan
13 1999
14 David Coulthard
15 Williams
16 Jackie Stewart
17 Damon Hill
18 Ferrari
19 False (He is his nephew)
20 Jacques Villeneuve
21 Mika Hakkinen
22 Alain Prost
23 Eddie Irvine
24 Damon Hill

25 1992
26 Roland Ratzenberger
27 Aged 36
28 Nigel Mansell
29 Murray Walker (It had to be!)
30 Japan
31 Nelson Piquet
32 True
33 Hungary
34 Monaco
35 Lotus
36 True
37 Jacques Villeneuve
38 Stewart
39 a) Heinz Harald Frentzen
40 A kidney
41 1988
42 Johnny Herbert
43 McLaren
44 Go karts
45 Nigel Mansell

30 Massive Machinery

It's only in the last few years that 'small' has become a design virtue in the world of motoring. Big has always been better, because big means powerful. And sometimes it just means big, but that's good too. Mankind needs to move stuff about, a lot, and for that it needs truly massive machines.

1 The Large Hadron Collider, the world's largest machine built by man, has such a large circumference that it crosses the border four times between France and which other country?

a) Italy
b) Switzerland
c) Germany

2 The oil tanker *Jahre Viking* was built where?

a) Japan
b) India
c) Sweden

3 American Ransom Eli Olds increased his car production from 425 cars in 1901 to how many a year later – all due to a massive assembly line?

a) 1,000
b) 2,000
c) 2,500

4 Bulldozers were originally built to replace which kind of power?

a) Mules
b) Bulls
c) Elephants

5 How were magnetically levitated trains more commonly known?

6 Which British nuclear submarine shares its name with a major naval battle?

a) Jutland
b) Trafalgar
c) Atlantic

7 Who said in a *Top Gear* Challenge, 'Based on no knowledge at

all we decided to push on in our three ton truck.' Was it Jeremy, Richard or James?

8 The Zamboni was created specifically to clear what?
a) Forests
b) Ice rinks
c) Minefields

9 *Samson* and *Goliath* are two massive cranes in which British port?
a) Southampton
b) Felixstowe
c) Belfast

10 The first Ferrari stretch limo was a version of which car?

11 The Komatsu D575A is a giant what?

12 The world's largest digger is over three hundred feet high. True or false?

13 Wabco became part of the Komatsu group but not before it made its colossal Wabco 3200B. How did you get into its cab?

14 For which piece of machinery have we Joseph Cyril Bamford to thank?

15 You would use the massive Liebherr T282 if you were in need of a what?
a) Crane
b) Chainsaw
c) Dumper truck

16 If you were driving a Big Bud you would most probably be part of which industry?

17 The Ukrainian aircraft the MRIA is named after the Ukrainian word for what?
   a) Magic
   b) Dream
   c) Sky

18 Which *Top Gear* presenter drove arguably the world's largest car, a version of the Dodge Power Wagon? Clue: That word power!

19 White became one of the major US truck manufacturers before being swallowed up by Volvo. It started out as the White Sewing Machine Co. True or false?

20 What name would be given in the UK to the vehicle an American would call a backhoe?

21 The awesome Bagger 288 is an earth mover but not a fast one. At what speed can it travel?
   a) 2 metres a minute
   b) 5 metres a minute
   c) 10 metres a minute

22 Canadian company Western Star built the Constellation 4964Fx B-train to transport which commodity for the building trade?
   a) Bricks
   b) Cement
   c) Piping

23 What kind of vehicle was the massive Knock Nevis?

24 Which space telescope was named after the US astronomer who identified that there were other galaxies beyond the Milky Way?

25 The supertanker *Seawise Giant* was so big she could not navigate the English Channel fully loaded. True or false?

26 In 2013, Hitachi revealed its ultra-large and impressive-sounding EX2600-6 at the international trade fair for the industry in Munich. What type of massive machine is it? An excavator or a pulveriser?

27 The *Top Gear* team will be queuing up to buy it! What is the Snakeliner President Suite?

28 Scania trucks in the 1990s introduced which innovation that allowed for ultra-long, international journeys?

29 How many gallons of oil can the average supertanker carry?
a) 75 million
b) 84 million
c) 99 million

30 What name is given to the massive tracked vehicles whose job it is to keep roads clear of snow and ice?
a) Snowdogs
b) Snowcats
c) Snowbears

31 It became the world's largest container ship and was named after which explorer?
a) Vasco da Gama
b) Ferdinand Magellan
c) Marco Polo

32 The Overburden Conveyor Bridges are used in Germany in which industry?
a) Car manufacture

b) Mining
c) Building

33 What was first used in the early years of the 20th century on tractors but was later used on many types of equipment including tanks?

34 The Midnight Rider is one of the world's largest what?
a) Motorcycles
b) Stretch limos
c) Trains

35 *Allure of the Seas* and *Oasis of the Seas* are both what type of ship?
a) Cargo ship
b) Cruise ship
c) Oil tanker

36 What was the nickname of the HEAO-2 satellite which housed an X-ray telescope in 1978?
a) Hubble
b) Einstein
c) Newton

37 The Strata 950 was used to carry out which high profile rescue in Chile?

38 Taisun is one of the world's largest what?
a) Diggers
b) Tanks
c) Cranes

39 How is the US's reusable spacecraft better known?

40 Which of the following is one of the world's largest dredger ships?
   a) *Queen of Great Britain*
   b) *Queen of the Netherlands*
   c) *Queen of Sweden*

41 Name the year
- JCB began painting their construction machinery in its distinctive yellow and black
- A Porsche was the first German car to be exhibited at the London Motor Show post WWII
- Austin and Morris agreed to merge

42 When complete, the HMS *Queen Elizabeth* will be the length of 28 London buses. What type of ship will she be?

43 What innovation could simulate the conditions experienced by an aircraft or high speed car and changed the design of these forever?

44 On its first successful run the first nuclear reactor produced enough energy to power what?
   a) Four electric heaters
   b) Four electric light bulbs
   c) Four electric cars

45 Who said, 'Our scientific power has outrun our spiritual power with guided missiles and misguided men'?
   a) Pope Francis
   b) Martin Luther King
   c) Mother Teresa

The Answers

1 b) Switzerland
2 a) Japan
3 c) 2,500
4 a) Mules
5 Maglev trains
6 b) Trafalgar
7 Jeremy
8 b) Ice rinks
9 c) Belfast
10 Modena 360
11 Bulldozer
12 True (That's about as tall as a 30 storey building)
13 Up a nine rung ladder (supplied)
14 JCB
15 c) Dumper truck
16 Farming (It's a tractor)
17 b) Dream
18 JC
19 True
20 JCB
21 a) 2 metres a minute
22 b) Cement
23 Oil tanker
24 Hubble
25 True
26 Excavator

27 One of the world's largest single storey caravans
28 Sleeper cabs
29 b) 84 million
30 b) Snowcats
31 c) Marco Polo
32 b) Mining
33 Caterpillar tracks
34 b) Stretch limo
35 b) Cruise ship
36 b) Einstein
37 Trapped miners
38 c) Cranes (It holds the world record for lifting – 20,133 metric tonnes)
39 Space shuttle
40 b) *Queen of the Netherlands*
41 1951
42 Aircraft carrier
43 Wind tunnel
44 b) Four electric light bulbs
45 b) Martin Luther King

31 Hot Hatches

Although the 1980s was responsible for some abysmal design ideas, it did give us the hot hatch, a game-changing car then and now. This was the idea that put performance into the hands of the average driver, and did so without compromising on a bit of practicality. The school run became a rally stage, the daily commute a qualifying lap.

1 Which terrifying hot hatch did Renault launch in 2001?

2 Who made the small but speedy Abarth, with a top speed of a staggering 128mph?

3 The tiny Subaru Justy had permanent four wheel drive. True or false?

4 Which car was Britain's first ever hatchback?

5 What year was the term hot hatch first used in the motoring press? Clue: it's also the name of a famous book
   a) 2001
   b) 1984
   c) 1968

6 The Ford Fiesta ST, with a top speed of 139mph, was originally tested on which German race track?

7 What was Ford's follow up in the hot hatch market to the Fiesta Supersport?

8 In 1982, which hot hatch became the last car without four wheel drive to win the RAC Rally?

9 Which Honda Civic had a top speed of 140mph?

10 The Vauxhall Astra VXR was designed by a Briton who shares his name with a brand of vacuum cleaner. What was his name?
   a) Dyson
   b) Bissell
   c) Hoover

11 What does the letter R stand for in the Austin Metro 6R4?

12 When *Top Gear* carried out their ultimate hot hatch test what was the average mpg of the Megane, Focus, Golf and Astra. Was it 30, 35 or 40?

13 The VW Rabbit was the US version of which hot hatch?

14 What was the name of Renaultsport's Clio 200?
a) The cat
b) The cup
c) The cool

15 A hot hatch with a hot price tag – how much would you expect to pay for an Audi RS3?
a) £30,000
b) £40,000
c) £50,000

16 The word Stradale was added to the Lancia Delta S4 to indicate where it could be driven. What does 'stradale' mean?

17 Which Renault became France's bestselling car in 1973, in no small measure due to its fuel economy in the wake of the Middle East oil crisis?

18 Who made the Chevette, initially a nippy hatchback but subsequently a successful rally car?

19 The Renault Clio Cup can do 141mph. True or false?

20 Ford's performance car the Focus ST has a top speed of what?
a) 120mph
b) 135mph

c) 154mph

21 Which was the first Japanese designed car to be built in Britain?

22 Which name did Peugeot resurrect when it entered the Sunbeam Lotus into the rally world?

23 What reputation did the Ford Escort XR3i have?
a) The most bought and sold hot hatch
b) The hot hatch with the most speeding tickets
c) The most stolen hot hatch

24 Which Renault GT Turbo was launched in 1986 and proved quite a match for 007 in a *Never Say Never Again* hot hatch/motorcycle race?
a) 4
b) 5
c) 8

25 The VW Golf GTI has a top speed of 100mph. True or false?

26 Name the year
- The Olympics were held in Moscow and were boycotted by some nations including the USA
- Sony launched the Walkman cassette player
- The Renault 5 Turbo was launched

27 The modest looking Peugeot 205 GTI has a top speed in excess of 110mph. True or false?

28 The Renaultsport Clio 200 Turbo has which sized engine?

29 Which Fiat started life as a family hatch in 1984 but reached hot hatch status a year later with a version with a bhp of 116 and a

top speed of 130mph?

30 Launched in 1986 which definitive Peugeot was *Car* magazine's car of the decade?

31 What was the alternative name of the Nissan Pulsar?

32 Which hot hatch was Peugot's big launch of 2013?

33 What was Kia's first hot hatch?

34 Which F1 team name did Renault add to their award winning Clio in 1993?

35 The Simca 1307 was the French version of which hot hatch?

36 Which small Hillman had models called a Californian and a Husky version?

37 Who made the hottest of hot hatches, the 205 GTI 1.6?

38 Which manufacturer developed suspension and steering technology called Perfohub for one of its flagship hot hatches?

39 The Golf GTi was the first ever hot hatch. True or false?

40 Which iconic name goes before Paceman John Cooper Works to name a hot hatch?

41 The Octavia vRS comes from which manufacturer?

42 Who made the Leon Cupra R a hot hatch of the early Noughties?

43 Ford's 2010 RS500 was part of which range?

a) Escort
b) Fiesta
c) Focus

44 Which company manufactured the Fabia vRS S2000 to mark its victory in the Intercontinental Rally Challenge?

45 Which Golf launched in 2012 became the fastest Golf to date?

The Answers

1 Clio V6
2 Fiat
3 True
4 Austin Maxi
5 b) 1984 (The novel was written by George Orwell)
6 Nurburgring
7 XR2
8 Lotus Sunbeam
9 Type R
10 a) Dyson
11 Rear engined
12 30
13 Golf
14 b) The cup
15 b) £40,000
16 Road or street
17 Renault 5
18 Vauxhall
19 True
20 c) 154mph
21 Honda Civic
22 Talbot
23 c) The most stolen hot hatch
24 b) 5

25 False (It will do an impressive 149mph)
26 1980
27 True (A hot hatch indeed, especially in the mid 1980s)
28 1.6 Turbo
29 Fiat Uno Turbo
30 205 GTI 1.9
31 Sunny
32 208 GTi
33 Kia Proceed GT
34 Williams
35 Chrysler/Talbot Alpine
36 Imp
37 Peugeot
38 Renault
39 False
40 Mini
41 Skoda
42 Seat
43 c) Focus
44 Skoda
45 VW Golf R

32 Le Mans Part 2

When the gentlemen in string-backed gloves gave way to the professional racers in fire retardant jumpsuits, the 24 hours of Le Mans became a very different affair. With serious commercial money pouring in to advanced aerodynamic improvements and increasingly enormous engines, cars began passing 250mph on the Mulsanne Straight, and every so often taking off. This was a truly dangerous time to be an endurance racer, as if there was ever a safe one.

1 What problem did the Porsche 956 suffer on the Sunday morning of the 1983 race?

a) Fuel leak
b) Burst tyre
c) Lost a door

2 In which decade did Ford take on the might of Ferrari et al at Le Mans?

3 Which Porsche was designed to conquer Le Mans and did so in 1970 and 1971?

4 The only British car to finish Le Mans in 1966 was a kit car. True or false?

5 Matra, a racing company with significant successes at Le Mans in the 1960s, were based in which country?

a) France
b) Italy
c) Portugal

6 Which Ford had a famous 1, 2, 3 in 1966?

7 Who am I?

- I was the first person to win the Indianapolis 500 and Le Mans
- I raced a turbine sports car at Le Mans in the 1960s with Jackie Stewart
- My son became a World Champion at F1

8 Jacky Ickx and Derek Bell won Le Mans in 1981 in this car's first year at the Sarthe circuit, having led from the start. What was it?

9 Which famous aircraft, which retired in 2011, shares its name with a 1980s Aston Martin which raced at Le Mans in 1982 finishing seventh?

a) Harrier
b) Nimrod
c) Spitfire

10 Which make of car ended Porsche's seven year winning streak in 1988?

a) Jaguar
b) Mazda
c) Peugeot

11 Which Maserati raced at Le Mans in the late 1960s but failed to finish despite being clocked at almost 200mph on the Mulsanne straight?

12 Which Porsche had an impressive 1/2 finish at Le Mans in 1970?

13 Name the year

- Buzz Aldrin was the second man on the Moon
- Fiat purchased a 50% stake in Ferrari
- Belgian Jacky Ickx and Brit Jackie Oliver were the fourth Ford team in a row to win Le Mans in a GT40

14 What was the relationship between the Andrettis who raced at Le Mans in 1983?

a) Brothers
b) Cousins
c) Father and son

15 The Shelby Cobra appeared at Le Mans in 1964 under what name?

16 The Porsche 917K was designed to win Le Mans in 1970. Did they succeed?

17 In 1972 which manufacturer was the first French one to win Le Mans since 1950?

a) Matra Simca
b) Citroen
c) Renault

18 Did Porsche have its first Le Mans win in the 1960s, 1970s or 1980s?

19 The Le Mans 24 Hour Race of 1967 saw one of the first examples of which post match celebration?

a) The press conference
b) Champagne spraying
c) On air interview with the winner

20 Who am I?

- I am Belgium's most famous driver
- I was F1 runner up in 1970 when I raced for Ferrari
- I won six Le Mans in between 1969 and 1982

21 Which Brit won his fourth Le Mans in 1986?

a) Andy Wallace
b) Derek Bell
c) Johnny Dumfries

22 It was named after another type of motor racing entirely but won Le Mans in its debut year. What was it?

23 In 1986 a Raphanel Cougar famously lost what at the Mulsanne corner?

a) A wheel

b) A leg
c) A door

24 1960 Le Mans winner Paul Frere had another career as what?
a) Vet
b) Painter
c) Journalist

25 In 1984 motor racing was divided as the dates for Le Mans clashed with the Canadian Grand Prix. True or false?

26 Name the year
- The CD audio system was launched
- The DeLorean plant in Northern Ireland was closed and John DeLorean was arrested in the US
- The Porsche Carrera GTR won its class at Le Mans

27 Only the second ever victory for a private entrant in Le Mans took place in the 1970s. True or false?

28 In which decade did Japanese cars enter the Le Mans arena?

29 In which decade did the start of the 24 Hour race move from a standing start to a rolling start?
a) 1960s
b) 1970s
c) 1980s

30 Roy Salvadari and which Scottish world drivers' champion came third at Le Mans in 1960?

31 Which was the last road car based model to win Le Mans in the 20th century?

32 Name the year
- The Renault A442 sports car won Le Mans
- Argentina won the World Cup on home soil
- Mario Andretti became world F1 racing champion

33 In 1984 Porsche earned their ninth Le Mans win equalling the tally of which rival manufacturer?
   a) Ferrari
   b) Jaguar
   c) Ford

34 Which team broke the Porsche stranglehold in 1988?

35 The 24 Hour Race usually takes place in June. Why did it take place in September in 1968?
   a) Bad weather
   b) Political unrest
   c) A drivers' strike over safety issues

36 In 1984 which manufacturer was at Le Mans for the first time in 20 years, with F1 ace John Watson behind the wheel?
   a) Jaguar
   b) Mazda
   c) Lancia

37 In 1985 Porsche took eight out of the first ten places. Who took the other two?

38 Who was the only British manufacturer to have a win during the 1960s, 1970s and 1980s?

39 Which Belgian/UK combination won Le Mans back to back in 1980/1981?

40 When Frenchman Paul Frere won Le Mans in 1970 what make of car was he driving?

a) Porsche
b) Ligier
c) Ferrari

41 Name the year

- The football World Cup was held in Britain
- The Road Safety Act was passed which led to the use of the breathalyser
- The Ford GT40 won Le Mans and also came 2nd and 3rd

42 In 1969 which Belgian driver protested about the dangers of Le Mans' famous running start by walking to his car and correctly fastening his seatbelt?

43 Which was the first Japanese make to be successful at Le Mans?

a) Toyota
b) Mazda
c) Nissan

44 How many times did Porsche win Le Mans in the 1980s?

45 What was the nickname of the Porsche 917/20 which raced back in 1971?

a) Pink Panther
a) Pink Pig
c) Pink Porsche

The Answers

1 c) Lost a door
2 1960s
3 917
4 True (It came in 15th)
5 a) France
6 GT40
7 Graham Hill
8 Porsche 956
9 b) Nimrod
10 a) Jaguar
11 Ghibli
12 917
13 1969
14 c) Father and son
15 Cobra 427
16 Yes (They won the following year as well)
17 a) Matra Simca
18 1970s (1970)
19 b) Champagne spraying
20 Jacky Ickx
21 b) Derek Bell
22 McLaren F1
23 c) A door
24 c) Journalist

25 True
26 1982
27 False (John Wyere was the very first in 1975)
28 1980s
29 b) 1970s
30 Jim Clark
31 McLaren F1
32 1978
33 a) Ferrari
34 Jaguar
35 b) Political unrest
36 a) Jaguar
37 Lancia
38 Jaguar (1988)
39 Jacky Ickx and Derek Bell
40 c) Ferrari
41 1966
42 Jacky Ickx
43 b) Mazda
44 Seven
45 b) Pink Pig

33 Moving to the Music

Pop songs are almost invariably about love. Or sex. Sex sells, and apparently makes people want to sing. But when a musician is tired of singing about love, or sex, he usually sings about cars. Perhaps because cars are sexy. Or perhaps just because musicians spend a lot of time on the road between singing and having sex. Music videos are chock full of cars too, although granted filling them with sex would be illegal.

1 *Top Gear*'s theme tune is a reworking of a tune named after which lady?

a) Jennifer
b) Jessica
c) Jezebel

2 In which song does country-pop star Taylor Swift sing about driving a new Maserati down a dead end street?

3 Which musician in the mega-selling band Queen shares his surname with a *Top Gear* presenter?

4 What type of vehicle features on the cover of Meat Loaf's album *Bat Out Of Hell*?

5 The Playmates recorded a tempo-changing novelty song about a race between a Cadillac and a Nash Rambler. What was it called?

a) 'Beep, Beep'
b) 'Honk, Honk'
c) 'Parp, Parp'

6 Whose 2003 song, American Life included the lines 'I drive my Mini Cooper, And I'm feeling super dooper'?

7 Who am I?

- My surname is Nelson
- I have been known as the Artist Formerly Known as…
- I sang about a Little Red Corvette in 1983

8 In Don McLean's 'American Pie' what did he drive to the levee but the levee was dry?

9 Which Gary had a No 1 hit with the moody synth-sound of 'Cars'?
   a) Gary Barlow
   b) Gary's Gang
   c) Gary Numan

10 Which super marque did Janis Joplin sing about?
   a) Ferrari
   b) Mercedes Benz
   c) Jaguar

11 'Drive' was fittingly a success for which Boston based band?

12 Which member of T Rex was killed in a Mini accident in 1977?

13 Name the year
- Flo Jo lit up the Seoul Olympics
- More than 150 workers were killed in an explosion at the Piper Alpha oil rig
- Billy Ocean had a major hit single with 'Get Outta My Dreams Get Into My Car'

14 Who famously matched the sound of roaring car engines to musical notes to create a unique version of the *Top Gear* theme?

15 Which New Jersey band recorded the album *Lost Highway*?

16 Which song with a motor-linked title was a hit for Rose Royce in the 1970s, 1980s and 1990s?

17 A massive digital download bestseller was 'Chasing Cars'. What is the name of the band that recorded it?

18 Grab a kaftan and think 1960s! What was the auto-linked name of the band featuring Stevie Winwood who had huge hits with 'Paper

Sun' and 'Hole In My Shoe'?

a) The Cones
b) Traffic
c) Yellow Lines

19 What was the name of C.W. McCall's novelty hit song about a group of American truckers banding together that led to a movie of the same name, made by Sam Pekinpah?

20 Who am I?

- I am a collector of classic cars
- Cars feature in my band's videos such as for 'White Knuckle Ride'
- I sing with Jamiroquai and I've been on *Top Gear* twice

21 In 1934 an electric musical instrument was deleveloped by a gentleman who shares his surname with a *Top Gear* presenter. What is the name of the instrument?

22 What type of classic car did rap star Nelly sing about in 2013?

23 'Drive My Car' appeared on which album by The Beatles?

a) *Help*
b) *Rubber Soul*
c) *With The Beatles*

24 Which early rock 'n' roller was 'Cruisin' and playing the radio, With no particular place to go'?

25 Which group famous for 'You Sexy Thing' declared in a song title that 'Heaven Is In The Back Seat Of My Cadillac'?

26 In a scheme worthy of a *Top Gear* project, Johnny Cash determined to smuggle parts out of the car factory where he

worked so he could assemble his own dream car. The song was called 'One Piece At A' what?

a) Day
b) Time
c) Shift

27 Bruce Springsteen aka the Boss has penned many songs about cars and driving. Which colour goes before Cadillac in one of his song titles?

28 Whose classic 'Driving Home For Christmas' features on his 1988 Christmas EP?

29 The man responsible for singing 'The Ballad of Davy Crockett' has a motor manufacurer as his last name. Which name follows Tennessee Ernie?

30 Returning with a No 1 album in 2013 after a break from releasing records, whose back catalogue includes 'Always Crashing In The Same Car'?

31 Which record label took its name from Detroit, Michigan, famous for building cars?

32 In the 1980s The Housemartins – featuring Norman Cook aka Fatboy Slim – had a No 1 single. The title included the name of a vehicle that is not close to Jeremy Clarkson's heart. What is the vehicle in question?

33 Which New Zealand Band shared its name with a Japanese car company?

a) The Hondas
b) The Toyotas
c) The Datsuns

34 'I've been drivin' all night, My hand's wet on the wheel,' are lyrics from which classic motoring song by Golden Earring?

35 What is the traffic-linked word that names Paul Weller's band who had No 1 hits including 'Going Underground' and 'Beat Surrender'?

36 Which band recorded the self penned song 'I'm In Love With My Car'?

37 Ric Ocasek just has to be in this section because of his band. What was it called?

38 Who were 'Road Trippin'' in 2001?
   a) Oasis
   b) Radiohead
   c) Red Hot Chilli Peppers

39 Pioneers of robot 'n' roll, Kraftwerk had which 1980s hit that honoured German motorways?

40 Which Route from Chicago to LA has been celebrated musically by Chuck Berry, Depeche Mode and others?

41 Name the year
- There is widespread fear that all computers will malfunction when the year ends
- Jeremy Clarkson leaves *Top Gear*
- A reissue of 'Born To Be Wild', Steppenwolf's biking song of the 1960s, finally reaches the UK top 20

42 Which Californian band had hits from the 1960s onwards which included 'Little Deuce Coupe' and 'Fun Fun Fun'?

43 Which hellish road is Chris Rea's 'Road to Hell' about?

44 Which high-flying band of the 1970s penned the lines 'It's a girl, my lord, In a flatbed Ford, slowing down to take a look at me'?

45 Who am I?

- I was born in India in 1940
- My 2005 hit single 'What Car' came nearly 50 years after my first hit
- My musical movie *Summer Holiday* featured a London bus

The Answers

1 b) Jessica
2 'Red'
3 Brian May
4 Motor bike
5 a) 'Beep, Beep'
6 Madonna
7 Prince
8 Chevy
9 c) Gary Numan
10 b) Mercedes Benz
11 The Cars
12 Marc Bolan
13 1988
14 James May
15 Bon Jovi
16 'Car Wash'
17 Snow Patrol
18 b) Traffic
19 'Convoy'
20 Jay Kay
21 Hammond organ
22 Porsche
23 b) *Rubber Soul*
24 Chuck Berry

25 Hot Chocolate
26 b) Time
27 Pink
28 Chris Rea
29 Ford
30 David Bowie
31 Motown
32 Caravan ('Caravan Of Love')
33 c) The Datsuns
34 'Radar Love'
35 The Jam
36 Queen
37 Cars
38 c) Red Hot Chili Peppers
39 'Autobahn'
40 Route 66
41 1999
42 The Beach Boys
43 M25
44 The Eagles
45 Cliff Richard

34 Embarrassing Crap

It's easy to forget, as we gaze through the annals of our motoring past, that for every little automotive gem carefully crafted from steel, wood and cured cow, there have been a hundred atrocities that ought to be erased from history lest we are visited by a superior alien species who find it all too appalling and kill us out of kindness. The Austin Montego could do that on its own. Burn this chapter after reading.

1 Why did its presence in the movie *Swordfish* with John Travolta and Hugh Jackman not help sales of the TVR Tuscan in the USA in 2001?

2 The Chevrolet Corvette Stingray had many unique design features. Sadly one got in the way of safer driving. What was it?
  a) A split rear screen
  b) Eye-dazzling chrome bonnet
  c) Wobbly tail fins

3 The TVR Tuscan was capable of terrifying speeds but had no airbags. True or false?

4 What was the day job of the person who invented the speed camera?
  a) Police officer
  b) Politician
  c) Rally driver

5 Which company reputedly lost money on the sale of each one of its Integra R Type Rs?
  a) Honda
  b) Toyota
  c) Nissan

6 The SsangYong was founded in the Republic of Korea in 1954. What does its name mean?
  a) Twin towns
  b) Twin dragons
  c) Twin peaks

7 Buyers of the exclusive Renault Clio Williams became irritated because of the car's success. Why?

8 What were Vauxhall Calibra Turbo 4x4 drivers advised to do if they had one flat tyre?

9 Largely due to fuel costs (again) sales of the Hummer H1 did what from 2007 to 2008?

a) Almost halved
b) Failed to increase
c) Stopped altogether

10 The Renault Twingo was available in pale/pastel shades with one notable exception. What was it?

11 Which member of the *Top Gear* team was the first to drive the Zenvo ST1?

12 In 2000 Ford recalled which model because of faulty tyres?

a) Focus
b) Explorer
c) Escort

13 Name the year

- The Austin Allegro made its debut
- A US scientist developed plastic bottles strong enough to hold fizzy drinks
- The government imposed a 50mph speed limit to save fuel

14 Owners of the GMC Typhoon were advised not to do what with it?

a) Try and float it
b) Drive it in snow and ice
c) Tow anything

15 How many exclusive Jankel Gold Label cars were built?

16 What was the principal drawback of Jeremy Clarkson's problem prone Ford GT?
a) Uncomfortable upholstery
b) Poor visibility
c) High fuel consumption

17 What happened to the last VW Beetle to be built?
a) Ridden round a race track in a blaze of glory
b) Pride of place at VW HQ
c) Stuck in a museum

18 Which 2002 VW bombed in the UK when it was launched?
a) Phaeton
b) 1 Litre
c) Corrado

19 The Jeep Hurricane could drive sideways. True or false?

20 How is the Honda Puyo a breeze for night driving?
a) Its chassis is luminous
b) All its fairy lights light up
c) It has a hi viz exterior

21 In 2010 Toyota recalled 8 million vehicles, mainly due to faulty what?
a) Accelerator pedals
b) Windscreen wipers
c) Handbrakes

22 Where did the much maligned Lada hail from?

23 How long was the AC 3000ME on the drawing board and the test track before it was in production?
a) 1 year

b) 3 years
c) 7 years

24 What joy did the Skoda Joyster produce when you folded out the fold out boot?
  a) A bed
  b) A cocktail bar
  c) Two picnic seats

25 In 1980 which Aston Martin stopped production before it had really started due to financial meltdown?

26 Name the year
- VW bought out Czech company Skoda
- The *Star Wars* follow up *The Phantom Menace* opened in cinemas
- Fatboy Slim had a No1 with 'Praise You'

27 The Mazda RX7 often ran just 20mpg. True or false?

28 The enclosure of the wheels on the Ferrari 512 S Modulo meant you couldn't do what to them?

29 Timing was a problem for the De Tomaso Longchamp. Was it the timing of its engine or the time it was produced?

30 Which perennial problem for car owners (especially those in the UK) was a mega problem for the Alfa Romeo Alfasud?
  a) Traffic warden
  b) Speed limit
  c) Rust

31 Which example of the Mini range was wholly out of place on home soil as it had no roof, no doors and no four wheel drive?

32 Which was the final De Tomaso model, production coming to a halt shortly before the death of the company's founder?

33 The Trabant 601 was East Germany's answer to which rival from the other side of the Iron Curtain?

34 The TVR 3000S did not sell as well as they'd hoped in the US so many were shipped back to base in the UK. Where was this base?
   a) Birmingham
   b) Brands Hatch
   c) Blackpool

35 Who made the 'mobile terrace' a vehicle to transport six people to their destination with a table coming up through the floor and swivel chairs all on board?

36 In 1991 Suzuki started building cars where – a country not famous at the time for car manufacture?
   a) Cambodia
   b) South Korea
   c) Vietnam

37 In 1927 Bugatti made only six of the vastly luxurious Type 41 Royales. With the arrival of the Depression how many did they sell?
   a) One
   b) Three
   c) All six

38 In the 1970s the Lancia Beta was withdrawn from sale to rectify a problem with which part of the car?
   a) Transmission
   b) Brakes

c) Air conditioning

39 What was the problem with the Citroen C3 Pluriel if you wanted to convert it into a pick-up?

40 The futuristic pod-like Nissan Pivo 2 can go in any direction, forwards, backwards and sideways. True or false?

41 Name the year
- Austin launched the Princess, not one of its most successful models
- British Leyland the last major British motor company passed into government ownership
- A colour TV licence was increased in price from £6 to £18 and a black and white one from £1 to £7

42 Which type of doors on the DeLorean DMSC-12 only added to its problems?

43 Which of these names is NOT one of the Tang Hua range of cars?
   a) Detroit Fish
   b) Purple Cloud
   c) Book of Songs

44 In 1999 Ford UK's highly limited performance model reputedly lost the firm money on every car. What was it called?
   a) The Racing Jaguar
   b) The Racing Cheetah
   c) The Racing Puma

45 Why could the TVR Speed 12 not enter Le Mans as had originally been intended?

The Answers

1 It wasn't for sale in the US at the time
2 a) A split rear screen
3 True
4 c) Rally driver
5 a) Honda
6 b) Twin dragons
7 They were so successful over 12,000 were built – no longer exclusive!
8 Change all four – costly!
9 a) Almost halved
10 White!
11 The Stig
12 b) Explorer
13 1973
14 c) Tow anything
15 Two (They were that exclusive!)
16 c) High fuel consumption
17 c) Stuck in museum
18 a) Phaeton
19 True
20 a) Its chassis is luminous
21 a) Accelerator pedals
22 USSR
23 c) 7 years

24 c) Two picnic seats (Joy indeed!)
25 Bulldog
26 1999
27 Expensively true
28 Steer!
29 The time it was produced (Oil prices rocketed and the Longchamp was costly on fuel)
30 c) Rust
31 Mini Moke
32 Guara
33 VW Beetle
34 c) Blackpool
35 Suzuki
36 b) South Korea
37 b) Three
38 b) Brakes
39 Doing this obscured the rear number plate making it road illegal
40 True
41 1975
42 Gullwing doors
43 b) Purple Cloud
44 c) The Racing Puma
45 Rule changes at Le Mans

35 The Silver Screen

Unlike its smaller, domestic counterpart, the cinema tends not to lend iconic status to terrible cars because of budget limitations. On the silver screen, where money oozes from every pore like sweat in a Turkish steam bath, great cars are everywhere, just made a little greater courtesy of a befitting star at the helm. The cinema is second only to the racetrack for showing off cars in their myriad magnificence, glittering in perfect foreign sun, resplendent on exotic locations. Obviously none of this applies to the Herbie franchise.

1 In *The Italian Job* the traffic jam to end all traffic jams was staged in which city?
   a) Rome
   b) Naples
   c) Turin

2 One of the most famous car chases sees driver Frank Bullitt screech around the streets of which city?

3 In *Grease* John Travolta sang 'Greased Lightning' with a Series 61 Cadillac as his co-star. True or false?

4 Which car, synonymous with the US, does Robert de Niro drive in *The Deer Hunter*?

5 Which 1971 movie takes its title from a world famous motoring event, and starred Steve McQueen?

6 In which car do Thelma and Louise make their getaway in the movie named after the girls?

7 Who am I?
- I was born Maurice Micklewhite in the 1930s
- I could afford a Rolls Royce before I could drive
- In one of my most famous films I said the line, 'You were only supposed to blow the bloody doors off!'

8 In *Collateral*, Vincent, played by Tom Cruise, hired what kind of driver to deliver him to the scene of five planned murders? Was it a truck driver or a cab driver?

9 David Lynch's 1999 road movie *The Straight Story* sees its hero Alvin crossing America to see his sick brother, driving what?

a) A Harley Davison
b) A Greyhound bus
c) John Deere lawn tractor

10 In which 1980s movie did Bill Murray star with Ecto-1, a Cadillac Miller-Meteor?

11 What type of car did Tom Cruise use to drive his autistic brother Raymond to Las Vegas in *Rain Man*?

12 In the 1968 movie *Bullitt* what did Steve McQueen famously drive?

13 *The Blues Brothers* with Dan Aykroyd, John Belushi and a Dodge Monaco had so many stunts and chases it ran up a bill of $33 million. True or false?

14 In the original movie *The Italian Job*, which factory loaned its space to film the 70mph leap between buildings?

15 Does Alfred Hitchcock give his heroine Tippi Hedren an Aston Martin or a Bentley in his classic movie *The Birds*?

16 In *Driving Miss Daisy*, the lady in the title crashes her Chrysler and is then driven around in what make of car by Morgan Freeman?
a) Cadillac
b) Hudson
c) Chevrolet

17 In *Four Weddings and a Funeral* which car is used by Hugh Grant and Charlotte Coleman to get to wedding No 1?

18 Which runaway vehicle is the star of the movie *Speed* with Keanu

Reeves and Sandra Bullock?

a) Plane
b) Car
c) Bus

19 In which 2008 movie does spy Maxwell Smart take the wheel of a Tiger Sunbeam with spectacular results?

a) *Get Carter*
b) *Get Smart*
c) *Getaway*

20 Who were we?

- We were a gangster duo in a 1967 movie
- We attempted to make our escape in a Ford V8
- We were so impressed with our car we wrote to Mr Ford to say how much we liked it!

21 Which car does Richard Gere borrow from his lawyer at the beginning of *Pretty Woman*?

22 In 2013 which make of car, driven by Steve McQueen in a 1971 movie about a 24 Hour race fetched $1.25 million at auction?

23 The 2004 movie *The Motorcycle Diaries* tells a tale of a journey across which region?

a) Latin America
b) Antarctica
c) Europe

24 The publicity poster for *Carry on Cabby* advertised which new Ford?

a) The Cortina
b) The Capri
c) The Popular

25 In 2013 the Batmobile sold for $4.2 million. True or false?

26 In the crime thriller *Ronin*, Robert de Niro chases Jonathan Pryce on which road?
a) Col de Turini
b) Peripherique de Paris
c) Stelvio Pass

27 What make of car owned by character Devereaux is used to import the drugs to the US in the classic 1970s movie *The French Connection*?

28 What is *The Fast Lady* in the title of the 1960s film? Is it a Bentley 3 litre or the name of a bend on the Brooklands circuit?

29 *Gone in 60 Seconds* starring Nicolas Cage is about what?
a) A retired racing driver
b) A retired car salesman
c) A retired car thief

30 In the movie *The Artist* which car driven by Berenice Bejo hits a tree in one of the final scenes of the movie?

31 In *The French Connection* what vehicle does Gene Hackman requisition to chase a train?

32 What colour is the taxi on the posters for the Robert De Niro movie *Taxi Driver*?
a) Yellow
b) Black
c) White

33 What links the car in *Chitty Chitty Bang Bang* with Bond cars?

34 What was the Swedish car of choice picked by Robert Redford playing the role of Watergate scandal discoverer Bob Woodward in *All the President's Men*?

35 In the 1970s movie *Gone in 60 Seconds*, a Ford Mustang was the first of this model to get a movie credit. What was she called?

a) Evie
b) Eleanor
c) Ethel

36 Why was it that most of the cars in *Bullitt* were Fords?

37 Which make of Sunbeam vanishes in the waters of the Tyne in the 1971 Michael Caine movie *Get Carter*?

38 What make of Austin was The Beatles' getaway car in *A Hard Day's Night*? Was it an Austin Princess or an Austin Cambridge?

39 Which vehicle appeared on the movie posters of the 1980s blockbuster *E.T.*? A spaceship or a bicycle?

40 F1 driver Graham Hill appeared in the movie *Grand Prix* as himself. True or false?

41 Name the year

- The Live Aid concert took place
- A gallon of petrol cost £1.88
- The gullwinged DeLorean DMC-12 was used in *Back to the Future* starring Michael J Fox

42 What colour was Mr Bean's Mini, apart from its black bonnet?

43 In the movie *Mona Lisa*, does petty criminal George chauffeur Simone around London in a Jaguar or a Rolls Royce?

44 What colour is the Deuce Coupe in the 1973 movie *American Graffiti*?

45 In *The Cannonball Run* is the race coast to coast or peak to peak?

The Answers

1 c) Turin
2 San Francisco
3 False (It was a DeLuxe Ford)
4 Cadillac
5 *Le Mans*
6 1964 Ford Thunderbird
7 Michael Caine
8 A cab driver
9 c) John Deere lawn tractor
10 *Ghostbusters*
11 Buick Roadmaster convertible
12 Ford Mustang Fastback
13 True
14 Fiat
15 Aston Martin
16 b) Hudson
17 Mini
18 c) Bus
19 b) *Get Smart*
20 Bonnie and Clyde
21 Lotus Esprit
22 Porsche 911S
23 a) Latin America
24 a) The Cortina

25 True!
26 b) Peripherique de Paris
27 Lincoln
28 Bentley 3 litre
29 c) A retired car thief
30 1935 Cadillac
31 Pontiac Le Mans
32 a) Yellow
33 Ian Fleming created *Chitty Chitty Bang Bang* and James Bond, 007
34 Volvo Amazon
35 b) Eleanor
36 The studio had a deal with the Ford Motor Company
37 Alpine
38 Austin Princess
39 Bicycle
40 False (He was in the film but he played the role of Bob Turner)
41 1985
42 Lime green
43 Jaguar
44 Yellow
45 Coast to coast

36 The Supercar Part 2

After a tentative first decade the supercar industry found its feet. In the vein of the Emperor's new clothes, somehow the manufacturers of these lethal, impractical, ruinously expensive and woefully unreliable luxury goods managed to convince right-thinking businessmen and film stars around the world that the definitive indication of their success was a car that started three times in ten and could only be parallel parked by a team of physicists. And they were right.

1 Which Ferrari was the great man's final flourish in the late 1980s?

2 Which two versions of the Porsche 911 2.7 Carrera went on sale in 1973?

3 The Alpine GTA was sold in the UK by which company – the parent of Alpine at the time?

4 The Alfa Romeo SZ was available in only one colour. What was it?

5 Which Aston Martin, the company's only supercar, displayed its British credentials in its name?
   a) The Lion
   b) The Bulldog
   c) The Britannia

6 How many rear seats did the Porsche 964RS have?

7 The Toyota MR2 was rebranded the MR in France as otherwise it sounded like a swear word. True or false?

8 Why did the Ferrari 288 GTO fail to win the Group B GT series it was designed for?

9 The Lotus Esprit was made chiefly of what?
   a) Plastic
   b) Aluminium
   c) Carbon fibre

10 Which BMW was the first with its engine behind the driver?

11 Ferrari replaced all the glass in the F40 with plastic to make it

lighter. True or false?

12 The De Tomaso Pantera was sold in North America through which dealerships?
   a) Chrysler
   b) Chevrolet
   c) Ford

13 Name the year
- The first London Marathon was held
- Motorcycle ace Mike Hailwood died
- Maserati introduced its BiTurbo

14 The striking Dodge Challenger R/T of 1970 had what capacity engine?
   a) 4,500cc
   b) 5,800cc
   c) 7,200cc

15 What is the Maserati Bora named after?

16 Which Maserati did the *Top Gear* team buy for £7,000 for their Italian Supercar Challenge, although it did not live up to the challenge during the show?

17 Which Porsche 911 took its name from a Sicilian race that stopped in the mid 1970s for safety reasons?

18 The Lancia Beta Monte Carlo had a much greater sting in its name in the USA. What was it called?
   a) Mosquito
   b) Scorpion
   c) Hornet

19 The badge on the De Tomaso Pantera, meaning 'panther', included a big cat ready to pounce. True or false?

20 When it was built in 1988 which Ferrari was the fastest and most expensive ever built?

21 Which British kit car was designed to be a match for the Miura and the Ford GT40?

22 The Maserati Khamsin took its name from a fierce wind in which terrain?
a) Mountains
b) Frozen tundra
c) Desert

23 Which Lamborghini was voted No 1 by *Top Gear Magazine* in its 100 Sexiest Supercars of All Time list?
a) Countach
b) Reventon
c) Espada

24 Which Lotus was originally to have been called the Kiwi?

25 Testarossa's is Italian for testosterone. True or false?

26 How many Aston Martin V8 Zagato's were built?
a) 52
b) 72
c) 102

27 Which Aston Martin was the world's first production car to have a digital instrument panel?

28 Which rally car with a supercar's transmission and engine was nicknamed the plastic dart?

29 Who sponsored Porsche when they had Le Mans victories in 1976 and 1977?

30 Was the engine of the Maserati Bora in front of or behind the driver?

31 Which Ferrari was the first road car able to top over 180mph?

32 The Vega in the name of the Chevrolet Cosworth Vega relates to what?

a) A bright star
b) A mis-spelling of Vegas
c) A fast moving rocket

33 What was the nickname of the Porsche 928?

a) Land crab
b) Land shark
c) Land wind

34 The Aston Martin Bulldog had five headlights. True or false?

35 Who created the Road Runner Superbird with a design of the cartoon character on its chassis?

36 What was the Ferrari Mondial Coupe named after?

a) Another car
b) A trophy
c) A race

37 What did the TVR Tasmin become better known as?

38 The Lamborghini Uracco had a top speed of 150mph. What does 'uracco' mean?
   a) Little bull
   b) Little swift
   c) Little shark

39 Which was the first supercar built by Maserati after Citroen took over the company?

40 The Porsche 959 was sold in 1986 for half what it cost to produce. True or false?

41 Name the year
- Clive Sinclair said petrol engines would be a thing of the past when he unveiled his C5
- Boris Becker won Wimbledon aged 17
- The BMW M3 was launched at the Frankfurt Motor Show

42 Which Ferrari had its distinctive slatted sides? Was it the Testarossa or the 288 GTO?

43 Who was tasked with building BMW's mid engine M1 supercar?
   a) VW
   b) Porsche
   c) Lamborghini

44 Which De Tomaso model was the last project of the company's founder? Was it the Pantera or the Guara?

45 The Renault Alpine was so called because it was made in a factory in the French Alps. True or false?

The Answers

1 F40
2 Tourer and Sport
3 Renault
4 (Alta) red
5 b) The Bulldog
6 None (It had no stereo either!)
7 True
8 The Group B GT series never got off the ground
9 a) Plastic
10 M1
11 True
12 c) Ford
13 1981
14 c) 7,200cc
15 Wind
16 Merak
17 Targa (from Targa Florio)
18 b) Scorpion
19 False (It was the branding mark of De Tomaso's cattle ranch)
20 F40
21 ADD Nova
22 c) Desert

23 a) Countach
24 Esprit
25 False (It means redhead)
26 a) 52
27 Lagonda
28 Lancia Stratos
29 Martini
30 Behind
31 288GTO
32 a) A bright star
33 b) Land shark
34 True
35 Plymouth
36 c) A race
37 350i
38 a) Little bull
39 Bora
40 True
41 1985
42 The Testarossa
43 c) Lamborghini
44 Guara
45 False (It was made in Dieppe)

➲

37 Top Gear *Telly 2: Bigger, Fatter, Older*

Top Gear in its current format is on series 20, so it'd be churlish not to have another chapter of pointless trivia about three fatheads and the daft excuse for a programme they have the audacity to refer to as a job. If you know the answer to even half of these you've been watching Dave too much and are probably getting a bit tubby. Go outside and have a kick about.

1 Which Band of Brothers recorded the song that became the *Top Gear* theme tune?

   a) The Blues Brothers
   b) The Allman Brothers
   c) The Righteous Brothers

2 In the Arctic race what was a Twin Otter? Was it a plane, a dog sled or a gigantic hotwater bottle?

3 At which circuit was the game of car football played?

   a) Ayr
   b) Bruntingthorpe
   c) Silverstone

4 Who was quoted in the *Guardian* as saying, 'I have sat in a car driving in the hills of St Tropez and I've thought, "Another day in the office"'?

5 Who won the biathlon in the *Top Gear* Winter Olympics?

6 In the closing credits of which road trip did the team assume the names Cletus Clarkson, Earl Hammond Jnr, Ellie May May and Rosco P Stig?

7 Who am I?

- I was the then youngest F1 champion when I won the F1 world championship in 2008
- I signed up for Mercedes for the 2013 season
- In 2013 I made a bid to be the fastest Star in a Reasonably Priced Car for the second time

8 When reviewing the Ford Fiesta what object did Jeremy use to demonstrate the space in the boot?

9 Which vehicle made it to France in the 'invention of the amphibious car' exploit?
   a) Toyota Hilux
   b) Volkswagen camper van
   c) Triumph Herald convertible

10 Who won the Arctic race? James and Jeremy in a truck or Richard on a dog sled?

11 A Lacetti that had given faithful service on the *Top Gear* track was crushed and laid to rest at which place in England with a rather grim sounding and perhaps apt name?

12 Which Richard Hammond book was the No 1 non-fiction bestseller of 2007?

13 Name the year
- Traces of horsemeat were found in some ready meals on sale in the UK
- Kimi Raikkonen won the opening F1 race of the season
- James May won the race to find the source of the river Nile

14 How many caravans were destroyed when Richard and James played a game of conkers using these much maligned vehicles?

15 When the Ferrari Enzo took on the Porsche 911GT2 on the *Top Gear* track, who came out the winner?

16 When the team became intrepid explorers and carried out their heroic polar trek, whose first name was used to replace all theirs during the closing credits?

17 Which waterway did the team have to negotiate in the Amphibious Car Challenge?

a) Lake Coniston
b) The Solway Firth
c) The English Channel

18 During the polar trek, what were skidoos?
a) Padded suits
b) Snowmobiles
c) Weapons to stun and immobilise polar bears

19 Which of the intrepid presenters said, 'Oh, this is torture, I will not be beaten by a washing machine'?

20 In May 2013 who did *Top Gear* approach to build a 130mph lawn mower?
a) Honda
b) Black & Decker
c) Qualcast

21 In their 2013 Africa epic the team chose a BMW, a Subaru and which other vehicle?

22 *Top Gear*'s top sports car of 2003 was made by whom: Ferrari, Aston Martin or Vauxhall?

23 Who yelled, 'I have never driven anything that accelerates so fast' when he drove the Ariel Atom 500 on *Top Gear*?

24 The drummer with which band lent his beloved Ferrari to *Top Gear* if they agreed to plug his book?

25 In the Winter Olympics the car and the bobsleigh raced down the same track. True or false?

26 Name the year

- Abba were No 1 with 'The Name of the Game' on 14 November, the 25th anniversary of the singles charts in Britain
- Queen Elizabeth II celebrated her Silver Jubilee
- *Top Gear* began as a regional TV programme

27 Which celebrity chef was the first to go on the new *Top Gear*? Was it Jamie Oliver, Gordon Ramsay or Gary Rhodes?

28 Which of the presenters said, 'What's the point of insuring an American's head? There's nothing in it!'?

29 In the Speed Skating section of the *Top Gear* Olympics what make of car was Jeremy driving? Was it a Jaguar, a Land Rover Discovery or a Mini?

30 An all-terrain skateboard triumphed over a Mitsubishi Lancer Evo Group N rally car in a downhill course in which country?

31 Who modified his vehicle by adding extra flashing lights in the Making a Better Police Car Challenge?

32 When Richard tried to add a Ducati 1098 motorcycle to the Cool Wall, what did Jeremy use to remove it?

a) His teeth
b) A crossbow
c) A chainsaw

33 Who was the first guest to make a return appearance to the new *Top Gear*? Clue: You can almost drive his surname.

34 Which presenter has had a Dodge Charger, a Ford Mustang and a Dodge Challenger in his own garage?

35 On a Comic Relief special, pop group McFly were challenged to produce a song that had to feature three words. Two of them were sofa and administration – what was the third word?

36 In series 5 a trial was made to see how many bouncy castles an ice cream van could jump over. How many could it clear?

37 Who tried – and failed – to break the land speed record for a caravan by towing it behind a Mitsubishi Evo 7?

38 Which car won the *Top Gear* Winter Olympics? Was it the Audi or the Volvo?

39 Which presenter was quoted as saying, 'There's a bit of Italian in my family and I do have a short fuse'?

40 What was the name given to the car that Jeremy and Richard designed for the elderly?

41 Which unfortunate sportsman had his garden restyled by the *Top Ground Gear Force* special for Sports Relief?
   a) Sebastian Coe
   b) Steve Cram
   c) Steve Redgrave

42 Which of the following was not a *Top Gear* charity special?
   a) *Top Gear of the Pops*
   b) *Top Ground Gear Force*
   c) *Top Gear Flog It!*

43 One of the presenters said, 'It's no wonder Michael Schumacher retired, he's slower than me.' Was it Jeremy, Richard or James?

44 Who drove a Ford GT round the *Top Gear* test track until it ran out of petrol?

45 Who am I?

- I am an actress who was born in California
- I provided the voice of Princess Fiona in the *Shrek* movies
- On the *Top Gear* track I recorded 1:45.2 in a Reasonably Priced Car

The Answers

1 b) The Allman Brothers
2 Plane
3 a) Bruntingthorpe
4 Richard
5 James
6 American road trip
7 Lewis Hamilton
8 A zebra's head (It was a prop!)
9 a) Toyota Hilux
10 James and Jeremy in a truck
11 Gravesend
12 *On the Edge*
13 2013
14 Six
15 Ferrari Enzo
16 Sir Ranulph (after the explorer Sir Ranulph Fiennes)
17 c) The English Channel
18 b) Snowmobiles
19 Jeremy
20 a) Honda
21 Volvo
22 Vauxhall (It was a VX220 Turbo)
23 Jeremy Clarkson
24 Nick Mason from Pink Floyd

25 False (The car drove down a road which finished at the same point as the bobsleigh run)
26 1977
27 Gordon Ramsay
28 Richard
29 Jaguar
30 Wales
31 Richard
32 c) A chainsaw
33 Jimmy Carr
34 Richard
35 Hyundai
36 None
37 James
38 The Audi
39 Richard
40 The James
41 c) Steve Redgrave
42 c) *Top Gear Flog It!*
43 James
44 Jeremy
45 Cameron Diaz

➜

38 The Micro Car and Other Nonsense

At some point in the latter half of the 20th century people began to realise that if we kept breeding and passing our driving tests at the current rate the world would quickly become one massive traffic jam, with nothing to do but listen to Ken Bruce until you died in your sleep against the steering wheel. So the micro car was invented. It hasn't solved the problem, but has enabled a few smug people to park in really, really small spaces in city centres.

1 How long was the original Mini?
   a) 72 inches
   b) 108 inches
   c) 120 inches

2 What kind of cars were Heinkels? Beetles or Bubble Cars?

3 In the 1958 Scootacar, driver and passenger sat astride what?
   a) The gear lever
   b) The engine
   c) The boot

4 What colour was the original Bond Bug, unveiled in 1970?

5 The Fiat 500, just three metres long, could seat how many adults?
   a) Two
   b) Three
   c) Four

6 On which island was the Peel P50 first made in 1963?

7 Who am I?
   - I played Charlene in *Neighbours* opposite Jason Donovan
   - My songs include 'Can't Get You Out of My Head'
   - I launched the Ford StreetKa

8 How many seats did the Peel P50 have?

9 Which Japanese company produced the first micro sports coupe?
   a) Toyota
   b) Datsun
   c) Honda

10 Where was the engine of the Fiat 126?

11 What was the engine capacity of the mighty midget the Suzuki Cappuccino?
   a) 550cc
   b) 657cc
   c) 755cc

12 What was the Riley version of the Mini called?
   a) The Elf
   b) The Fairy
   c) The Goblin

13 Name the year
- *Top Gear* Star in a Reasonably Priced Car Simon Cowell was born
- The Morris Mini Minor went on sale for £500
- Three point seat belts were developed by Volvo

14 The Reliant Robin could originally be driven with just a motorcycle licence. True or false?

15 Who designed the Morris Minor? Clue: He's also very famous for designing the Mini.

16 Why did the Bond Minicar of 1948 have a cheaper tax bill than some of its contemporaries?

17 In the name of the diminutive Alfa MiTo, what does MiTo signify?

18 Which tiny Fiat was nicknamed the Bambino due to its small size?

19 The BMW Isetta did not have a reverse gear. True or false?

20 What made driving the Fiat Topolino embarrassing for macho Italian men?

21 The plastic body of the Bond Bug had a boot lid made from what?

22 What was Mary Quant talking about when she said 'neither is longer than is necessary'?

23 The Citroen 2CV launched a special Cocorico version in 1986 to support their national side in what?

24 What was the name of the 1950s Morris Minor which had a fold down rear seat for extra space and a distinctive wooden trim?

25 In the Messerschmitt KR200 Kabinenroller you had to stop the car to go into reverse. True or false?

26 In 2005 Jeremy Clarkson managed to drive the Peel 50 into a lift but which BBC news presenter had to push him out again?
- a) Sian Williams
- b) Sophie Raworth
- c) Fiona Bruce

27 In which part of the UK was the Hillman Imp built?

28 Which UK manufacturer ceased production of its micro car in 1998?
- a) Reliant
- b) ACCars
- c) Berkeley

29 What was the first British car to sell over a million?

30 Where was the Goggomobil TS-250 built?

31 Vespa created extra space in the 400 by having rolldown plastic windows. True or false?

32 About which Mini did Dame Edna Everage on a visit to Stratford on Avon comment, 'even the cars here are half timbered'?

33 What did the K stand for in the Australian Mini K?
a) Koala
b) Kookaburra
c) Kangaroo

34 How did you get into a Messerschmitt 500?
a) Through the roof
b) From the back
c) From the front

35 How many wheels did Bond Minicars have?

36 What did the first m.Go cars run on?
a) Diesel
b) Unleaded petrol
c) Electricity

37 The 360 was the first car Subaru built. What did the 360 refer to?
a) Engine size
b) The number which first rolled off the assembly line
c) The price

38 The TV and internet Ad about the 'tall girl' was marketing which micro car?

39 What was the upmarket Wolseley Mini called?

a) Wasp
b) Mosquito
c) Hornet

40 The Fiat 126 was built exclusively in Italy. True or false?

41 The short lived Vignale Gamine had a wheel base of just what?
a) 48 inches
b) 72 inches
c) 84 inches

42 How many doors did the Peel P50 have?

43 The Corbin Sparrow only had a single seat. True or false?

44 Which Mini was free from purchase tax when it was first launched on the grounds that it could be used for business?

45 The TWIKE micro car is pedal assisted. True or false?

The Answers

1 c) 120 inches
2 Bubble Cars
3 b) The engine
4 Orange
5 c) Four
6 The Isle of Man
7 Kylie Minogue
8 One
9 c) Honda
10 Boot
11 b) 657cc
12 a) The Elf
13 1959
14 True
15 Alec Issigonis
16 It only had three wheels
17 Mi for Milan and To for Torino (Turin)
18 500
19 True
20 At home its name meant Mickey Mouse
21 Plywood
22 The Mini and a mini skirt
23 Football World Cup
24 Traveller

25 True
26 c) Fiona Bruce
27 Scotland
28 a) Reliant
29 Morris Minor
30 Germany
31 False (The windows were fixed but it had a roll back roof)
32 Mini Traveller
33 c) Kangaroo
34 a) Through the roof
35 Three
36 b) Unleaded petrol
37 a) Engine size
38 VW Up!
39 c) Hornet
40 False (It was built in Poland until 2000)
41 b) 72 inches
42 One
43 True
44 Mini van
45 True

39 007

No quiz book is complete without a chapter on James Bond. Even a quiz book about 17th-century European marquetry needs some reference to the world's favourite bed-hopping secret agent. Happily a quiz book about cars can readily accommodate a man who spends quite a lot of his waking life at high speed behind the wheel of a subtly fettled Aston Martin. Get any of these wrong and you have an excuse to watch all the films again in the name of research.

1 Out of the first 23 Bond films (*Dr No* to *Skyfall*), how many have included Aston Martins?

a) 8
b) 11
c) 16

2 In *Moonraker*, a Bond vehicle becomes a speedboat then a hovercraft. What did it start out as?

3 In which Bond movie that starred Pierce Brosnan as 007 was there an invisible car?

4 In *For Your Eyes Only* which car took 007 and Melina Havelock to safety?

a) A Peugeot 206
b) A Citroen 2CV
c) A Mini Cooper

5 The 19th Bond movie *The World Is Not Enough* opens with a chase in what vehicle?

a) Plane
b) Car
c) Boat

6 Which type of deathly vehicle concealed the Three Blind Mice as they lay in wait for 007 in *Dr No*?

7 In *Goldeneye*, 007's Aston Martin is overtaken by ex-Soviet fighter pilot Xenia Onatopp driving which make of superfast car?

8 In which Bond movies does the V12 Aston Martin DBS appear?

9 In *Octopussy*, how did Bianca transport the minijet Acrostar without attracting attention?

10 What saved Bond's life when his Rolls Royce Silver Cloud was submerged in a lake?

11 In *Tomorrow Never Dies*, Q presents Bond with a beautiful new car in Hamburg, which has all manner of gadgets and modification, including remote control. What make is it?

12 In *Quantum of Solace*, which cars ambush 007 as he drives Mr White to a safe house in the boot of his Aston Martin DBS?

13 Name the year

- The Beatles had a hit with 'A Hard Day's Night'
- The plasma screen was invented
- Bond's Aston Martin DB5, his favourite and the archetypal Bond car, was registered

14 In *Tomorrow Never Dies*, 007 and Wai Lin escape Elliot Carver's Saigon HQ handcuffed together driving what?

15 In *Dr No* which group of people drive black Mk 2 consuls?

a) Police
b) Taxi drivers
c) Villains

16 Which is the only Bond film where his Bentley appears?

17 In *Casino Royale*, with Daniel Craig as 007, how did Bond slow down the tanker he was driving, a tanker which was in fact a mobile bomb?

18 Which vintage 1937 gold car does Goldfinger own in the film of the same name?

a) Bentley
b) Rolls Royce
c) Jaguar

19 The DB5 in *Goldfinger* was the most popular model made by Corgi toys. True or false?

20 Q unveiled Bond's new car in *Die Another Day* in MI6's top secret base located where?

21 Which make of car was dangled from a helicopter in *You Only Live Twice*? Clue: The action takes place in Japan.

22 In *Live and Let Die*, which very British vehicle did Bond and Solitaire use to make their escape to the coast?

a) A Mini
b) A Rolls Royce
c) A Routemaster bus

23 In *Thunderball*, raising the Aston Martin's bullet proof shield revealed what?

a) Water jets
b) Front firing rockets
c) Nail guns

24 In *Casino Royale*, which Caribbean island's name appears on the Aston Martin number plate?

25 In *You Only Live Twice*, the 2000GT Spider used in the movie was specially built as Sean Connery was too tall for the coupe. True or false?

26 Name the year

- British Leyland launched the Morris Marina range and Rolls Royce went bankrupt
- Rod Stewart and T Rex had No 1 hits with 'Maggie May' and 'Get It On' respectively
- The Bond car did its famous two wheel stunt in *Diamonds Are Forever*

27 In *Thunderball* what did assassin Fiona Volpe ride?

28 In *Goldfinger*, 007 asks Q where his car is. It's not the famous DB5 this time. What is it?

29 To what was 007 referring when he said, 'Q's not going to like this!' in *The World Is Not Enough*?

a) Helicopter blades had torn his BMW Z8 in half
b) He commandeered Q's prototype speedboat
c) His BMW Z8's remote control refused to work

30 When Bond drove the Lotus Esprit into the sea in *The Spy Who Loved Me*, what happened next?

31 Which model Bentley did Bond drive prior to *Goldfinger*?

32 In *Die Another Day*, Bond's Aston Martin V12 Vanquish accelerated from 0 to 62 in how many seconds?

a) 4.4
b) 6.8
c) 7.9

33 Bond drives a Sunbeam in the movie of *Dr No* replacing which vehicle that appeared in the original novel?

34 Where did Bond take a tuk tuk taxi ride after he outswindled

Kamal Khan in *Octopussy*?

35 In *On Her Majesty's Secret Service* what kind of race did Bond and Tracy Vicenzo join to escape form Blofeld's henchmen?

a) A bicycle race
b) A stock car race
c) A motorcycle race

36 In which Bond movie did M incredulously say, 'A car that sprouted wings, and Miss Goodnight was in the boot!'? Was it *The Man With The Golden Gun* or *The Spy Who Loved Me*?

37 In *A View to a Kill* which make of taxi did Bond hijack to chase a mysterious parachutist who had leapt from the Eiffel Tower?

38 Which modifications did Bond's Aston Martin NOT have in *Goldfinger*?

a) Dashboard moving map display
b) Thermal imaging system
c) Passenger ejector seat

39 Which car did Bond steal from a showroom in *The Man With The Golden Gun*, a car which was later used to leap across a collapsed bridge?

40 In *Diamonds Are Forever*, what was 007's first escape vehicle from WW Tectronics?

a) An autogyro
b) A moonbuggy
c) A Harley Davison

41 In *The Living Daylights*, Bond tells Q, 'just taking the Aston Martin out for a spin'. Q replies, 'Be careful 007 it's just had a new' what?

a) Set of tyres

b) Ejector seat
c) Coat of paint

42 In *Skyfall* what is M's company car?

43 In *Diamonds Are Forever,* in which vehicle, borrowed from Tiffany Case, did Bond outwit and outchase the Las Vegas Police Dept?

44 In *You Only Live Twice*, where was the gunmen's car dropped when the Japanese Secret Service switched off the magnet which was holding it in place?

45 How many movies have included the Aston Martin DB5 before *Skyfall*?

The Answers

1 b) 11
2 Gondola
3 *Die Another Day*
4 b) A Citroen 2CV
5 c) Boat
6 Hearse
7 Ferrari (Spider 355 GTS)
8 *Casino Royale* and *Quantum of Solace*
9 In a horsebox (There were horse trials taking place nearby)
10 Air in one of its tyres
11 BMW 750iL
12 Alfa Romeo 159s
13 1964
14 BMW R1200 bike
15 a) Police
16 *From Russia With Love*
17 Drove it into a line of police cars
18 b) Rolls Royce (Phantom III)
19 True
20 Disused London Underground station
21 Toyota (Crown S40)
22 c) A Routemaster bus
23 a) Water jets

24 Bahamas
25 True
26 1971
27 BSA A65L Lightning
28 Bentley
29 a) Helicopter blades had torn his BMW Z8 in half
30 It turned into a mini submarine
31 Mk IV
32 a) 4.4 seconds
33 Hillman Minx
34 Delhi
35 b) A stock car race
36 *The Man With The Golden Gun*
37 Renault
38 b) Thermal imaging system
39 AMC Hornet X (in red!)
40 b) A moonbuggy
41 c) Coat of paint
42 Jaguar XJL
43 Red Ford Mustang Mach 1
44 Tokyo Bay
45 Four

40 The 200mph Club

At the end of the 1980s something very silly indeed happened. It became possible to buy a road car that could pass 200mph. This was, and still is, something you are unlikely to find yourself doing on your way to get a KitKat, but it set a precedent that has remained the willy-waving high water mark for countless manufacturers who should know better. Nowadays hundreds of cars can pass 200mph and none of them ever, ever do. But it's nice to know you could.

1 Which production car was the first to pass 200mph?

2 Which Ferrari was named after the company's founder?

3 In the Lamborghini Murcielago LP640 how do the doors open?
  a) Up
  b) Out
  c) Down

4 When Volkswagen shoehorned a 6 litre, 12 cylinder engine into the Golf W12, where in the car did they manage to squeeze it?

5 How big is the engine in the Bugatti Veyron?
  a) 6 litre
  b) 7 litre
  c) 8 litre

6 The Mercedes SLS was styled on which stylish 1960s sports car?

7 Who am I?
- I have driven for Ferrari in F1
- My brother Ralf is also a famous racing name
- I played my part in the design of the Ferrari F430 Scuderia

8 The Ferrari P4/5, a mere snip at a £3 million, uses the same chassis as which other Ferrari supercar?

9 The Bugatti EB110, that reached a top speed of 212mph, charged you a top price of what in 1991?
  a) £120,000
  b) £150,000
  c) £180,000

10 The Ferrari FXX was only eligible for competition and was not allowed on normal roads. True or false?

11 What was Britain's first 200mph supercar with four wheel drive?

12 The M600, with a top speed of 225mph, is made by which manufacturer?

13 What was the top speed of the Lamborghini Murcielago?

14 The so-called baby Ferrari shares its name with which US state?

15 Where was the Saleen S7 made?

16 Which letter did Aston Martin add to the Vanquish when they turned it into a 200mph club member?

17 The very British Bristol Fighter was powered by which make of engine – a massive 8.3 litre V10?

18 The SSC Ultimate Aero, once the fastest car in the world reaching a mind-boggling 256mph, was built where?
   a) Italy
   b) Germany
   c) USA

19 The Brabus Biturbo Roadster was a powerful Italian convertible. True or false?

20 Name the year
- EuroDisney opened in Paris
- Windows 3.1 was released
- The McLaren F1 hit the supercar world with a top speed of 240mph

21 How much would a Mercedes CLK GTR have set you back when it was launched back in 1998?
a) £600,000
b) £900,000
c) £1.1 million

22 Which of the following is not a 200mph Aston Martin?
a) The Vanquish
b) The Vantage
c) The Victor

23 Which super supercar did Bugatti develop when the Veyron was superseded as fastest car in the world by the SSC Ultimate Aero?

24 Who made the Flying Spur, a 6-litre 12 cylinder super limousine?

25 Which member of the 200mph club was Ferrari's first four wheel drive? Clue: All those F's might just help you to the answer!

26 Fewer than 20 Zenvo ST1 supercars were ever made, but where?
a) Sweden
b) Finland
c) Denmark

27 The Ascari A10 will set you back around £350,000 but it doesn't have a stereo or air conditioning. True or false?

28 Which 2009 Bentley superseded the Speed, and topped 200mph into the bargain?

29 Which Porsche claimed to hit 60mph in a mere 3 seconds but having a staggering mpg of 94?
a) Panamera
b) 918 Spyder

c) 997 GT3

30 Does the 661bhp V12 Lamborghini LP670-4SV have gullwing doors or scissor doors?

31 Which Gumpert model, one time record holder round the *Top Gear* track, aptly shares its name with a US space programme?

32 What speed can the Chevrolet Corvette ZR 1 reach in first gear alone?
a) 45mph
b) 55mph
c) 65mph

33 What was the nickname of the RUF CTR, in its day the fastest car in the world?
a) Bluebird
b) Yellowbird
c) Redbird

34 The Ferrari 599 GTB will get to 100mph in less than eight seconds. True or false?

35 The Porsche 911 GT1 was designed specifically to win which race, although a few were turned into road cars?

36 What does the abbreviation mean in Chrysler's 240mph ME Four-Twelve?

37 How many Ferrari Enzos were made?
a) 250
b) 400
c) 550

38 In the US the Dodge SRT-10 has a name with a lot more venom. Is it Viper or Cobra?

39 Who owned Maserati when the MC12 was made?

40 The Koeninsegg CCX was made in Germany. True or false?

41 Name the year

- Tony Blair stood down as PM after 10 years in the job
- It was discovered that silicon had been found in unleaded petrol and had damaged thousand of cars
- The Ferrari F430 went on sale

42 In which decade did the Lamborghini Countach see the light of day? 1960s, 1970s or 1980s?

43 The Lexus LFA was made by Nissan. True or false?

44 What was the Lamborghini Reventon named after?

a) A bull
b) A horse
c) A cat

45 Who was the boss at McLaren when they embarked on the project which became the McLaren F1?

The Answers

1 Ferrari F40
2 The Enzo
3 a) Up
4 Where the back seats were meant to be
5 c) 8 litre
6 300SL Gullwing
7 Michael Schumacher
8 Enzo
9 c) £180,000
10 False (It wasn't allowed on either. Hopefully you found this out before handing over around £1.3 million)
11 Jaguar XJ220
12 Noble
13 210mph
14 California
15 USA
16 S
17 Chrysler
18 c) USA
19 False (It was made in Germany)
20 1992
21 c) £1.1 million
22 c) The Victor
23 Bugatti Veyron Supersport

24 Bentley
25 Ferrari FF
26 c) Denmark
27 True
28 Continental Supersports
29 b) 918 Spyder
30 Scissor doors
31 Apollo
32 c) 65
33 b) Yellowbird
34 Amazing but true!
35 Le Mans 24 Hour Race
36 Mid Engine Four turbo Twelve cylinder
37 b) 400
38 The Viper
39 Ferrari
40 False (It was made in Sweden)
41 2007
42 1970s
43 False (It is made by Toyota)
44 a) A bull
45 Ron Dennis

41 The Star in a Reasonably Priced Car

Ever since *Top Gear* reappeared in a sweaty shed next to an airfield the highlight of every show has been seeing which minor celebrity is sufficiently needy to pound a cut-price Korean shopping cart round a Mickey Mouse race track in a dicey trade off between total humiliation and promoting their next daytime drama/comeback album. Who do you remember? 'Nobody' will score you a point.

1 Which comedian was the first ever Star in a Reasonably Priced Car?

a) Jimmy Carr
b) Jack Dee
c) Harry Enfield

2 In series 1 where had Jeremy Clarkson cooked food for Gordon Ramsay?

3 Which manufacturer designed the track where the stars are put through their paces?

a) Jaguar
b) Lotus
c) Rolls Royce

4 Which Doctor Who drove an automatic Liana as he didn't have a manual licence?

a) David Tennant
b) Christopher Eccleston
c) Matt Smith

5 When the Suzuki Liana became the Reasonably Priced Car how much did it cost?

a) £5,999
b) £9,999
c) £15,999

6 What do the stars have to endure before watching their fastest lap?

7 Which politician, once famous for owning two Jags, was just beaten by Alice Cooper?

8 The third make of Average Car hailed from which country?

9 Who was the first Dame to appear as the Star? (And we mean a real lady not a bloke in a dress.)

10 When Harry Enfield was the Star, which car that he once owned was brought into the studio?
   a) Vauxhall Cavalier Convertible
   b) Porsche 911 GTI
   c) Toyota Hilux

11 Which F1 driver was fastest in the Liana?
   a) Rubens Barichello
   b) Mark Webber
   c) Lewis Hamilton

12 Which Irish-born knight and nominee for the Nobel Peace Prize was a star in series 17?

13 Name the year
- James Bond drove an invisible Aston
- Everton's Wayne Rooney was BBC Young Sports Personality of the Year
- The Star in a Reasonably Priced Car made its debut

14 For series eight which car replaced the Suzuki Liana?

15 The Liana suffered a dented boot and a broken suspension in the hands of which Irish presenter? Was it Patrick Kielty or Graham Norton?

16 Two of the fastest stars, F1 racing driver Rubens Barichello and comedian John Bishop averaged what speed around the track?
   a) 60mph

b) 80mph
c) 100mph

17 Who coaches the stars before they drive the cars?

18 In his interview with Gordon Ramsay who or what did Jeremy and Gordon complain about?
a) Women drivers and vegetarians
b) Caravan owners and speed limits
c) Organic gardeners and professional actors

19 When the Liana first appeared, who took a test drive around the track with Jeremy and Richard?

20 Who am I?
- I was known as a member of the Crazy Gang when I played for Wimbledon
- I starred in the movie *Lock Stock and Two Smoking Barrels*
- I was described on *Top Gear* as a decidedly scary Star in a Reasonably Priced Car

21 Time-travelling Doctor David Tennant drove faster than age-reversing Simon Cowell. True or false?

22 Who am I?
- I was born in Jamaica in 1986
- I was beaten by tennis ace Boris Becker on the *Top Gear* track
- I won Olympic golds on another track during the summer of 2012

23 Which celebrity chef took his own VW Camper on to the track?

24 The late Richard Whiteley averaged which speed on the *Top Gear* track?

a) 50mph
b) 60mph
c) 70mph

25 The acerbic Anne Robinson admitted to having which accessory in her car when she was interviewed as a star?
a) A jacuzzi
b) An espresso machine
c) A television

26 Name the year
- Fernando Alonso won the British Grand Prix
- *Life on Mars* was first screened
- The Lacetti replaced the Liana as the Reasonably Priced Car

27 Which famously be-hatted star and renowned supercar owner was only two seconds behind The Stig?

28 How long is the *Top Gear* track?
a) 2.82km
b) 3.14km
c) 5.99km

29 What did Jeremy Clarkson call the part of the leaderboard with times lower than 1:51 as there were so many actors appearing there?
a) The Thespian Zone
b) The Luvvie Zone
c) The Darling Zone

30 What happened to Jimmy Carr the second time he appeared as the Star?

31 The Chicago part of the track is named after one of The Stig's favourite bands. True or false?

32 Who was the first knight in a Reasonably Priced Car?
- a) Sir Jackie Stewart
- b) Sir Michael Gambon
- c) Sir Terry Wogan

33 Which Maserati driving supermodel was superfast in series 2 in the Suzuki Liana?
- a) Kate Moss
- b) Jodie Kidd
- c) Naomi Campbell

34 For which group of drivers was the Liana pulled out of retirement and back on to the *Top Gear* track?

35 What happened to the car when it was driven by Motown star Lionel Richie?

36 Sir Michael Gambon negotiated the bend which is now called Gambon Corner in his honour on how many wheels?

37 The *Top Gear* track is in the shape of which number? Is it 0, 8, or 9?

38 What happened to Jools Holland in his first attempt on the *Top Gear* track in the Chevrolet Lacetti? Did he spin off the track without braking or did he reverse into the vehicle driven by the camera crew?

39 Who was the Star when the car was decorated with a Starsky-and-Hutch-style flashing light and a white stripe down the side?

40 What did the team do to destroy the second Reasonably Priced Car?

41 Name the year

- Bentley launched the Mulsanne
- Volcanic ash from an Icelandic volcano disrupted travel all over Europe
- Tom Cruise lapped the *Top Gear* circuit in 1.44.2, a second faster than his then co-star Cameron Diaz

42 When Simon Cowell was first a Star in a Reasonably Priced Car he was involved with which of his famous TV talent shows?

43 Which oddly punctuated car was introduced at the start of series 15?

44 Which comedian appeared as the star with L plates as he hadn't passed his driving test?

a) Dara O Briain
b) Johnny Vegas
c) Al Murray

45 What did Jeremy point out to Usain Bolt about his victory in Beijing? Were his shoelaces undone or had he got his shoes on the wrong feet?

The Answers

1 c) Harry Enfield
2 Under the bonnet
3 b) Lotus
4 b) Christopher Eccleston
5 b) £9,999
6 An interview with Jeremy
7 John Prescott
8 South Korea
9 Dame Helen Mirren
10 a) Vauxhall Cavalier Convertible
11 a) Rubens Barichello
12 Sir Bob Geldof
13 2002
14 Chevrolet Lacetti
15 Patrick Kielty
16 a) 60mph
17 The Stig
18 a) Women drivers and vegetarians
19 Jason Dawe
20 Vinnie Jones
21 False (Mr Cowell was nearly three seconds faster than Time Lord Tennant)
22 Usain Bolt
23 Jamie Oliver

24 a) 50mph
25 c) A television
26 2006
27 Jay Kay
28 a) 2.82km
29 a) The Thespian Zone
30 He spun off the track
31 True
32 b) Sir Michael Gambon
33 b) Jodie Kidd
34 F1 drivers past and present
35 Wheel fell off
36 Two
37 8
38 He spun off the track without braking
39 David Soul
40 Crushed it under a demolished chimney
41 2010
42 Pop Idol
43 Kia Cee'd
44 b) Johnny Vegas
45 His shoelaces were undone

42 Hybrids and All That

While busily warring around the globe for the few remaining dregs of oil, the developed world has been looking into some contingency plans. Hybrids are commonplace now, and the all-electric alternative is finally available, if a bit useless. It's cutting edge stuff this though, and vital to the survival of the car as we know it. It does all seem a bit un-*Top Gear*, but if the likes of Ferrari and Porsche are getting involved then we've got nothing to worry about. Have we?

1 The first hybrid car available worldwide came from which country?
   a) Sweden
   b) Switzerland
   c) Japan

2 The Vauxhall Ampera is an electric/petrol engine hybrid which calls on both fuels when tackling hills. True or false?

3 The Mitsubishi Lancer Evo XI is a hybrid of electricity and what?
   a) Bio fuel
   b) Petrol
   c) Diesel

4 Which were the first two manufacturers to put hybrids on the market?

5 Which Mercedes launched in 2010 has hybrid options?
   a) F800
   b) 450 SEL
   c) Grosser 770K

6 Which company made the first V8/electric hybrid?
   a) Lexus
   b) Toyota
   c) Suzuki

7 The Ginetta G50 electric car has a top speed of what?
   a) 100mph
   b) 120mph
   c) 140mph

8 The Opel Flextreme will travel 37 miles on its battery before what

kicks in to start recharging it?

9 The Honda FCX Clarity has to refill at a hydrogen pump. True or false?

10 How is the Opel Ampera known under the Chevrolet marque? Clue: Think electricity.

11 The Columbia electric coach in 1899 ran on four sets of batteries numbering how many in all?
  a) 36
  b) 40
  c) 44

12 The Prius is the first hybrid from which manufacturer?

13 Name the year
- England won the Rugby World Cup for the first time ever
- The final VW Beetle was built having been in production for almost 60 years
- The Prius was first used to ferry celebs at the Oscars

14 The Peugeot BB1 has how many electric motors to power its 75 mile range?

15 The Stanley Runabout of 1901 was a true hybrid as it used wood or any combustible material to produce the steam that powered it. True or false?

16 Which manufacturer unveiled the hybrid 599HY-KERS at the Geneva Motor Show in 2010?
  a) Ferrari
  b) Porsche
  c) Jaguar

17 What was Honda's first hybrid called?

18 The Ginetta could be recharged from the car's cigarette lighter socket. True or false?

19 Toyota built how many airbags into the iQ micro car to maximise safety?

20 Which sporty VW has the surprisingly low carbon emissions of 110g/km?

21 How is the Prius powered in slow traffic?

22 In which UK county was the Tesla Roadster partly built, producing a supercar with zero emission?

23 The bulky GMC Yukon Denali runs on what?

  a) Unleaded petrol
  b) E85 ethanol
  c) A combination of the two

24 Who launched the first hybrid SUV on the market?

  a) Ford
  b) Land Rover
  c) Toyota

25 The economical Tata Nano has only one windscreen wiper and just one wing mirror. True or false?

26 Name the year

- Fraser Nash produced a concept car with rotary and electric power
- England beat Australia to win the Ashes
- Jenson Button became Britain's 10th World F1 Champion

27 The Prius Mk II had a petrol engine, an electric motor and which other feature?

28 What does ZEV stand for in vehicles such as Peugot's Hybrid4?

29 Who made the electric sports car the C5?
   a) Lexus
   b) Lancia
   c) Lamborghini

30 Which Peugeot, a close relative of the Partner, was offered as a hybrid and marketed as either a van or a passenger vehicle?

31 Which manufacturer showcased the Leon Verdi in 2013?

32 The Nissan Leaf was first manufactured in Japan and which two other countries?

33 What was the fate of the electric powered General Motors EV1, first leased to owners in 1996?

34 The Lexus RX 400h, an electric motor/V6 hybrid, was a collaboration between Japan and whom? Was it the UK or the USA?

35 In 2010 Porsche added a hybrid to its Cayenne range. True or false?

36 Which of the following does the P-NUT offer?
   a) Petrol
   b) Hybrid
   c) Electric

37 The oil level sensor in the Honda Insight checks oil level and what else?

38 Which General Motors full size hybrid was launched in 2005?

39 Which US-built hybrid was the first from a US manufacturer?

40 What could you do to the wheels in the Renault Zoom to aid parking?

a) Put them in the boot
b) Fold them forwards
c) Lock them inside the car

41 In the name of the P-NUT the letter U stands for what?

a) Utility
b) Urban
c) Unleaded

42 What is the fuel tank capacity of the innovative Tata Nano?

43 There are two types of hybrid. One is series the other is what?

44 The Ford Escape was used as a NYC taxi. True or false?

45 Which company sold its millionth hybrid in 2009?

a) Nissan
b) Toyota
c) Seat

The Answers

1 c) Japan
2 True
3 c) Diesel
4 Honda and Toyota
5 a) F800
6 a) Lexus
7 b) 120mph
8 Diesel engine
9 True
10 Chevrolet Volt
11 c) 44
12 Toyota
13 2003
14 Two
15 True
16 a) Ferrari
17 Insight
18 Definitely false (But they could be recharged from a standard domestic electricity socket)
19 Nine
20 Scirocco Blue Motion
21 Electric motor
22 Norfolk
23 c) A combination of the two

24 a) Ford
25 True
26 2009
27 The battery recharged when the car was on the move
28 Zero Emission Vehicle
29 a) Lexus
30 Berlingo
31 Seat
32 UK and USA
33 They were recalled and crushed!!
34 USA
35 True
36 It offers all three!
37 Oil condition
38 Chevrolet Tahoe
39 Ford Escape
40 b) Fold them forwards
41 b) Urban
42 4 gallons
43 Parallel
44 True
45 b) Toyota

➲

43 Jeremy – Too Much Info

How many questions you can answer in this section will vary depending on how much of your time you have spent reading tabloid newspapers. No one wants to know half as much about Jeremy Clarkson as they do, but somehow it just seems to seep in. If you learn anything you didn't want to we apologise in advance.

1 Who was quoted in the *Daily Mail* as saying, 'Remarkably, Jeremy is quite a courteous driver, even though he's very rude in every other respect'?
   a) David Cameron
   b) David Coulthard
   c) James May

2 According to Gwen Russell's biography of JC, whose picture did he have on the steering wheel of his first car, Debbie Harry or Suzi Quatro?

3 Name the year
   - The Olympic Games were held in Seoul, South Korea
   - Bruce Willis starred in the first *Die Hard* movie
   - Jeremy Clarkson first appeared on *Top Gear*

4 Jeremy Clarkson's grandfather invented a glass preserving jar with a rubber seal. True or false?

5 JC's first journalistic job was on which paper?
   a) *The Rotherham Advertiser*
   b) *The Royston Crow*
   c) *The Colne Times*

6 JC shared a flat in the same block as which future Royal?
   a) Sarah Ferguson
   b) Diana Spencer
   c) Sophie Rhys-Jones

7 What type of car did Jeremy drive into a swimming pool in series 6 of *Top Gear*?

8 Who did Jeremy Clarkson nominate as a 'Great Briton' in the TV

series of the same name?

a) Alec Issigonis
b) Winston Churchill
c) Isambard Kingdom Brunel

9 When JC put an EEL F1A jet fighter in his garden he had to have it removed despite his protestations that it was what?

a) A waste disposal unit
b) A leaf blower
c) A garden ornament

10 What was Jeremy Clarkson's luxury choice when he was a castaway on radio's *Desert Island Discs*?

a) Jet ski
b) Ferrari
c) An endless supply of champagne

11 Jeremy Clarkson is obviously well known as a respecter of authority and a stickler for political correctness. His mother was once a magistrate. Is that last statement true or false?

12 As part of his first screen test for *Top Gear* JC was asked to bring along a car of his choice to talk about. What did he bring – a Range Rover or a Ferrari?

13 Name the year

- The first Blu-ray discs went on sale
- The use of hand held cell phones while driving was made illegal in the UK
- Jeremy Clarkson was a passenger on the last ever BA Concorde flight

14 Jeremy attended the same school as *Charlie and the Chocolate Factory* author Roald Dahl. True or false?

15 When JC appeared on the comedy show *Room 101* which wheeled vehicle did he consign to oblivion?

16 When the *Top Gear* team did their race across London from West London to City Airport, what means of transport did JC use?

17 Who replaced Jeremy Clarkson when he left the series – temporarily as it turned out – at the beginning of 1999?

18 Jeremy's mother had a toy-manufacturing business. Which Bear was its first creation?
   a) Rupert
   b) Paddington
   c) Bungle

19 The book *Driven to Distraction* is a collection of articles published in which newspaper?

20 Who are we?
- We are a rock band formed in the 1960s
- Our drummer is Phil Collins
- JC wrote the sleeve notes for *Selling England by the Pound* on our box set

21 In the finale to *Top Gear*'s autumn 2009 series, which car did Jeremy describe as 'wonderful, wonderful, wonderful'?

22 JC has gone on record as saying, 'England's only true spectacular road…' is where?
   a) The Derbyshire Peaks
   b) The Yorkshire Dales
   c) The west Pennines

23 In the Race to the North Jeremy was in a Tornado. What type of

vehicle was that?

a) Jet propelled racing car
b) Motorcycle
c) Steam train

24 Who said on Chris Evans's Radio 2 show in February 2013 that he would love to appear in the Reasonably Priced Car, only for Clarkson to take to Twitter with 'Never'?

25 Jeremy's first car was an MGB GT. True or false?

26 In the race from Italy to London when JC drove a Bugatti Veyron the challenge was to deliver which items?

27 What is Jeremy's star sign?

a) Aries
b) Taurus
c) Virgo

28 Which *Top Gear* producer, who also presented some programmes, gave JC his screen test for the programme?

a) Jon Bentley
b) Tiff Needell
c) Quentin Wilson

29 On which TV programme did JC make comments about the UK public sector strike of November 2011?

30 Jeremy moved to which village in the Cotswolds?

a) Cheesewold
b) Chipping Norton
c) Much Ranting

31 Which animal – apart from Jeremy – appears on the cover of the

book *Born to Be Riled*?

32 Which county, not a Clarkson favourite, is the home of Lotus cars?

33 What did Jeremy drive a Toyota Hilux into near a Somerset church in 2004? Was it the church, a tree or the vicarage?

34 Jeremy Clarkson was hit in the face with a banana meringue when he was attending a ceremony to receive an honorary degree from which university?

a) Oxford Brookes
b) University of East Anglia
c) Birmingham

35 What make of car did JC drive round in when visiting India for the 2011 Christmas Special?

36 After an attempted makeover by Trinny and Susannah on *What Not to Wear*, JC declared that instead of appearing on the show again he would rather eat what?

a) His drumsticks
b) His own hair
c) The Hamster's socks

37 JC was a fan of the Ford Escort. True or false?

38 On which Isle were there problems involving a right of way near Clarkson's second home?

a) Isle of Man
b) Isle of Wight
c) Isle of Capri

39 According to an often quoted statement made by Jeremy, what

'has never killed anyone'?

40 Which independent school did JC attend – Lancing or Repton?

41 Name the year
- Malcolm Campbell took new £1 million car Bluebird on its first test run
- Olympic Games were held in Rome
- Jeremy Clarkson was born

42 Jeremy's book of 2011 was titled *Round the* what? Was it *Round the Bend*, *Round the Corner* or *Round the Horn*?

43 In which town in December 2007 was JC involved in an altercation with a group of youths while waiting outside a snow dome where his daughter was attending a birthday party?

44 Ben Tongue featured in an offroad challenge in series 5 involving a Land Rover Discovery that caused controversy. At the time who or what was Ben Tongue?
a) Leader of the Scottish Ramblers Association
b) A Scottish mountain
c) A Scottish MP and landowner

45 'I've got absolutely no repeatable views to express on Mr Jeremy Clarkson' was a quote attributed to which political figure following JC's remarks about Gordon Brown made in 2009?
a) David Cameron
b) Tony Blair
c) Peter Mandelson

The Answers

1 c) James May
2 Debbie Harry
3 1988
4 True
5 a) *The Rotherham Advertiser*
6 b) Diana Spencer
7 Rolls Royce
8 c) Isambard Kingdom Brunel
9 b) A leaf blower
10 a) Jet ski
11 True
12 A Range Rover
13 2003
14 True (But not at the same time!)
15 Caravan
16 Power boat up the Thames
17 James May
18 b) Paddington
19 *The Sunday Times*
20 Genesis
21 Aston Martin V12 Vantage
22 b) The Yorkshire Dales
23 c) Steam train
24 Piers Morgan
25 False (It was a Ford Cortina)
26 Truffles

27 a) Aries
28 a) Jon Bentley
29 *The One Show*
30 Chipping Norton
31 A dog
32 Norfolk
33 A tree
34 a) Oxford Brookes
35 Jaguar
36 b) His own hair
37 True (It was the Cosworth with four wheel drive, a turbo Cosworth engine and a top speed in excess of 130mph)
38 a) Isle of Man
39 Speed
40 Repton
41 1960
42 *Round the Bend*
43 Milton Keynes
44 b) A Scottish mountain (JC drove up it!)
45 c) Peter Mandelson

44 Formula 1 Part 4

Modern Formula 1 is a lavish, bewildering circus of money, technology, glitz and more money, roaming the world with its exclusivity and extravagance threatening to obscure the very reason it's all there in the first place. You need a PhD in aeronautical engineering to understand how the cars work, the patience of a saint to find and then sit through the coverage of a race – in which almost nothing happens from green light to chequered flag – and all the while you have to look at Eddie Jordan and David Coulthard in tight white jeans.

It may have disappeared up its own behind some time ago, but F1 is still the pinnacle of design, of driving and of showmanship, a combination that keeps bringing us back for more.

1 Who was only the second F1 driver to win a hat trick of F1 titles?
   a) Michael Schumacher
   b) Ayrton Senna
   c) Lewis Hamilton

2 In October 2012 Kimi Raikkonen confirmed he would race for which manufacturer in 2013?

3 Who was Russia's first F1 driver?

4 Who was the only F1 driver to compete in every F1 championship between 1993 and 2011, after which he moved to Indy Car?

5 In 2009 Mark Webber sustained a broken leg which hampered his pre season training. How did he do it?
   a) Cycling
   b) Skiing
   c) Foot caught in a rabbit hole as he was walking his dog

6 In 2012 the Brazilian Grand Prix was the last on the calendar but which Grand Prix came last alphabetically?

7 Who am I?
- I was born in Ireland in 1948
- I gave Michael Schumacher his first F1 start in Belgium in 1991
- I became BBC pundit for motor racing in 2009

8 Which South American was number 2 driver to Michael Schumacher when first joining Ferrari. Was it Rubens Barrichello or Felipe Massa?

9 Which pseudonym did Kimi Raikkonen use when he entered

a dangerous snowmobile race just days before his debut with Ferrari?

a) Damon Hill
b) James Hunt
c) Jackie Stewart

10 This F1 team was renamed Renault in 2002. What was its previous name?

a) Benetton
b) Bugatti
c) Burberry

11 In 2008 which member of the team drove the amazing Renault R25 round the Silverstone track? Was it Jeremy, Richard or James?

12 In 2009 the KERS system was introduced to F1. K stands for Kinetic, R stands for Recovery and S stands for System. What does E stand for?

13 Name the year

- Barack Obama became President of the USA
- Jeremy Clarkson lost money after publishing details of his bank account in his newspaper column
- Sebastian Vettel became the youngest Grand Prix winner

14 Where is Red Bull racing based?

15 Which F1 driver's nickname is the Iceman? Is it Kimi Raikkonen or Mika Hakkinen?

16 The manufacturer Toro Rosso's two drivers for the 2013 season (their second for the Italian team) come from which two countries?

17 Which driver was born in Hyogo, Japan, in 1986 and made his debut at the Brazilian Grand Prix in 2009?

18 Which airline featured in the name of the 2012 Abu Dhabi Grand Prix?

a) British Airways
b) Virgin Atlantic
c) Etihad Airways

19 The Abu Dhabi Grand Prix is raced at midnight. True or false?

20 Who am I?

- I was born in Frome in Somerset in 1980
- At the age of 17 I became the youngest driver to win the European Formula Super A championship
- I became F1 World Champion in 2009

21 The Sauber team is based in which country?

22 In 2008 Lewis Hamilton brought his team their first drivers' championship of the millennium. Which team was it?

23 Which team's garages were damaged by fire following the 2012 Spanish Grand Prix?

a) Williams
b) Mercedes
c) Toro Rosso

24 Kamui Kobayashi had his first podium place at which Grand Prix?

25 Following his successful F1 career Juan Pablo Montoya went on to have a successful career racing what?

a) Motorcycles
b) Horses

c) Stock cars

26 Name the year

- The Summer Olympics were held in the country Ferdinand Alonso hails from
- A gallon of petrol cost £2.13
- Lewis Hamilton aged 12 first appeared on *Blue Peter* driving a go kart

27 Jenson Button was named after the Jensen sports car. True or false?

28 Which Scandinavian won the last two F1 World Championships of the 20th century?

29 In 2009 Nelson Piquet Jr was dropped by Renault. Who replaced him?

a) Romain Grosjean
b) Kimi Raikkonen
c) Jacques Villeneuve

30 Which Italian's first F1 win was in Monaco in 2004. Was it Jarno Trulli or Giancarlo Fisichella?

31 In 2007 Lewis Hamilton lost the world championship by just one point to which Ferrari driver?

32 Where is the Yas Marina circuit?

a) San Marino
b) Brazil
c) Abu Dhabi

33 Adrian Newey was design chief in 2012 with which manufacturer?

a) Ferrari

b) Red Bull
c) Williams

34 Italian ex-Formula 1 driver Alessandro Zanardi, who lost both legs following a crash in 2001, won Paralympic gold at London 2012 in which event? Was it handcycling or wheelchair Rugby?

35 In 2012 what was Team Lotus called?

36 In 2009 Lewis Hamilton won in Hungary and which other Grand Prix?

37 Which manufacturer was accused of stealing Ferrari's technical secrets in 2007?

38 In 2009 what dropped off the car in front of Felipe Massa and went through his helmet?

39 In the 2011 season Jenson Button and Lewis Hamilton clocked up the same number of Grand Prix wins for McLaren. How many?

40 In 2011 which Grand Prix, due to open the season, was postponed because of civil unrest?

41 Name the year

- *The King's Speech* won Best Picture at the Oscars and also provided Colin Firth with the Best Actor award
- The *News of the World* closed down in the wake of the phone hacking scandal
- The Delhi circuit was first used for Formula 1

42 How much would you typically expect to spend on an F1 steering wheel?

43 In 2009 when Nelson Piquet Jr deliberately crashed to alter the outcome of a race, he was driving for which team?

44 Who was faster on the *Top Gear* track? Was it Lewis Hamilton or Mark Webber?

45 Who am I?

- I was born in Heppenheim in Germany
- In 2001 I won the German and European Junior Karting titles
- In 2012 I became the youngest back to back triple F1 Champion in history

The Answers

1 a) Michael Schumacher
2 Lotus
3 Vitaly Petrov
4 Rubens Barichello
5 a) Cycling
6 United States
7 Eddie Jordan
8 Rubens Barichello
9 b) James Hunt
10 a) Benetton
11 Richard
12 Energy
13 2008
14 Milton Keynes
15 Kimi Raikkonen
16 Australia (Daniel Ricciardo) and France (Jean-Eric Vergne)
17 Kamui Kobayashi
18 c) Etihad Airways
19 False (It is a twilight race)
20 Jenson Button
21 Switzerland
22 McLaren
23 a) Williams
24 Japanese Grand Prix

25 c) Stock cars
26 1992
27 False (He was named after a family friend whose surname was Jensen)
28 Mika Hakkinen
29 a) Romain Grosjean
30 Jarno Trulli
31 Kimi Raikkonen
32 c) Abu Dhabi
33 b) Red Bull
34 Handcycling
35 Renault
36 Singapore
37 McLaren
38 Suspension spring
39 Three
40 Bahrain
41 2011
42 £50,000!
43 Renault
44 Lewis Hamilton
45 Sebastian Vettel

45 The Green Agenda

The environment is a subject close to *Top Gear*'s collective heart, mostly because every time it rains in August or a polar bear chips a nail effigies of Jeremy made of hemp and lentils are burned in zero impact communes in the Californian desert. Which is good of course. But warmer weather impedes the performance of turbochargers and wet weather reduces grip in high speed corners. Disaster.

1 The Peel P50 claimed to have an mpg of what?
   a) 100mpg
   b) 150mpg
   c) 200mpg

2 Which country had a cycling-only day at the time of the Middle East oil crisis of the early 1970s?
   a) Netherlands
   b) Sweden
   c) Switzerland

3 The Volkswagen 1 litre was so called because it had an economical 1 litre fuel tank. True or false?

4 The eco-minded VW Bluesport can hit a top speed of 140mph. But what is its mpg?
   a) 40mpg
   b) 45mpg
   c) 50mpg

5 The Tesla Roadster people claim their car will do how many miles on a single charge?
   a) 150
   b) 200
   c) 250

6 In 1985 which company announced variable inlet geometry to promote fuel economy?

7 Which amphibious Rinspeed vehicle did Richard try out in series 5?

8 The Elettra was a version of which popular car by Fiat?

9 The Tama Electric car was made where?

10 In France who uses the Citroen Berlingo Electrique?
a) Police
b) Ambulance service
c) Post office

11 In which country was the Smart developed?
a) UK
b) USA
c) Germany

12 Great Wall's Haval ran on liquid gas in which country?
a) China
b) Malaysia
c) Italy

13 Name the year
- Toyota launched the economical iQ, the world's smallest four seater production car
- Ford celebrated the centenary of the Model T
- Oil costs a hundred dollars a barrel for the first time

14 What was described by *Top Gear* as 'the most important car since the car was invented'?

15 What is the world's first mass produced electric car with zero emissions?

16 The electricity powered Mitsubishi i-MiEV is exempt from road tax and the London congestion charge. True or false?

17 What happens to the Vauxhall Ampera when the electricity runs out?

a) It stops
b) It switches to a petrol engine
c) It runs on batteries

18 What is the normal range of a battery powered vehicle?
a) 200 miles
b) 300 miles
c) 400 miles

19 The Volvo C30 Electric has two exhaust pipes. True or false?

20 Prince Charles's Aston Martin has been modified to run on what?
a) Diesel
b) Biofuel
c) Electricity

21 Where was the Fisker Karma, marketed as the first luxury electric car, developed?

22 Which optional extras do the makers of the Renault Twizy recommend for driving in wet weather?
a) Windscreen wipers
b) Screen washers
c) Doors

23 As early as 1988 General Motors developed a vehicle capable of speeds of 48mph powered on what alone?

24 Where did the Rinspeed UC originate?
a) Switzerland
b) Austria
c) Belarus

25 The Veritas RS3 has its own electricity supply. True or false?

26 Which company, legendary in the development of the petrol powered car, unveiled a plan for the SLS AMG E Cell in 2012?

27 What powers the air conditioning in the Hyundai i-flow?
a) Batteries
b) Wind turbine
c) Solar panels

28 The Sinclair C5 ran on what?

29 The Murray T25 takes up a third of the parking space of a conventional car, but how many people can get inside?
a) One
b) Two
c) Three

30 What name was given to the Mondeo of 2012, which gave a nod to green/eco credentials?

31 What does the ZE stand for in the Twizy ZE?

32 The Tesla Roadster has the shell of which Lotus?
a) Elise
b) Elan
c) Elite

33 Where is the REVA/G-Wiz made?
a) China
b) India
c) Japan

34 What is the only emission from a Honda FCX Clarity?

35 What did the wind-cheating Volkswagen 1 litre have instead of

wing mirrors?

36 What was the name of Renault's 1992 green concept car?
  a) Whizz
  b) Zoom
  c) Cool

37 What was the bestselling electric car of the first decade of the 21st century?

38 The electric powered Ginetta G50 EV was the first car to drive through what? Was it the Channel Tunnel or the Seikan in Japan?

39 In the Volvo C30 Electric, where is the electric motor housed?
  a) In the boot
  b) Under the bonnet
  c) Between the rear seats

40 Japan's Kyocera SCU-O was solar powered. True or false?

41 Name the year
- Daimler built the first Mercedes car
- The Automobile Club of America met to discuss putting signposts on main highways
- On the green front, the first electric tram was launched

42 The all-electric supercar the Tesla Roadster returns an equivalent of what?
  a) 100mpg
  b) 135mpg
  c) 160mpg

43 The Renault Twizy has no doors and the passenger sits behind the driver. Does he/she need a crash helmet by law?

44 Which electric car did *Top Gear* vote to be Luxury Car of the Year in 2011?

45 How many motors does the Audi e-tron have?

The Answers

1 c) 200mpg
2 a) Netherlands
3 False (It could travel 100km on 1 litre of fuel)
4 c) 50mpg
5 b) 200
6 Ford
7 Rinseed Splash
8 Cinquecento
9 Japan
10 c) Post office
11 c) Germany
12 c) Italy
13 2008
14 Honda FCX Clarity
15 Nissan Leaf
16 True
17 b) It switches to a petrol engine
18 b) 300 miles
19 False (It has none)
20 b) Biofuel
21 USA
22 c) Doors
23 Sunlight
24 a) Switzerland

25 True
26 Mercedes Benz
27 c) Solar panels
28 Electricity
29 c) Three
30 Ecoboost 240
31 Zero emission
32 a) Elise
33 b) India
34 Pure water
35 Rear facing cameras
36 b) Zoom
37 REVA/G-Wiz
38 Channel Tunnel
39 b) Under the bonnet
40 True
41 1901
42 b) 135mpg
43 No
44 Fisker Karma
45 Four, one for each wheel

➲

46 Ferrari through the Ages

There is one marque above all others as universally desirable as it is recognisable. The scarlet paint, the prancing horse, the distinctive holler of its frenzied engines. Admittedly the baseball caps and coasters have diluted the exclusivity a smidgen recently, but Ferrari remains the manufacturer with the purest performance lineage. Still a formidable force in F1, still the cars to beat on the road, and now with the added benefit of starting at least six days out of seven.

1 Ferrari made its first road vehicle when it had been in business for how many years?
  a) Five
  b) Ten
  c) Twenty

2 The *Top Gear* team showed a picture of which model of a Ferrari abandoned in Dubai?
  a) Enzo
  b) F40
  c) Testarossa

3 Which Italian company bought a 50% stake in Ferrari in 1969?

4 In which century was the founder of Ferrari born, 19th or 20th?

5 Pininfarina is a name inextricably linked with Ferrari. What was Pininfarina?
  a) A design company
  b) An F1 driver
  c) A financial backer

6 Which Austrian F1 champion crashed his Ferrari in the German Grand Prix in 1976?

7 Who am I?
- My own company was called Ginger Productions
- My TV shows included *The Big Breakfast* and *Don't Forget Your Toothbrush* and now you can hear me on Radio 2
- I appeared on *Top Gear* in 2010 when I had added a Ferrari 250 GTO to my collection

8 What is the logo on the Ferrari badge?

9 How many seats did the Ferrari Dino have? Two or four?

10 The background to the Ferrari badge is yellow as this is the colour symbol of Ferrari's home town of Modena. True or false?

11 How many titles in a row had Michael Schumacher won with Ferrari when he announced his retirement from F1 in 2006?

12 In series 18, Jeremy tested the new Ferrari FF on which surface?

13 Name the year
- Silicon rubber was invented
- The Home Guard, Dad's Army, was formed
- Ferrari founded his Auto Avio Costruzione

14 The Ferrari F40 was launched to mark the Ferrari company's 40th birthday. True or false?

15 Which Ferrari shares its name with a US state?

16 Which rock legend and musician is *not* a famous Ferrari owner?
   a) Brian May
   b) Eric Clapton
   c) Justin Bieber

17 In 1920 Enzo Ferrari became a driver for which company? Was it Alfa Romeo or Fiat?

18 Who left the F1 Stewart team in 1999 and joined Ferrari alongside Michael Schumacher?
   a) Rubens Barrichello
   b) Felipe Massa
   c) Eddie Irvine

19 Where in Italy is the Ferrari base? Is it Modena, Milan or Maranello?

20 Who am I?
- I owned a Ferrari Enzo which appeared on *Top Gear*
- When I appeared on *Top Gear* I had just written a book about my band
- I was the drummer with Pink Floyd

21 When it was launched in 2005 this model was said to be 'the world's fastest convertible'. What was it?

22 Which Ferrari driver led the F1 championship by a staggering 40 points going into the summer break in 2012?

23 In 1979 who was the last Ferrari driver for 21 years to take the driver's title?

24 When the Enzo was first released how many models were produced?
a) 200
b) 400
c) 600

25 What name is given to the prestigious event hosted by Ferrari for its most important clients?
a) Ferrari Confederation
b) Ferrari Celebration
c) Ferrari Cavalcade

26 Name the year
- Prince William married Kate Middleton at Westminster Abbey
- Apple Mac founder Steve Jobs died
- Alonso won the British Grand Prix for Ferrari at Silverstone

27 Enzo Ferrari raced horses before he became a car manufacturer. True or false?

28 Which Ferrari was *Top Gear*'s Supercar of the Year in 2006?

29 Ferrari post race meetings (especially where the team did not do well) were dubbed what?
   a) The museum of mistakes
   b) The hall of hell
   c) The haven of hope

30 The Ferrari 375 MM Coupe Speciale was made especially for an Italian movie director. True or false?

31 Which engineer joined Ferrari in in 1996 at the same time that Schumacher became a Ferrari driver?

32 When Ferrari launched his own company they made parts for farm machinery. True or false?

33 Which country issued a set of eight stamps showing eight famous Ferrari Grand Prix models to mark the centenary of Ferrari's birth and 50 years of Ferrari victories?
   a) San Marino
   b) Monaco
   c) Italy

34 Ferrari named one of its cars after which creature?
   a) Cat
   b) Eagle
   c) Spider

35 The Ferrari America series were built during which two decades?

36 The awful-looking Ferrari Mondial Cabriolet appeared during which decade?

37 She has been Patsy in *Ab Fab*, Purdey in *The New Avengers* and a Star in a Reasonably Priced Car. She has also owned a Ferrari GTS Targa. Who is she?

38 The F40 was the last Ferrari to be produced during the company's founder's lifetime. Is that true or false?

39 In 2012 *Top Gear* drove Ferrari's fastest ever road car. What was it called?

40 All Ferrari F50s were made in which decade?

41 Name the year

- Kelly Holmes won two golds at the Athens Olympics in the 800m and 1500m
- Ferrari took its 6th constructor's title
- Michael Schumacher took his fifth driver's title with Ferrari

42 The Ferrari F40, launched in 1987 was originally going to be manufactured in very small numbers. When did production in fact cease?

a) 1990
b) 1992
c) 1996

43 In the Ferrari colour palette what colour is Rosso Corsa?

44 The Ferrari FF, launched in 2012, is so called because FF stands for what?

a) Ferrari Forte
b) Ferrari Four
c) Ferrari Furioso

45 Who am I?

- I am a world famous guitarist
- My nickname is 'Slowhand'
- In 2012 *Top Gear* reported that Ferrari were making me my very own model, the SP12EC

The Answers

1 c) Twenty
2 a) Enzo
3 Fiat
4 19th, in 1898
5 a) A design company
6 Niki Lauda
7 Chris Evans
8 Horse
9 Four
10 True
11 Five
12 Ice
13 1940
14 True
15 California
16 a) Brian May
17 Alfa Romeo
18 a) Rubens Barrichello
19 Maranello
20 Nick Mason
21 575 Superamerica
22 Alonso
23 Jody Scheckter
24 b) 400

25 Ferrari Cavalcade
26 2011
27 False (He raced cars)
28 Fiorano
29 a) The museum of mistakes
30 True (Roberto Rossellini)
31 Ross Brawn
32 False (They manufactured parts for the aircraft industry)
33 a) San Marino
34 c) Spider
35 1950s and 1960s
36 1980s
37 Joanna Lumley
38 True
39 F12 Berlinetta
40 1990s
41 2004
42 b) 1992
43 Racing red
44 b) Ferrari Four
45 Eric Clapton

47 Celebrity Garage

If you're rich and famous, chances are you have a nice car. What else are you going to spend your money on after all? There's something fascinating about stars and their cars, perhaps because cars can reveal so much about a person. Wayne Rooney's Cadillac Escalade, James May's Fiat Panda… Better still is when they do something memorable in them. Brian Harvey, we're mostly talking about you.

1 Who called his Porsche 550 Spyder 'Little Bastard' and died at its wheel after owning it for less than two weeks?

2 Who advertised the Lexus 200h in 2011?
   a) Kylie Minogue
   b) Jessie J
   c) Adele

3 Which Beatle's 1965 Rolls Royce Phantom V was finished in psychedelic paintwork and sold for $2,299,000 in New York in 1985, five years after his death?

4 Which former Everton, and now England and Man Utd star bought a Mercedes Benz G55 AMG?

5 Which British car was the official car of choice for British Prime Ministers from Harold Wilson (who had a specially large ashtray fitted) to Margaret Thatcher?
   a) Rolls Royce Silver Shadow
   b) Rover 3.5 litre P5B
   c) Standard Vanguard

6 On which occasion did Prince Charles receive an Aston Martin DB6 Volante from his parents in 1969?
   a) His 21st birthday
   b) His marriage
   c) When he founded the Prince's Trust

7 Who am I?
- I owned a Rolls Royce Silver Cloud
- My daughter was once the wife of Michael Jackson
- My famous home was Graceland in Memphis Tennessee

8 Twiggy passed her driving test in 1968 driving a which iconic 1960s car?

9 Which controversial US boxer bought a glass topped Bentley SC Sedanca?

10 Which US football star in a Ford Bronco was pursued by police on the LA highway in full view of TV cameras?

11 Which veteran host of Radio 4's *Just A Minute* boasted of being the proud owner of an Alvis TD21?

12 Which founder member of Pink Floyd has competed in the Le Mans 24 Hour race no less than five times?

13 Who am I?
- A singer, I also launched a perfume collection
- My first hit was 'Baby One More Time'
- I bought a 360 Modena Spider for my husband

14 When the Pope visited the UK in 1982 the government commissioned two Popemobiles for him to travel in. What classic vehicles were they?

15 What happened to Elvis Presley's first Pink Cadillac?
   a) It crashed into a tree
   b) It caught fire
   c) It was stolen never to be seen again

16 Nelson Mandela's autobiography was called *Long Walk to Freedom*. In which make of car was he driven from jail after his years of imprisonment?
   a) Toyota

b) Renault
c) Mercedes

17 Where did soccer superstar Cristiano Ronaldo crash his Ferrari in 2009?
a) Milan
b) Manchester
c) Monte Carlo

18 Which Beverley Hills Cop owns a Mercedes Benz SLS AMG with a top speed of nearly 200mph?

19 A Chicago company provided a Ford Excursion Diplomat for Eminem. What makes it special?
a) It's armoured
b) Its offroad ability
c) It's a stretch limo

20 Who am I?
- I starred in the movies *Titanic* and *The Beach*
- I won a Golden Globe for playing Howard Hughes in *The Aviator*
- I bought *Top Gear Magazine*'s luxury car of the year the Fisker Karma in 2011

21 Why did Elvis Presley shoot his Pantera in the bumper?
a) It was nothing but a hound dog
b) It wouldn't start
c) It was cheaper if it wasn't road worthy

22 Which former film star and Princess of Monaco was killed in a car crash near Monte Carlo in 1982?

23 What is the name of the limo assigned to the President of the USA?
   a) Lincoln 1
   b) Chevrolet 1
   c) Cadillac 1

24 Which Finnish rally driver and F1 star said his prize possessions were his wife and his Ferrari Enzo?

25 Which F1 boss bought a Mercedes Benz 540K at auction in in 2007 for around £5 million?

26 When Pope Benedict XVI revisited his native Germany in 2006 what make was his Popemobile?
   a) Mercedes
   b) BMW
   c) Audi

27 Which star of *Ocean's Eleven* owned a 1959 Chevrolet Corvette C1?

28 The Pegaso Z-102 Thrill was a two seater coupe owned by the woman who was the subject of the musical *Evita*. Who was she?

29 The Prince Royal was the first car built in the Prince/Emperor's own country. Where was this?
   a) Ethiopia
   b) Japan
   c) China

30 US President Roosevelt used gangster Al Capone's old car as he needed an armoured vehicle at short notice. Is this true or false?

31 Which make of car is a favourite of the Duke and Duchess of Cambridge?
   a) Audi
   b) Peugot
   c) VW

32 Which car did Bruce Springsteen buy after he signed his first record deal and which inspired the words of the song, 'Tramps like us, baby, we were born to run'?

33 At the 2012 Paris Motor Show, Infiniti unveiled a supercar named after which racing driver?

34 Which TV detective and later agent 007 personally bought a Volvo P1800 as he enjoyed driving it so much in the TV show?

35 The Sultan of Brunei bought the first of these elegant British exports, launched in 1991 with an eye-watering price tag of £199,750? What was it?

36 After his success in films such as *Alfie*, Michael Caine was advised to buy a Rolls Royce as an investment. Why did he not drive it?

37 Which car, which shares its name with a sword in the legend of King Arthur, had celebrity owners such as Sonny & Cher, Frank Sinatra and Tony Curtis?

38 Which world famous Ferrari has numbered Jay Kay and Rod Stewart among its devoted owners?

39 Which star of *Gambit* has raced at the annual Toyota Pro/Celebrity race at the Grand Prix of Long Beach?
   a) Colin Firth

b) Alan Rickman
c) Cameron Diaz

40 Which US chat show host bought not one but two Lotus Elan sports cars to add to his collection
a) Jerry Springer
b) Jay Leno
c) David Letterman

41 Who am I?
- I was born in Austria and was a former Mr Universe
- In the movie *Terminator* I famously said 'I'll be back!'
- I was seen at the wheel of my Hummer H1 when campaigning to be Governor of California in 2005

42 What is special about the Tesla Roadster, other than the fact Brad Pitt and Matt Damon are among its owners?

43 Which US classic and favourite of the King took him to his final resting place in 1977?

44 Which famous mother of four, with homes in London, Scotland and Norfolk, bought a Rover P5 Coupe in 1967?

45 Who am I?
- I am a singer songwriter born in Middlesbrough
- I sang 'Do You Own A Ferrari' on my album *La Passione*
- My other songs include 'The Road to Hell Part 2'

The Answers

1 James Dean
2 a) Kylie Minogue
3 John Lennon
4 Wayne Rooney
5 b) Rover 3.5 litre P5B
6 a) 21st birthday
7 Elvis Presley
8 Mini
9 Mike Tyson
10 O.J. Simpson
11 Nicholas Parsons
12 Nick Mason
13 Britney Spears
14 Range Rovers
15 b) It caught fire
16 a) Toyota
17 b) Manchester
18 Eddie Murphy
19 c) Stretch limo
20 Leonardoo DiCaprio
21 c) It wouldn't start
22 Grace Kelly (Princess Grace of Monaco)
23 c) Cadillac 1
24 Kimi Raikkonen

25 Bernie Ecclestone
26 a) Mercedes
27 George Clooney
28 Eva Peron
29 b) Japan (It was made by Nissan)
30 True
31 a) Audi
32 Chevrolet Bel Air
33 Sebastian Vettel
34 Roger Moore
35 Bentley Continental R
36 He was a learner driver and could not be insured
37 Excalibur
38 Enzo
39 c) Cameron Diaz
40 b) Jay Leno
41 Arnold Schwarzenegger
42 All-electric supercar
43 Cadillac
44 HM Queen Elizabeth II
45 Chris Rea

48 Chelsea Traction

For about the last decade there have been two popular growth areas in car design. One is for economy driven city cars to cope with our congested streets, the other is for impossibly massive, four wheel drive, fuel banging Behemoths, affectionately dubbed SUVs. The car as status symbol lost all perspective when size became key. The last time this happened was in postwar America where gas stations attendants paid you to take petrol away. It won't wash today, but you try telling that to the wife of an RBS banker.

1 Who built the first 'ute' or utility vehicle after a request from a farmer's wife for a vehicle which could be used for going to church on Sunday and to the market with the pigs on Monday?

2 Which early SUV from Lada has a name which means 'crop field'?

3 The Willys Jeep could run on road or railway track. True or false?

4 The Toyota Land Cruiser was originally used in which war?
   a) Vietnam War
   b) WWII
   c) Korean War

5 The Rancho was a joint venture between Matra and which manufacturer?

6 The Land Rover was already world famous when the Land Cruiser appeared. Who was guilty of this shameless plagarism?

7 What am I?
- I was first exhibited at the London Motor Show in Earl's Court in 1970
- Two examples of me were used in 1972 for the British Trans Americas Expedition
- I was the original Chelsea Tractor

8 Which Renault was considered Europe's first MPV?

9 Which Porsche is hotter by name than nature?
   a) Chilli
   b) Cayenne
   c) Vindaloo

10 What was an optional extra in the first Land Rovers?

a) Brakes
b) Glove compartment
c) Roof

11 Which Toyota was the first passenger vehicle to be exported, in 1952?

12 Who made the Jimny LJ10 which dates back to 1970?

13 Name the year

- Satellite TV was launched in Britain
- Ford acquired Jaguar Motors
- The Land Rover Discovery was launched

14 Which Jeep, then largely known as a military vehicle in 1963, was the world's first luxury SUV?

a) Willys
b) Wagoneer
c) Wrangler

15 In 1999 the Lada Niva achieved a world altitude record for a vehicle above which mountain base camp?

a) Everest
b) The Matterhorn
c) Mt Kilimanjaro

16 Whose first offroader in 1974 was the Taft?

a) Nissan
b) Toyota
c) Daihatsu

17 What was the nickname of the Lamborghini LM002?

a) Mambo Lambo

b) Rambo Lambo
c) Tambo Lambo

18 Which offroad icon was Jeep's SUV for the 1980s?
a) The Jangler
b) The Strangler
c) The Wrangler

19 GMC limited the top speed of the Typhoon to 100mph. True or false?

20 Which of the following is not part of the Land Rover range?
a) Defender
b) Discovery
c) Director

21 Who made the 4.4 litre V8 engine found in the Volvo Xc90?
a) Suzuki
b) Yamaha
c) Volvo

22 Where in the US was the very roomy and very powerful Cadillac Escalade built?
a) California
b) Alaska
c) Texas

23 Not really designed for Chelsea terrain the URI Desert Runner was first built in Namibia and later where?
a) South Africa
b) Zambia
c) Zimbabwe

24 To address the problem of economy, in 2009 Porsche offered the

Cayenne as a diesel or an electric car?

25 The Subaru Forester was available as a petrol and a diesel offroader when it was launched in 1997. True or false?

26 Name the year

- Margaret Thatcher became PM, arriving at No 10 in a very British Rover car
- US government bailed out Chrysler with a loan of just $1.5 billion!
- Daihatsu launched 4x4 diesel engine SUV called the F50

27 The Lada Niva had its own toolkit. True or false?

28 Which ground breaking sporty SUV by Spyker is named after an endurance rally where its predecessors competed in the early 20th century?

29 The Range Rover sport had a chassis based on which other model in the Range Rover stable?

a) Overfinch
b) Discovery
c) LE Defender

30 The VEPR Commander is an offroad vehicle from which country? Clue: Boxer Vitali Klitschko drove it during a promotion.

31 Which world leader had a Mercedes Benz M Class SUV with moveable glass cabin which has bulletproof plastic glass and a separate air supply in case of chemical attack?

32 What was Audi's first SUV?

33 The GMC Yukon Denali has which of the following?

a) A high speed rating
b) A high fuel economy rating
c) A high safety rating

34 Which famous female was a design consultant on the Range Rover Evoque?
a) Colleen Rooney
b) Victoria Beckham
c) Christine Bleakley

35 The Jeepster is a retro SUV made by Chinkara in which country?

36 Which Jeep, first made by Chrysler in 1984, shares its name with a native American people?

37 Which is larger, the Audi Q5 or the VW Tiguan?

38 Which AMC crossover SUV shared its name with a bird of prey?
a) Falcon
b) Vulture
c) Eagle

39 The Lamborghini LM002 had two sets of tyres. One normal set, and an extra set for which terrain?
a) Mud
b) Ice
c) Desert

40 The Trooper was made by Mitsubishi. True or false?

41 Name the year
- George W Bush became US President
- The Olympic Games were held in Sydney
- Mercedes Benz launched their barn storming ML 55 AMG

42 Who developed the Compass?
- a) Land Rover
- b) Jeep
- c) BMW

43 The special exhaust of the Troller T4 allows it to cope with which driving hazard?
- a) Floods
- b) Extreme cold
- c) Extreme heat

44 Skoda produced a SUV called the Yeti. Is this abominable statement correct?

45 Who am I?
- I am the daughter of actor Jon Voight, star of *Midnight Cowboy*
- In *Lara Croft Tomb Raider* I drove a Land Rover LE Defender
- I am the partner of fellow actor Brad Pitt

The Answers

1 Ford
2 Niva
3 True
4 c) Korean War
5 Simca
6 Toyota
7 Range Rover
8 Espace
9 b) Cayenne
10 c) Roof
11 Land Cruiser
12 Suzuki
13 1989
14 b) Wagoneer
15 a) Everest
16 c) Daihatsu
17 b) Rambo Lambo
18 c) The Wrangler
19 False (It could reach a whopping 124mph)
20 c) Director
21 b) Yamaha
22 c) Texas
23 a) South Africa
24 Diesel

25 False (A diesel model was not available)
26 1979
27 True
28 (D12) Peking to Paris
29 b) Discovery
30 Ukraine
31 Pope Benedict XVI
32 Q7
33 c) A high safety rating
34 b) Victoria Beckham
35 India
36 Cherokee
37 Audi Q5
38 c) Eagle
39 c) Desert
40 False (It was made by Isuzu)
41 2000
42 b) Jeep
43 a) Floods
44 Yes
45 Angelina Jolie

49 The Hamster's Wheels

Somehow more omnipresent than even Jeremy, Richard Hammond has become a household name by appearing in every living room in the land and flatly refusing to go away. This resilience has enabled him to survive a 300mph car crash, however, and put up with a decade of relentless abuse from Clarkson and May. Clearly he's going to outlive us all so we'd better get used to him and his suspiciously white teeth.

1 Richard Hammond's first car was a Toyota Corolla Liftback. True or false?

2 Which creature was lurking in the river when Richard's car sank crossing a river in Botswana?
   a) Crocodile
   b) Hippo
   c) Elephant

3 Which car was Richard driving in a race against a powerboat, which also involved a detour to an Italian police station?

4 Which book did Mr and Mrs Hammond write about the Hamster's car crash?

5 Richard Hammond was born in motor city Detroit. True or false?

6 When the team did their race across London, from West London to City Airport, in series 10 what means of transport did RH use?

7 Who is it?
- He was a famous motor racing driver throughout the 1950s
- He was severely injured in a crash at Goodwood in 1962
- He was the subject of a TV special where he was interviewed by Richard

8 In 2006, Richard Hammond was critically injured in a car crash near which city?
   a) Leeds
   b) Hull
   c) York

9 What type of car did Richard Hammond travel in in Botswana – an Opel or a Skoda?

10 In the Hammond household what were Buster, Lollipop, Molly and Gertie?
  a) Dogs
  b) Horses
  c) Land Rovers

11 What did Richard do with a picture of a BMW M6 in a disagreement about positioning on the Cool Wall?

12 While racing his motorhome, Richard had a problem when what got stuck?
  a) The accelerator
  b) Gear lever
  c) Window controls

13 Name the year
- Neil Armstrong became the first man to land on the Moon
- Concorde made its maiden flight
- Richard Hammond was born

14 On the *Top Gear* Bolivia special it was discovered Richard Hammond had a phobia of what?
  a) Cats
  b) Birds
  c) Insects

15 While testing the Bowler Wildcat in series 2 Richard was heard to shout out in triumph, 'I am a driving' what?

16 Who won when Richard took on some French skiers in an Audi RS6?

17 What fate did Richard's van meet in the challenge to keep ahead of a chasing police car?

a) Blew up
b) Engine stalled
c) Rolled over

18 Which musical instrument did Richard take up and play in a *Top Gear* Special?

a) Bass guitar
b) Flute
c) Violin

19 On which airfield did the 2006 high speed crash take place?

20 What colour was Richard's motorcycle painted on the Vietnam road trip?

21 Richard took a Suzuki Vitara and tried to turn it into a what?

a) Amphibious vehicle
b) Police car
c) Tank

22 What did Richard name his car for the African Challenge? Was it Fagin, Nancy or Oliver?

23 In the quiz show *Petrolheads*, Richard pranged his own Ferrari while attempting to parallel park. What was done to him to make the manoeuvre more difficult?

24 In the Miami to New Orleans challenge did Richard drive a Corvette or a pick-up?

25 Which car did Richard stall eight times while trying to pull away?

26 Richard bought himself a second-hand Robinson R44 which is what type of machine?

27 Jeremy removed Richard's microphone on air after the latter had decided that which cars should be moved to Uncool on the Cool Wall?

28 Which word completes Richard's quote from a *Top Gear* clip featuring a table football game played against Jeremy: 'I have not had my teeth…'?

29 At which circuit was Richard shunted off track while driving a Bugatti Veyron in the 2007 Britcar 24-hour race?

30 In Cyprus, Richard raced a Porshe Cayenne Turbo S against a man using what form of transport?

31 Who won when Richard in a Tomcat 4x4 tried to go round an Icelandic lake before an engine powered kayak crossed the stretch of icy water?

32 True or false? Richard has started to produce a range of marmalades and preserves branded as Hamsterjam.

33 How much time did Richard give Jeremy in his Daihatsu Terios before hunting him on horseback with a pack of baying hounds?
a) Two minutes
b) Five minutes
c) Ten minutes

34 Which car did Richard describe as, 'a wretched, awful, miserable, spluttering, puttering, slow, noisy, ugly piece of hateful misery'?

35 'Country and western is rubbish'. The Hamster painted this on

Jeremy's car during a road challenge in which country?

36 In a drag race Richard beat Jeremy in an Audi R8. The Hamster was in his own car. What type was it?

37 What was the name of the jet powered vehicle that nearly claimed Richard's life in the high speed 2006 crash?

38 Although a petrolhead, he's a country boy at heart. In fact in 2009, Richard was President of the Hertfordshire County Fair. True or false?

39 Richard made a documentary in the US in 2007 about which legendary motorcycle stunt man just weeks before the great man's death?

40 When Richard was born which monster hit by The Archies was in its eighth and last week at No 1 in the British single charts?

41 How many miles were raced when Richard in a Bugatti Veyron took on a Eurofighter Typhoon? Was it two miles, twelve miles or twenty miles?

42 What is the name of the production company that Richard set up? Clue: Think of his nickname and something found on a car.

43 Musicals from the golden age of Hollywood used to festoon staircases with hundreds of showgirls. How many girls lined the stairs to welcome Richard back to *Top Gear* after his high speed accident of 2006?

a) Six
b) Twenty-six
c) Sixty

44 Richard Hammond has a daughter who shares her name with which tree?

a) Rowan
b) Willow
c) Linden

45 To which person did Richard say: 'Now you've confused yourself, you poor old goat'?

The Answers

1 True
2 a) Crocodile
3 Ferrari Daytona
4 *On the Edge*
5 False (He was born in a motor city – Birmingham)
6 Carbon fibre racing bike
7 Stirling Moss
8 c) York
9 Opel (Kadett)
10 c) Land Rovers
11 Ate the picture
12 a) The accelerator
13 1969
14 c) Insects
15 God
16 The skiers
17 c) Rolled over
18 a) Bass guitar
19 Elvington Airfield
20 Pink
21 b) Police car
22 Oliver
23 He was blindfolded
24 Pick-up

25 A Renault F1 car
26 Helicopter
27 Aston Martins
28 Whitened
29 Silverstone
30 A parachute
31 Kayak
32 False
33 a) Two minutes
34 VW Beetle
35 USA
36 Porsche 911 Carrera 2S
37 Vampire
38 True
39 Evel Knievel
40 'Sugar, Sugar'
41 Two miles
42 Hamster's Wheel
43 a) Six
44 b) Willow
45 James May

50 Absolutely Enormous and Amazing Numbers

All good quiz books have big numbers in them. This one only deals with Absolutely Enormous and Amazing Numbers. Which makes it a much, much better quiz book. If you know the answers to most of these questions you probably need some sort of professional intervention, but well done anyway. If you don't, learn them and bore your friends half to death.

1 What kind of vehicle is *Midnight Rider*, which is 70ft long and weighs in excess of 22,000 kg?

a) Train
b) Ship
c) Limousine

2 The 13,200 tonne Big Muskie was too expensive to run but if it did it removed dirt from what? Was it coal or gold?

3 Which country had the largest battleships in WWII?

a) UK
b) Japan
c) USSR

4 In 2004 which iconic US truck hit a top speed of over 150mph, then the fastest ever for a pick-up?

5 A 100 feet long limousine needed how many wheels to keep its Californian passengers rolling?

a) 12
b) 26
c) 38

6 According to the *Guinness Book of Records*, David Morgan from the UK has the biggest collection of which motoring memorabilia?

a) Parking meters
b) Traffic cones
c) RAC badges

7 In 2004 Dave Willwock achieved a water speed in excess of 220,000mph in which craft?

a) *Miss Stella*
b) *Miss Budweiser*

c) *Miss Guinness*

8 Pelorus and Le Grand Bleu are yachts in excess of 370 feet long owned by which football club owner?
a) Roman Abramovich
b) The Glazer family
c) V H Group

9 How many of Porsche's Kubelwagens, Beetle based military vehicles, were built in just five years in WWII?
a) 10,000
b) 30,000
c) 50,000

10 What type of vehicle was the *Knock Nevis* – also known as the Happy Giant – which weighed in at a massive 564,764 tons?

11 Only 200 two seater Mercedes 60hp were made. How much did one fetch in a sale in 1991?
a) £500,000
b) £1 million
c) £1.6 million

12 In 1980 a traffic jam on the Paris to Lyon road was how long?
a) 50 miles
b) 75 miles
c) 100 miles

13 How many litres of fuel will an F1 team use during a typical season for testing and racing?
a) 20,000
b) 200,000
c) 2,000,000

14 Approximately how many bricks did James May use to build an entire house from Lego?

a) 32,000
b) 320,000
c) 3.2 million

15 *Freedom of the Seas* is (unsurprisingly) a sea going vessel with a tonnage of over 150,000. What kind of ship is it?

a) Aircraft carrier
b) Cruise ship
c) Oil tanker

16 In the early years of car production the Ford Model T is a legend. How many were made?

a) 10.5 million
b) 12.5 million
c) 16.5 million

17 In 2007, two motorists drove their modified Suzuki Samurai to a record altitude of 6,688 metres in which country?

a) Chile
b) USA
c) Australia

18 As the ultimate in luxury, which diamond encrusted car accessory (quite mundane to most of us) can be customised for a Bentley at a cost of £5,000?

a) Keys
b) Gear knob
c) Hubcap

19 One of the world's largest screwdrivers is over a metre long. True or false?

20 In 1972 a 10.5mph record was achieved where?
   a) Antarctica
   b) In a vat of baked beans
   c) The Moon

21 Approximately how many tyres were used in the 2012 F1 season?
   a) 13,000
   b) 23,000
   c) 33,000

22 In 2010 a diesel Passat covered how many miles without refuelling?
   a) 1,000
   b) 1,500
   c) 2,000

23 In 2004 which ship became the largest passenger ship of all time with a passenger capacity of over 3,000?
   a) *Queen Elizabeth II*
   b) *Queen Mary 2*
   c) *Crown Princess*

24 In 2011 in Australia, which piece of furniture was fitted with an engine and created a world record by being driven at 101.36mph?
   a) A bed
   b) A sofa
   c) A wardrobe

25 The Pan American Highway is 15,000 miles long. True or false?

26 What is the F-111 Aardvark that is capable of speeds of 1,850mph?
   a) Bomber

b) Research aircraft
c) Jet fighter

27 The steam in the British Steam Car which broke the steam land speed record in 2009 was heated to which temperature – 200, 300 or 400°C?

28 Jeremy is a tall chap, but approximately how many Jeremys would match the depth of the Grand Canyon?
a) 1,600
b) 2,100
c) 2,600

29 In 1961 the Chrysler Imperial was the biggest standard car other than a limo. How long was it?
a) 13 feet
b) 16 feet
c) 19 feet

30 In 2012 the record for the number of people in a Mini was broken when how many crammed into a Mini Cooper?

31 The 5 tonne Big Green Machine was capable of cutting an acre of grass in how many minutes?
a) One
b) Three
c) Five

32 Crawler Transporters which weigh around 6 million lbs unloaded are used to move what?
a) Tanks
b) Earth and rocks
c) Space shuttles

33 The Leopard Roadster costs £100,000 in its country of manufacture, the most expensive car it produces. Where does it come from?

34 In June 2009 an airspeed of 155mph was reached in which type of aircraft?

a) Glider
b) Electric only
c) Propeller driven

35 What kind of vehicle was the Texas Titan 33-19? Its fuel tank held 5,910 litres (1,300 gallons).

36 A Lincoln Continental limo built in 1968 weighed in at almost six tons, half of which was what?

a) Extra heavy mudguards
b) Armour plating
c) Audio equipment

37 A record breaking tallest rideable motorcycle was built in 2005 in the USA with tyres which were how high in themselves?

a) 2 feet
b) 4 feet
c) 6 feet

38 Weighing in at nearly 5 tonnes the Harzer Bike Schmiede is what?

a) A ten bike tandem
b) A motorcycle
c) A sidecar

39 In 2011 a 1903 Ford Model A sold for how many dollars, quite a bit for a car that was nearly 110 years old?

a) $55,000

b) $77,000
c) $99,000

40 The *Top Gear* live stunt team did the first ever double loop the loop on a motorcycle, therefore completing how many degrees?

41 Name the year

- West Germany won the World Cup beating Holland in the final
- UK motorways had a 50mph speed limit
- General Motors introduced its Terex Titan, capable of carrying 312 tons

42 How many passengers could the DAF Super City Train buses carry, both seated and strap hanging?
a) 250
b) 350
c) 450

43 The massive fire engines made by the US company Oshkosh Trucks are designed to be used at which fire sensitive locations?
a) F1 racing tracks
b) Airports
c) Rocket launch sites

44 The fastest mobility scooter can break the speed limit on a UK motorway. True or false?

45 In 2007 the French TGV reached which top speed?
a) 250mph
b) 300mph
c) 350mph

The Answers

1 c) Limousine
2 Coal
3 b) Japan (Although the 72+tonne Musashi and Yamato were sunk in 1944 and 1945 respectively)
4 Dodge Ram
5 b) 26
6 b) Traffic cones
7 b) *Miss Budweiser*
8 a) Roman Abramovich
9 c) 50,000
10 Oil tanker
11 c) £1.6 million
12 c) 100 miles
13 b) 200,000
14 c) 3.2 million
15 b) Cruise ship
16 c) 16.5 million
17 a) Chile
18 a) Keys
19 True (You would need the world's biggest toolbox to keep it in!)
20 c) The Moon
21 b) 23,000
22 1,500
23 b) *Queen Mary 2*

24 b) A sofa
25 True
26 a) Bomber
27 400°C
28 c) 2,600
29 c) 19 feet
30 28 people
31 a) One
32 c) Space shuttles
33 Poland
34 b) Electric only
35 Dumper truck
36 b) Armour plating
37 c) 6 feet
38 b) A motorcycle
39 c) $99,000 (£63,800)
40 720
41 1974
42 b) 350 (There was a first and second trailer, and it weighed 28 tonnes without passengers)
43 b) Airports
44 True (71.50mph, not exactly an enormous number in itself but it is for a mobility scooter!)
45 c) 350mph

51 The Stig(s)

The Stig is one of the great enigmas of the post-modern media age. Or at least he was until he got sacked and wrote a book about it. Still, they found a new one pretty easily, proving that it's better to be a salaried enigma for years than a celebrity in WH Smiths for a fortnight.

1 How is The Stig usually described?
   a) *Top Gear*'s cool racing driver
   b) *Top Gear*'s tame racing driver
   c) *Top Gear*'s secret racing driver

2 What colour did the original Stig wear?

3 Which presenter chased The Stig in his version of a police car whose wheel fell off?

4 Which Stig featured in the Big Lorry Challenge?
   a) German Stig
   b) Rig Stig
   c) Black Stig

5 When the team did their race across London, from West London to City Airport, in series 10 what means of transport did The Stig use?

6 Which of The Stig's relatives was dubbed the Big Stig?
   a) The Stig's African Cousin
   b) The Stig's American Cousin
   c) The Stig's Australian Cousin

7 Who am I?
- In October 2012 when I was a Mercedes F1 driver I announced my retirement from F1 (again) at the age of 43
- I had previously raced for Ferrari
- In 2009 I was the face revealed in The Stig's helmet when I appeared on the show

8 The name The Stig came about as it was a term used for new boys at JC's old school. True or false?

9 When first appearing, The Stig's gloves did not match his outfit? What colour were his gloves?

10 Which racing driver was the first to beat The Stig's time for a lap in a Reasonably Priced Car?

a) Michael Schumacher
b) Rubens Barrichello
c) Damon Hill

11 Which presenter was the first to have their own car driven by The Stig on a power lap?

12 Published in 1963, Clive King wrote a children's book titled *Stig of the Dump*. Is that true or false?

13 In a newspaper column Jeremy explained that The Stig is not permitted to talk because 'the opinions of all racing drivers are completely...' what?

a) Bonkers
b) Unreliable
c) Worthless

14 What did the Vegetarian Stig have on his helmet?

15 In which Challenge did The Stig become Ronnie Stigs?

16 Which corner on the *Top Gear* track, the second to last, is named in honour of The Stig's love of easy listening music?

a) Henry Mancini
b) James Last
c) Burt Bacharach

17 In the Winter Olympics which vehicle did The Stig drive in the ski jump?

18 Which two words usually introduce a nugget of information about The Stig?
   a) It's whispered
   b) Rumour suggests
   c) Some say

19 At Jeremy's 50th birthday bash which famous person from the world of politics posed as The Stig in a video film?
   a) Barack Obama
   b) David Cameron
   c) Gordon Brown

20 Who am I?
- I have been World Snooker Champion on more than one occasion
- The Stig challenged me in series 4 on the *Top Gear* track
- My nickname is the rocket

21 Which Stig tested *Top Gear*'s homemade electric car in 2009?

22 What was the name of the aircraft carrier where the Black Stig had his final challenge?

23 The new White Stig was introduced to *Top Gear* to which music?
   a) '2001: A Space Odyssey'
   b) 'Thriller'
   c) 'Bohemian Rhapsody'

24 According to Jeremy, The Stig suffers from which syndrome? Clue: Think of a famous name from F1.

25 What was the title of the first *Top Gear* book devoted to activities involving The Stig?
   a) *What Is Stig?*

b) *Where's Stig?*
c) *Who Is Stig?*

26 Which F1 driver was the first to be presented with a T-shirt declaring 'I Am The Stig'?

27 In the Build Your Own Car Challenge who caught The Stig speeding?
a) The Metropolitan Police
b) Suffolk Constabulary
c) The Scottish Constabulary

28 At the start of series 12 Stig was driving a Lamborghini Gallardo LP560-4 on the *Top Gear* track. He had given up a background of music and was now listening to what?

29 At the 2008 British National Television Awards, The Stig collected a prize on behalf of *Top Gear*. What saved him from making a speech?
a) Transmission ended
b) There was a power cut
c) He gave an acceptance letter to the host to read

30 What was the title of an autobiography published by Harper Collins that was subject of a court case involving the BBC?
a) *I Am Stig*
b) *The Man Inside Stig's Helmet*
c) *The Man In The White Suit*

31 Which attribute does The Stig share with Harpo Marx and Marcel Marceau?

32 What make of car did the Black Stig drive into the sea in his last appearance?

a) Ferrari
b) Jaguar
c) Porsche

33 The Stig's Swedish cousin wrote a bestselling thriller *The Girl with the Dragon Tattoo*. Is that true or false?

34 What colour outfit did The Stig's Communist Cousin wear?

35 In which country was the African Stig first discovered?

36 When The Stig in a Saab took on a Harrier jump jet on the TG track, who won?

37 What was the first car that saw Stig go careering off the *Top Gear* track?

38 What was the name of the driver who acted as the Black Stig in the early episodes of the new *Top Gear*?

39 The demise of the first Stig shown at the beginning of series 3 was in the waters off which country?

40 The Russian Stig was called Stigushka. True or false?

41 What speed did the Black Stig clock up on his last *Top Gear* ride?
a) 109mph
b) 129mph
c) 199mph

42 Stig Mk II's first test was in which make of car?
a) BMW
b) Porsche
c) Ferrari

43 What happened to the veggie Stig shortly after testing the Hammerhead Eagle iThrust 2009?

44 Which Stig tested the 'ultimate track day cars' at the EuroSpeedway in 2010?

45 Who is he?

- He's an experienced racing driver who was involved in car stunts for the Bond movies
- His autobiography infamously claimed he was the The Stig
- Richard Hammond called him Jilly Cooper on screen

The Answers

1 b) *Top Gear*'s tame racing driver
2 Black
3 Jeremy Clarkson
4 b) Rig Stig
5 Public transport (He even had an Oyster card!)
6 b) The Stig's American Cousin
7 Michael Schumacher
8 True
9 Green
10 b) Rubens Barrichello
11 Jeremy
12 True (But this Stig was a prehistoric caveman)
13 c) Worthless
14 Solar panels
15 Making a Better Police Car Challenge
16 Burt Bacharach
17 Snowmobile
18 c) Some say
19 David Cameron
20 Ronnie O'Sullivan
21 Vegetarian Stig
22 HMS *Invincible*
23 a) '2001: A Space Odyssey'
24 Mansell Syndrome

25 b) *Where's Stig?*
26 Mark Webber
27 c) The Scottish Constabulary
28 Morse code
29 c) He gave an acceptance letter to the host to read
30 c) *The Man In The White Suit*
31 Not speaking
32 b) Jaguar
33 False (The author was Stieg Larsson who is no relative!)
34 Red
35 Botswana
36 The jet
37 Koenigsegg CCX
38 Perry McCarthy
39 Portugal
40 True
41 a) 109mph
42 a) BMW
43 He died
44 German Stig
45 Ben Collins

52 Circuit Training

Motorsport is only half about the cars and drivers. The other critical element is the tracks on which the drama unfolds. A circuit can make or break a series, creating incredible spectacles of human endeavour or mindless processions, depending on the skill of their design. Some of the great corners carry as much importance as the drivers who have tackled them. And some are named after the luvvies who nearly died going round them in the name of light entertainment. Thank you Sir Michael.

1 The Nordschleife was banned in the 1970s for being too dangerous. It is part of which famous track?
   a) Nurburgring
   b) Osterreichring
   c) Hockenheim

2 At Brooklands in 1922 who was responsible for maintaining the scoreboard?
   a) Boy Scouts
   b) Metropolitan Police
   c) Household Cavalry

3 On which circuit was the first 200km/h record broken?
   a) Monza
   b) Hockenheim
   c) Silverstone

4 In which US state does the Sebring race take place?
   a) Florida
   b) Arizona
   c) Alaska

5 Which corner on the *Top Gear* track shares its name with a US city and a musical – and all that jazz?
   a) Oklahoma
   b) Chicago
   c) New York

6 On the *Top Gear* circuit the first part of the track where some cars start to struggle is named after which one time *Top Gear* presenter?
   a) Woollard
   b) Willson

c) Edmonds

7 Where were the Fork and the Railway Straight?

8 The F1 championship rotated between Silverstone, Brands Hatch and which other track between 1955 and 1986?

9 Jonathan Ross and Harry Enfield posted circuit times in series 1 of new *Top Gear*. Both later returned, but who came out on top?

10 Which part of the *Top Gear* track shares its name with a type of shark?

11 The Daytona Beach circuit is in which US state?
   a) California
   b) Florida
   c) Massachusetts

12 Name the year
- The Olympic Games were held in West Germany
- Films released this year included *The Godfather* and *Straw Dogs*
- It's not exactly a circuit, until you lose your way on it, but Spaghetti Junction opened

13 Where would you race on the Mulsanne Straight?

14 The Milk Race was a round Britain race on which vehicles?
   a) Bicycles
   b) Motorcycles
   c) Tractors

15 Which 1990s Bentley takes its name from a famous bend on the Le Mans 24 Hour circuit?

16 Which car took longer to go round the *Top Gear* track, the Bugatti Veyron or the Caterham Superlight 500?

17 In which country is the Spa 24 Hour race held?

18 In which US state is the infamous Pikes Peak, a 12 mile hill climb?
   a) Colorado
   b) Arizona
   c) Nevada

19 Which fast circuit had the Abbey Curve?

20 During which rally did you negotiate the Epreuve de Regularite?

21 How long does the Sebring race last?

22 Which is the oldest race still staged on a regular basis?

23 Which Grand Prix track has the Tabac Corner?
   a) Monaco
   b) French
   c) Belgian

24 Why was Brooklands not a good choice for a 24 Hour race in the late 1920s, which many people wanted to inaugurate?

25 The Moroccan Grand Prix first took place in Casablanca in 1925. True or false?

26 In which year of the 20th century did the Indianapolis 500 begin?
   a) 1901
   b) 1911
   c) 1921

27 The Targa Florio was held on which island?
   a) Cyprus
   b) Corsica
   c) Sicily

28 In which city was the Avus track, where Opel's rocket car hit 143mph in 1928?

29 Where would you drive round the Parabolica?
   a) Monza
   b) Spa
   c) Hockenheim

30 In which city was the Montjuich Circuit?
   a) Madrid
   b) Seville
   c) Barcelona

31 On which island would you find the Willaston Corner?
   a) Isle of Wight
   b) Isle of Man
   c) Guernsey

32 How many laps of the *Top Gear* track did the Suzuki Liana complete before being replaced by the Chevrolet Lacetti as the reasonably priced car for a whole host of stars?
   a) 1,000
   b) 1,300
   c) 1,600

33 Which circuit had the elitist sign 'the right crowd and no crowding'?
   a) Silverstone
   b) Brooklands
   c) Brand's Hatch

34 At which Grand Prix would you negotiate the Station hairpin?

35 How long does the Daytona endurance race last?

36 On the *Top Gear* track, what was Gambon Corner originally called?

a) Carpenters
b) Bee Gees
c) Rolling Stone

37 Which track boasts the infamous Death Curve?

38 On the *Top Gear* track who is the Bentley Bend named after? Was it the founder of Bentley cars, W.O. Bentley, or a former *Top Gear* presenter and producer, Jon Bentley?

39 Where was the British Grand Prix held in 1955, 1957 and 1959?

a) Brooklands
b) Aintree
c) Brand's Hatch

40 Where was Byfleet Bridge?

41 Name the year

- The Korean War began
- Giuseppe Farina was GP World Champion
- The Sebring race was first held

42 In the late 1950s how many laps were there on the Monaco track?

a) 85
b) 90
c) 105

43 On which circuit is Tertre Rouge?

44 What was the name of the first purpose-built race circuit in the world?

45 Were was the Ards Circuit?

The Answers

1 a) Nurburgring
2 a) Boy Scouts
3 a) Monza
4 a) Florida
5 b) Chicago
6 b) Willson
7 Brooklands
8 Aintree
9 Harry Enfield
10 Hammerhead
11 b) Florida
12 1972
13 Le Mans
14 a) Bicycles
15 Arnage
16 Caterham Superlight 500
17 Belgium
18 a) Colorado
19 Silverstone
20 Monte Carlo (It's in Monaco)
21 12 Hours
22 RAC Tourist Trophy on the Isle of Man
23 a) Monaco
24 You couldn't race at night

25 True
26 b) 1911
27 c) Sicily
28 Berlin
29 a) Monza
30 c) Barcelona
31 b) Isle of Man
32 c) 1,600
33 b) Brooklands
34 Monaco
35 24 Hours
36 a) Carpenters
37 Santa Monica
38 Jon Bentley
39 b) Aintree
40 Brooklands
41 1950
42 c) 105
43 Le Mans Sarthe circuit
44 Brooklands
45 Ireland

53 Jeremy, James or Richard

A test of memory here, or logical deduction. Or, in fact guess work. You have at least a one in three chance of getting even the difficult ones right. You should score highly here. If you don't you clearly haven't been watching enough Dave Ja Vu.

1 Which of the trio made a TV special about Bond cars?
   a) JC
   b) JM
   c) RH

2 Which of the three became a patron of Help For Heroes?
   a) JC
   b) JM
   c) RH

3 Which *Top Gear* presenter drove the then world's smallest car, the Peel P50, into work – literally?
   a) JC
   b) JM
   c) RH

4 Who introduced the *Top Gear* track to the *Top Gear* audience?
   a) JC
   b) JM
   c) RH

5 Comedian Sean Lock, in the comedy show *Room 101*, consigned which *Top Gear* presenter to oblivion?
   a) JC
   b) JM
   c) RH

6 Who was the first of the three to obtain a light aircraft pilot's licence?
   a) JC
   b) JM
   c) RH

7 Who presented *Motor Week* for a year, starting in 1998?

a) JC
b) JM
c) RH

8 Which *Top Gear* presenter's grandparents worked in the motor trade in Birmingham car making factories?

a) JC
b) JM
c) RH

9 Who was born furthest west in England?

a) JC
b) JM
c) RH

10 Which of the three presented a BBC documentary about his father in law and other recipients of the Victoria Cross, or VC?

a) JC
b) JM
c) RH

11 In 2006 the show's producer Andy Wilman co-wrote *What Not to Drive* with which of the show's presenters?

a) JC
b) JM
c) RH

12 Who presented the British Parking Awards at the Dorchester Hotel?

a) JC
b) JM
c) RH

13 Who fronted a prank show where victims were filmed by a hidden camera, including a prince from Malvania?
- a) JC
- b) JM
- c) RH

14 In the Making a Better Police Car Challenge who drove a Lexus?
- a) JC
- b) JM
- c) RH

15 In the *Top Gear* Winter Olympics who won the ice hockey challenge?
- a) JC
- b) JM
- c) RH

16 In the Africa Challenge who drove the Lancia Beta?
- a) JC
- b) JM
- c) RH

17 Who had a two series spin off called *Motorworld*?
- a) JC
- b) JM
- c) RH

18 When the team set off for Europe's greatest driving road who was driving the Aston Martin?
- a) JC
- b) JM
- c) RH

19 Who shares a birthday with Cerys Matthews and Joss Stone?

a) JC
b) JM
c) RH

20 Who said, 'I could say "Maserati" before I could say "Mummy"'?
a) JC
b) JM
c) RH

21 Who has a CV including stints working on Radio Cleveland, Radio York and Radio Cumbria?
a) JC
b) JM
c) RH

22 Who wrote an autobiography called *As You Do*?
a) JC
b) JM
c) RH

23 Who drove the Mercedes in the Botswana Challenge?
a) JC
b) JM
c) RH

24 Who had the fastest tractor in the Grow Your Own Petrol Challenge?
a) JC
b) JM
c) RH

25 Who was the proud owner of a Ford GT with a top speed of 205mph?
a) JC

b) JM
c) RH

26 Who was particularly impressed with the Pagani Zonda Roadster F?
a) JC
b) JM
c) RH

27 Who decided to buy a Morgan Aeromax?
a) JC
b) JM
c) RH

28 Who wrote *Car Fever*?
a) JC
b) JM
c) RH

29 Who has been quoted as saying, 'When I was five I sat on my father's lap and asked him how many days it was before I could take my driving test'?
a) JC
b) JM
c) RH

30 Who described the Mercedes SL Black as 'the most uncomfortable car in all of human history' even though it cost around a quarter of a million pounds?
a) JC
b) JM
c) RH

31 Who is a huge fan of the Porsche 911 GT3?

a) JC
b) JM
c) RH

32 Who shares a birthday with Andre Michelin of tyre fame?
a) JC
b) JM
c) RH

33 Who triumphed in a Triumph in the challenge to build an amphibious vehicle?
a) JC
b) JM
c) RH

34 In the Polar Challenge who travelled on a dog sled?
a) JC
b) JM
c) RH

35 Which of the trio worked on the *Rochdale Observer* and the Wolverhampton based *Express & Star*?
a) JC
b) JM
c) RH

36 Who presents his own *Man Lab* on TV?
a) JC
b) JM
c) RH

37 Who made a programme called *Toy Stories*?
a) JC
b) JM

c) RH

38 Who wrote an autobiography called *Or Is That Just Me*?
a) JC
b) JM
c) RH

39 Which of the trio has the middle name Daniel?
a) JC
b) JM
c) RH

40 Who won the Making a Better Police Car Challenge?
a) JC
b) JM
c) RH

41 Who has written a regular column in the *Daily Telegraph*?
a) JC
b) JM
c) RH

42 Who was most smitten by Kristin Scott Thomas when she appeared on the show?
a) JC
b) JM
c) RH

43 Which of the three has Capricorn as their horoscope sign?
a) JC
b) JM
c) RH

44 Who bought a Lamborghini Gallardo Spyder?

a) JC
b) JM
c) RH

45 Who described driving the BMW Z8 as, 'like trying to get a wardrobe up a fire escape'?
a) JC
b) JM
c) RH

The Answers

1 c) RH
2 a) JC
3 a) JC (He drove it into the BBC's West London offices)
4 c) RH
5 a) JC
6 b) JM
7 c) RH
8 c) RH
9 b) JM (Bristol)
10 a) JC
11 c) RH
12 c) RH
13 c) RH (*Richard Hammond's Secret Service*)
14 b) JM
15 c) RH
16 a) JC
17 a) JC
18 b) JM
19 a) JC
20 a) JC
21 c) RH
22 c) RH
23 b) JM
24 a) JC

25 a) JC
26 b) JM
27 c) RH
28 b) JM
29 c) RH
30 a) JC
31 c) RH
32 b) JM
33 b) JM
34 c) RH
35 a) JC
36 b) JM
37 b) JM
38 c) RH
39 b) JM
40 c) RH
41 b) JM
42 a) JC
43 b) JM
44 a) JC
45 a) JC

54 War on Wheels

The natural progression from big things that go Vroom is to big things that go Bang. Here's a chapter on military hardware, not all of it with wheels on because that would make war a bit boring. If you know all the answers here you've probably accessed classified information and are likely to be arrested before you finish the first page.

1 How was the 'Truck, GS, SAS, three quarter ton, 4x4 Rover 11' better known?
  a) Red devil
  b) Pink panther
  c) Yellow peril

2 It featured prominently in the Cold War rather than a world war but the LuAZ 967 was what kind of vehicle?
  a) Armoured car
  b) Amphibious jeep
  c) Military ambulance

3 Which Korean company starting out making jeeps for the US army in the mid 1950s?

4 Zil was a manufacturer of military vehicles, trucks and armoured cars in which Cold War country?

5 Lamborghini's first 4x4 the LM002 was originally intended for which military market?
  a) Italy
  b) US
  c) Iraq

6 What was the pared down, jeep-like Mini called, a model which was designed originally for military use?

7 What was the first viable stealth fighter aircraft called?
  a) Nightowl
  b) Nightingale
  c) Nighthawk

8 The Hummer began life as the Humvee during which war?

a) Vietnam
b) Iraq
c) Bosnia

9 The Delahaye VLR-D was developed in France to improve on which world famous US vehicle?

10 What is special about the wings of the Tornado aircraft?

11 The Chevrolet Maple Leaf series of 3 ton 4x2 trucks was exported to Australia from where?

12 Which Swedish manufacturer made the Sugga or Sow named in honour of its snout shaped front?

13 Name the war
- Ballistic missiles were first used
- Cluster bombs became part of military warfare
- The Enigma machine was part of wartime strategy

14 The Jeep Wrangler TJ-L, a US/Egyptian joint venture could either have two rows of seats in the rear to carry troops or what?

15 Bazookas were developed to combat which vehicles?
a) Aircraft
b) Submarines
c) Tanks

16 What is a Russian BMP-1 used in the Chechen disturbances in the early years of the 21st century?

17 Who on *Top Gear* tested the ten ton military vehicle the Marauder?

18 Which country has the F-22 Raptor fighter jet?

19 What is the British Army's main utility/patrol vehicle?

20 The Westland Apache can operate day and night. What is it?

21 The massive MZKT 74135 from Belarus is supplied with which extra to handle its spare wheels?

22 Where does a DPV patrol?

23 What is a Rigid Raider?
a) Submarine
b) Fighter jet
c) Boat

24 Which British Army vehicle is highly mobile and flexible and can carry a machine gun?
a) Husky
b) Pointer
c) Bloodhound

25 The Taranis does not need human input to make a strategic decision. True or false?

26 The armoured patrol vehicle the Foxhound is designed to provide protection particularly from what?
a) Aircraft
b) Roadside bombs
c) Mines

27 The paint used on the first stealth aircraft could absorb radar signals. True or false?

28 What is the four legged military robot developed by US engineers?
   a) Big Cat
   b) Big Dog
   c) Big Bull

29 What was the nickname of the US tank, a mere six tonnes in weight with the ability to roll over cars?
   a) The Roller
   b) The Crusher
   c) The Flattener

30 What is another name for a UAV or unmanned aerial vehicle?
   a) Queen
   b) Worker
   c) Drone

31 What has been given to the supersonic, radar dodging Eurofighter?
   a) Mistral
   b) Typhoon
   c) Hurricane

32 What is an APC?

33 Where does a CERV travel, land, sea or air?

34 The Finnish-made Sisu E11T HMTV is a high-mobility tactical vehicle designed by which car maker, better known for its small family cars or its motor racing stable?

35 The Czech Tatra T813 Kolos (meaning Colossus) could run on petrol, diesel and which other fuel?

36 What was the Hunting-Percival Harrier?
 a) A jet
 b) A folding car
 c) A hovercraft

37 Towards the end of WWII Leyland built the Hippo, the Lynx and the Retriever. Which was the heaviest?

38 What name is given to the technology which deflects enemy radar in order to remain undetected?

39 The Renault TRM 700-100T was designed to be used as a transporter for the Leclerc, which is what?
 a) Helicopter
 b) Tank
 c) Missile launcher

40 Leyland built an artillery tractor called the Martian. True or false?

41 In the *Top Gear* battle between the Marauder and the Hummer who won?

42 How many military vehicles will Great Britain leave when it pulls out of Afghanistan?
 a) 300
 b) 1,500
 c) 3,000

43 In which country did the Santana company start building Land Rovers?
 a) Spain
 b) Portugal
 c) Italy

44 Which branch of the British armed services was the only one to use the Mini Moke, which was originally designed as a military vehicle?

a) Royal Navy
b) RAF
c) Army

45 The prototype of which military vehicle was developed by McLaren and BMW in 2010?

a) Ocelot
b) Lemur
c) Bobcat

The Answers

1 b) Pink panther
2 b) Amphibious jeep
3 SsangYong
4 USSR
5 b) US
6 Mini Moke
7 c) Nighthawk
8 b) Iraq
9 The Jeep
10 Variable sweep wings depending on use
11 Canada
12 Volvo
13 WWII
14 Machine gun
15 c) Tanks
16 Armoured personnel carrier
17 Richard Hammond
18 USA
19 Land Rover
20 Helicopter
21 A crane
22 Desert
23 c) Boat
24 a) Husky

25 True
26 b) Roadside bombs
27 True
28 b) Big Dog
29 b) The Crusher
30 c) Drone
31 b) Typhoon
32 Armoured Personnel Carrier
33 Land
34 Renault
35 Aviation jet fuel (kerosene)
36 b) A folding car
37 The Hippo
38 Stealth bomber
39 b) Tank
40 True
41 The Marauder
42 c) 3,000
43 a) Spain
44 a) Royal Navy (It could be used on aircraft carrier decks)
45 a) Ocelot

55 Le Mans Part 3: Diesel Dominance

A few years ago if you'd suggested that Le Mans would be won, repeatedly, by a car with a diesel engine, they'd have taken off your shoelaces and locked you in the attic. Nowadays it's just logical that a frugal, hardwearing diesel drive train, with thunderous in-gear acceleration, should be the dominant force of endurance racing. Audi singlehandedly changed the face of racing and even made diesel sexy. In a manner of speaking.

1 Which was the first Japanese team to win Le Mans?
   a) Toyota
   b) Honda
   c) Mazda

2 Mario Andretti had his first Le Mans start in 1966 and his last one in an Olympic Year. Where were the Olympics?
   a) Seoul
   b) Barcelona
   c) Sydney

3 How long is one lap of the Le Mans circuit?

4 At the beginning of the 21st century which manufacturer won 9 out of the 11 Le Mans 24 Hour races between 2000 and 2010?

5 Which French cars came first and second in 2009, breaking a monopoly by one other manufacturer?
   a) Renault
   b) Peugeot
   c) Citroen

6 Which Bentley, launched in 2009, is named after the longest straight at Le Mans?

7 Who am I?
- I'm a French racing driver and made my F1 debut for Tyrrell in 1989
- I have raced for Ferrari, Benetton and Sauber among others
- I started Le Mans in 1989 and again 21 years later in 2010

8 When BMW gave their M3 GT2 to artist Jeff Koons to decorate before the race what design did he choose?

a) Stripes
b) Stars
c) Random circles

9 Peugeot won in 2009. How many years since their previous triumph?
a) 10 years
b) 16 years
c) 21 years

10 Bentley had a famous 1/2 in 2003. True or false?

11 Which 1998 Nissan was built with the manufacturer's eyes set firmly on victory at Le Mans?

12 McLaren won Le Mans in 1995 with whose engine powering their car?
a) BMW
b) Porsche
c) Jaguar

13 Name the year
- The movie *Titanic* won 11 Oscars
- France won the World Cup on home turf, in a tournament where David Beckham got sent off
- The Porsche 911 GT1 was a 1/2 Le Mans winner

14 Which Audi won three successive Le Mans races in the late Noughties?

15 The Aston Martin DBR9 won on its debut at Sebring in 2005. How many years later did it win Le Mans?

16 Who created the first diesel car to win at Le Mans in 2006?

17 After winning Le Mans in 1992 Martin Brundle was signed by which team the following season?
a) Peugeot
b) Renault
c) Ligier

18 Despite winning Le Mans in 1991, why was Bertrand Gachot not able to continue the following season?

19 How many times did diesel cars win Le Mans before the first hybrid took the chequered flag?

20 Bentleys were famous at Le Mans in the roaring twenties. They only roared to victory again in the 1980s, 1990s or 2000s?

21 In 2010 the race was won by which make of car, covering a record breaking 3,246 miles in the 24 Hour period?

22 Which Italian driver, who died while preparing a car for Le Mans in 2001, won the race in 1997?

23 Johnny Herbert won Le Mans in 1991 but with which team did he make his F1 debut in Brazil in 1989?
a) Arrows
b) Porsche
c) Tyrrell

24 In 1990 on which straight were two extra chicanes installed to slow things down?

25 Keke Rosberg took part in his first Le Mans in 1991. True or false?

26 The tricolore of France traditionally starts Le Mans. What was the

first year of the new millennium that the tricolore belonged to a winning team?

27 Which was the first constructor to win in the 1990s?
a) Jaguar
b) Porsche
c) Peugeot

28 Which Italian manufacturer has had most wins?
a) Alfa
b) Ferrari
c) Lancia

29 Up to and including 2012, which tyre manufacturer has enjoyed most Le Mans winning success?
a) Michelin
b) Pirelli
c) Dunlop

30 Which driver, who became a racing pundit, won Le Mans in 1990 with John Nielsen and Price Cobb in a Jaguar XJR-12?

31 In 2012 Audi and which other manufacturer entered a hybrid in the LMP1 class?
a) Peugeot
b) Toyota
c) Jaguar

32 In 1996 Alexander Wurz was the youngest Le Mans victor. How old was he?
a) 22
b) 24
c) 26

33 In the GTE class at Le Mans, what does the E stand for?

34 The 2009 Lola Aston Martin had whose code letters on its side?

35 In 2013 the Automobile Club de l'Ouest recreated the Pontlieu hairpin in honour of which anniversary of the Sarthe track?

36 In 2010 what happened to all the Peugeots which had put up a challenge to Audi?

37 Which Derek won Le Mans in 1992? Bell or Warwick?

38 Which Frenchman won Le Mans in 1992, 1994 and 1995, each time with a different make of car?

39 What colour was the BMW M3 GT2 which raced at Le Mans in 2010?
   a) Red
   b) White
   c) Blue

40 In 2011 which team's drivers were involved in major crashes but could walk away from the wreckages?

41 Name the year
- The euro was officially launched
- Nissan launched its final Skyline, the GT-R R34
- BMW had its first win at Le Mans

42 In 2011 and 2012 Le Mans was won by a team made up of a French driver, a German driver and a driver of which other nationality?

43 How long do the qualifying sessions last prior to the race weekend?

44 In the 2012 race Anthony Davidson crashed on which section of the track?

45 Whose hybrid took the chequered flag at Le Mans in 2012?

The Answers

1 c) Mazda
2 c) Sydney
3 8.5 miles
4 Audi
5 b) Peugeot
6 Mulsanne
7 Jean Alesi
8 a) Stripes
9 b) 16 years
10 True
11 R390
12 a) BMW
13 1998
14 R10
15 Two
16 Audi
17 c) Ligier
18 He was involved in a court case in the UK
19 Six
20 00s (2003)
21 Audi R15
22 Michele Alboreto
23 c) Tyrrell
24 Mulsanne Straight

25 True
26 2009
27 a) Jaguar
28 b) Ferrari
29 c) Dunlop
30 Martin Brundle
31 b) Toyota
32 a) 22
33 Endurance
34 007's
35 90th
36 All had to retire
37 Warwick
38 Yannick Dalmas
39 b) White
40 Audi
41 1999
42 Swiss
43 2 hours
44 The Mulsanne Straight
45 Audi

56 May Day May Day

James May. What to say. He's the weird one with the renaissance hairdo and 1970s pornographer's shirts. He's also a musical scholar who likes taking old things apart and beer. Despite earning the moniker Captain Slow, he has now turned blokishness into an art form, a trait that is putting him in danger of superseding Hammond as the man most likely to be on your telly at any given time of day.

1 What was the name of Channel 4's motoring show launched in 1988 where James started his presenting career?

a) *Car Club*
b) *Driven*
c) *Wheelspin*

2 It would be handy if someone with the moniker of May was actually born in the month of May. Was he?

3 What is James May's preferred tipple?

a) Beer
b) Red wine
c) Italian vermouth

4 In the challenge to resurface a stretch of road, what was the first task for James to deal with?

a) Organise the tea rota
b) Organise a road diversion system
c) Organise waste removal from the site

5 James May was presented with an honorary Doctor of Letters degree from Lancaster University. True or false?

6 When the team did their race across London from West London to City Airport, what means of transport did JM use?

7 James had the ingenious notion of building a stretch limo combining a Saab with which other type of car?

a) Alfa Romeo
b) Fiat Panda
c) Opel Kadett

8 James claims to have been dismissed from the staff of which

motoring magazine after his subbing left a cheeky message appearing in print?

9 What was the name of his pet that James described as 'Standoffish and grumpy, just like me'?
   a) Jezza
   b) Fusker
   c) Hamster

10 Who appeared first on *Top Gear* – James May or Richard Hammond?

11 How many times did James take his driving test before passing?

12 James was the bright spark who devised the idea of motorhome racing. Is this true or false?

13 Name the year
- It was announced that Rio de Janeiro would host the 2016 Summer Olympics
- *Slumdog Millionaire* won 8 Oscars
- James May built an entire full size house from Lego

14 Which subject did James study at university?
   a) Architecture
   b) Fashion design
   c) Music

15 The Race to the North pitted a steam engine against a motorbike and a car. James got the car and went for a stylish classic made by which manufacturer?
   a) Bentley
   b) Jaguar
   c) Rolls Royce

16 What name did James suggest for Jeremy's manly smoothie concocted in a blender powered by a V8 engine?

17 James's famous caravan airship flew round the skies of East Anglia, but which county had he intended to travel to and meet up with the Hamster?

18 Which form of transport do both James and Richard often use for commuting?
  a) London bus
  b) Folding bike
  c) Helicopter

19 Captain Slow has presented dog show *Crufts* on TV. True or false?

20 On the team's caravan holiday what did James drive into when trying to reverse and park the caravan?
  a) An old lady
  b) A tent
  c) A tree

21 Ever the detached English gentleman, how did James show his euphoria when the Hamster returned on the set following the near-fatal crash of 2006?

22 Which airport was involved in the *Top Gear* 'emergency' as an airship with a caravan beneath it flew over the area?

23 In the Basel to Blackpool race which car did James choose?
  a) Porsche Cayenne Turbo S
  b) BMW M6
  c) Subaru Legacy Diesel

24 Which Hollywood star who appeared on *Top Gear* in 2011 was snubbed for a handshake with The Stig while James was carrying on an interview?

25 James had a nasty accident in 2010 when he fell backwards and hit his head on a rock in which country?

26 In the Man with a Van Challenge, why could James not tailgate Jeremy's van?
   a) Could not catch up with it
   b) Stuck in reverse
   c) Out of fuel

27 James drove a Ferrari California Spider on busy public roads and met an L-plate traffic jam. Which celebrity owned the car?
   a) Chris Evans
   b) Elton John
   c) Wayne Rooney

28 Captain Slow has taken part in the Rock Paper Scissors World Championship. True or false?

29 In the road trip across the western side of the US involving all three presenters, which car did James choose to drive?

30 Name the year
- The Beatles had their first British No 1 hit single
- President Kennedy was assassinated in Dallas
- James May was born

31 What was the bespoke interior colour scheme of James's brand new Porsche Boxster that 'caused much derision among my colleagues'?

32 In a 2007 Brylcreem poll James was named as Worst Celebrity what?

33 James adopted a Reliant Robin in the challenge to cross the Channel. True or false?

34 In which car did Captain Slow make a mockery of his nickname and clock up a top speed of 253mph?

35 In which city did James in a Peugot 207 take on parkour experts who were moving across the roofs of buildings?

36 In the mini-cabbing challenge in South London, James's first customer had some specialist equipment to squeeze into the boot. What was it?
- a) A keyboard
- b) Fencing swords
- c) Ladder

37 Flute, piano and trumpet – which of these does James not play?

38 At which circuit did James get some handy driving hints from Sir Jackie Stewart?

39 Who was the unfortunate singer that JM was meant to be driving to the BRIT awards, only to get lost en route?

40 His first job after graduating was in the archive department of what type of establishment?
- a) Animal refuge centre
- b) Museum
- c) Women's hospital

41 James, in an Alfa Romeo, had to drive round roads on the Humber estuary before his challenger crossed the river directly by what means?

42 In which city did James in a Fiat 500 race two BMX bikers through the streets?

43 In which American state did Ken Block introduce JM to airfield rallying?
   a) California
   b) Texas
   c) Vermont

44 Which word completes this James May quote? 'Cars that drive themselves were invented years ago. They're called…'

45 Who taught Captain Slow how to skid and slide while loose surface driving in Finland?

The Answers

1 b) *Driven*

2 No (He was born in January)

3 a) Beer

4 b) Organise a road diversion system

5 True

6 Mercedes 'Chelsea Tractor' 4x4

7 a) Alfa Romeo

8 *Autocar*

9 b) Fusker

10 James May

11 Two

12 False (It was Richard)

13 2009

14 c) Music

15 b) Jaguar (An XK120)

16 The Bloody Awful

17 Kent

18 b) Folding bike

19 False (Richard Hammond has!)

20 b) A tent

21 Shook Richard's hand

22 Norwich

23 c) Subaru Legacy Diesel

24 Tom Cruise

25 Syria
26 a) Could not catch up with it
27 a) Chris Evans
28 True (In 2013)
29 Aston Martin Vanquish
30 1963
31 Brown and black
32 Haircut
33 False (He used a Triumph Herald)
34 Bugatti Veyron
35 Liverpool
36 b) Fencing swords
37 Trumpet
38 Oulton Park
39 Lemar
40 c) Women's hospital
41 Waded through the water
42 Budapest
43 a) California
44 Taxis
45 Mika Hakkinen

57 *International* Top Gear

Top Gear has managed to upset a spectacular number of countries in the last decade, often without even leaving the studio. The road trips themselves have caused the odd diplomatic incident too, but generally speaking everyone goes home happy. Until they turn on the telly to see endless repeats of series 1 on grainy satellite channels and realise they've got it all to come.

1 In the spring of 2013 the team were seen in search of the source of which river?
   a) Amazon
   b) Nile
   c) Orinoco

2 The USA Road Trip Challenge ended in New Orleans. Where did it start?

3 In the Japan challenge, which make of car did Jeremy race James and Richard in?

4 In the World's Best Driving Road Challenge did Richard Hammond drive a Porsche, a Ferrari or a Jaguar?

5 How did the team mainly travel from Ho Chi Minh City to near Hanoi on their Vietnam trek?
   a) Motorbikes
   b) Bicycles
   c) Rickshaws

6 Which country launched its own *Top Gear* in 2008?
   a) Australia
   b) USA
   c) South Africa

7 In the closing credits of which Special did the team assume the first names Francis Ford? Clue: think Good Morning Francis Ford Coppola!

8 James was beaten by a downhill mountain biker in which city on the Iberian peninsula?

9 Which car was pitted against an America's Cup yacht in the long-distance race in New Zealand?

10 How many Canadian Inuit dogs were in the team pulling the sled for the Polar Special? Was it six, ten or twenty?

11 In the Japan Challenge which type of transport did James and Richard use?

12 In the *Top Gear* Winter Olympics which member of the team took part in the Snowmobile Ski Jump?

13 In series 16 the presenters tested luxury cars in less than luxurious surroudings. In which country were a Rolls Royce, a Bentley and a Merc put through their paces?
   a) Albania
   b) Greece
   c) Latvia

14 In the closing credits of which road trip did the production crew all assume the first names Billy Bob?

15 When the team did their World's Best Driving Road Challenge, why did they have a problem in Liechtenstein where the road was closed?

16 'Lazy, feckless, flatulent, overweight' were some of the words Richard used when he thought about cars that came from which country?

17 In the *Top Gear* Winter Olympics which car took part in the Ski Jump?

18 In the USA Road Trip the presenters got involved in a drive by shooting contest. The target was a cardboard replica of which famous celebrity?

a) Jeremy Clarkson
b) Piers Morgan
c) The Stig

19 Who stripped out the air conditioning from his car before setting off to find the world's best road?

20 When they filmed the Botswana Challenge what was the budget per car?

a) £1,500
b) £2,500
c) £3,500

21 In the *Top Gear* Winter Olympics which make of car did Jeremy Clarkson drive in the Biathlon?

22 On the Africa road trip what was the penalty if one of the cars broke down?

23 What type of vehicle was used when the presenters decided to build their own snow plough in Norway?

a) Combine harvester
b) Jeep
c) Tank

24 What did James and Jeremy (controversially) have to drink at the end of the North Pole Challenge?

25 In which American state did Richard sample stock car racing US style at a NASCAR rally?

a) California

b) Kentucky
c) Texas

26 In the World's Best Driving Road Challenge James May drove a Range Rover? True or false?

27 In which country did Richard try out the Marauder, a ten ton military vehicle?

28 In the closing credits of which Challenge did the team assume the names Bjorn, Benny, Agnetha or Anni-Frid?

29 Who had the honour of switching on the Blackpool Illuminations after the race that started in Switzerland?

30 In the *Top Gear* Winter Olympics which make of car did James May drive in the Biathlon? Was it an Audi or a Mercedes?

31 When Jeremy Clarkson raced a Bugatti Veyron across Europe from Italy to London, what were James and Richard racing against him in?

32 In the North Pole challenge Jeremy and James used an ultra-high tech Toyota Hilux. What did they give Richard?

33 In the *Top Gear* Winter Olympics in which event did Jeremy drive a Jaguar XK competing against Eskil Ervik?
a) Nordic skiing
b) Snowboarding
c) Speed skating

34 What was strapped to the back of the German rollerskater who raced against an Aston Martin V8-driving Richard Hammond?

35 With only a single ticket up for grabs for a football match, the trio had to race from Wembley to the San Siro stadium in which Italian city?

a) Milan
b) Rome
c) Turin

36 In the Africa Challenge which make of car did James May drive?

37 Which country were the guys driving through when they came across the destruction caused by Hurricane Katrina?

38 Which Olympic gold medal winner raced on a skeleton bobsled on the frozen downhill track at Lillehammer against a Mini Rally car with James on board?

39 In which South American country did the team complete a famous long road trip?

40 In the Middle East Special, James should have brought a gift of frankincense. What did he use as a substitute?

41 Jeremy once strapped which animal to the roof of his car?

a) Cow
b) Horse
c) Hippo

42 Ewen Page, Steve Pizzati and Shane Jacobson represented which country in a challenge against the UK presenters?

43 In the closing credits of which Special did the team all have the first name Archbishop Desmond?

44 In which country were the *Top Gear* Winter Olympics held?
  a) Norway
  b) Sweden
  c) Switzerland

45 What colour was Richard Hammond's car on the *Top Gear* Challenge to Botwsana?

The Answers

1 b) Nile
2 Miami
3 Nissan
4 A Porsche
5 a) Motorbikes
6 a) Australia
7 Vietnam
8 Lisbon
9 Toyota Corolla
10 Ten
11 Train
12 The Stig
13 a) Albania
14 American road trip
15 There was a cycle race!
16 Mexico
17 Mini
18 c) The Stig
19 James May
20 a) £1,500
21 Volvo
22 Complete the journey in a Volkswagen Beetle
23 a) Combine harvester
24 Gin and tonic

25 c) Texas
26 False (He drove an Aston Martin)
27 South Africa
28 Winter Olympics
29 The Stig
30 Audi
31 Cessna light aircraft
32 Dog sled
33 c) Speed skating
34 A rocket jetpack
35 a) Milan
36 Mercedes Benz
37 America
38 Amy Williams
39 Bolivia
40 Shampoo
41 a) Cow
42 Australia
43 Africa Special
44 a) Norway
45 Yellow

58 The Challenges

The thing that really makes Britain's favourite oafs tick, apart from a united suspicion of hairdressers and post-1980s tailoring, are the challenges. Pitting man and machine against an assortment of always arbitrary and occasionally genuinely dangerous demands for the benefit of our Sunday evenings in the safe embrace of the sofas has created some classic telly.

1 In the North Pole Challenge who declared that he did not like snow (a severe handicap for that particular quest)?

2 In attempting to destroy a Toyota Hilux, Jeremy's first plan was to drive the car down what?
   a) A fairground slide
   b) A flight of steps
   c) A white water raft course

3 What served as the bullseye in the game of car darts?

4 When the team did their race across London from West London to City Airport in series 10 who won?

5 Which of the team managed to outmanoeuvre an Apache helicopter gunship?

6 In an early *Top Gear* challenge, how many motorcycles did a double-decker bus jump over?

7 Name the year
- Swedish car makers Saab filed for bankruptcy
- Matt Smith became the fastest Doctor Who in a Reasonably Priced Car
- The *Sweeney* movie was released with the help of the *Top Gear* team

8 What rather vibrant colour was Richard's Porsche 911 GT3 RS that he used for the challenge to find the world's best driving road?

9 In the HGV challenge Jeremy had to do a hill start with who or what parked directly behind his lorry?

a) Keira Knightley
b) Jeremy's drum kit
c) a Porsche

10 What name was given to the car built by the team to rival the G-Wiz electric car?
a) Petrolhead
b) Hammerhead
c) Chargerhead

11 Which cars took place in the five-a-side hockey game?

12 Who managed to reverse his tractor into an Astra in the Grow Your Own Petrol Challenge?

13 What name was given to Jeremy's amphibious Toyota?
a) Flotilla
b) Knightley
c) Toybota

14 When the team made a people carrier into a convertible which model of car did they use?

15 Which of the three presenters was in the Mercedes GL500 in the race through London's rush hour?

16 Where in London was the finishing line for the Bugatti v Cessna race?

17 In which country did James and Richard find themselves separated as they were in a bullet train that split in half?

18 In the Making a Better Police Car Challenge did Richard Hammond drive a Suzuki or a Nissan?

19 Which challenge did the team take up on the 40th anniversary of a manufacturer based originally in Lancashire, to prove that they did make good cars?

20 Which manufacturer makes the Aygo used in the game of car football?

21 In the hunting challenge where Jeremy was the prey, what was tied to the bumper of his foxy Daihatsu Terrier?
   a) James May's shoe
   b) Rag soaked in fox urine
   c) Part of an animal carcass

22 The Race to the North started down south in London and ended up in which city?
   a) Edinburgh
   b) Glasgow
   c) Newcastle

23 In series 8 episode 4 Richard competed in a Porsche Cayenne Turbo S against a British army parachutist. Who won?

24 Which stadium was the venue for the 2013 game of car rugby where Captain Slow took on Jezza?

25 Which popular comic actor who died in 2013 provided the voice-over for the sat nav in the challenge to provide a car for the elderly?

26 After their challenge to make stretch limos where did the team have to drive the stars to?

27 On the American challenge who painted 'NASCAR sucks' on James's car?

28 In the Making a Better Police Car Challenge who decided that a paint gun system would be a splendid addition to his vehicle?

29 Greyhound racing took on a new meaning when a speedy canine beat a MX-5 that was driven by which presenter?

30 Which car did JC use to make a stretch limo?
a) Mini
b) Ford Fiesta
c) Fiat Panda

31 With the *Top Gear* train challenge what was the lowest class for passengers of the caravan-carriage train?

32 Which Eric played his electric guitar through the speakers of the KIA C'eed?
a) Eric Clapton
b) Eric Idle
c) Eric Sykes

33 The presenters decided that the best driving road in the world was from Davos in Switzerland to the Stelvio Pass in which other country?

34 During the Building a Convertible Challenge where were the boys required to drive in order to prove their confidence in their creation?
a) A carwash
b) A safari park
c) A nasty part of town

35 In the Making a Better Police Car Challenge Jeremy Clarkson drove a Fiat. True or false?

36 To prove that cars are more popular than traditional art the *Top Gear* trio decided to fill a gallery with motor-related work in which city?

a) London
b) Middlesbrough
c) Swansea

37 What was unusual about the Icelandic mountain that James drove up in a modified Toyota Hilux?

38 In the Making a Better Police Car Challenge did Richard Hammond borrow his siren from an ice cream van or an old air raid warning system?

39 Jeremy managed to get injured in the challenge to try to be a HGV driver when he drove in to a wall. Is that true or false?

40 In a surprising show of agreement between the presenters, who was declared to be the winner in the challenge to build a new motorhome?

41 When Jeremy was challenged to race across the width of Britain in the hours from sunset to sunrise he set off from Land's End and finished where?

a) Clacton
b) Dover
c) Lowestoft

42 Which presenter's team won the game of car football?

43 How long did the team have to resurface a mile and a half of the D54871 road in Warwickshire?

a) 24 hours
b) Two days

c) One week

44 During the Grow Your Own Petrol Challenge, which animals had to be cleared from a field – bulls or sheep?

45 James and Richard in a Porsche Panamera raced what from the Scilly Isles to the Orkneys?

The Answers

1 James
2 b) A flight of steps
3 Caravan
4 Richard
5 Jeremy
6 Three
7 2012
8 Green
9 b) Jeremy's drum kit
10 b) Hammerhead
11 Suzuki Swifts
12 Richard
13 c) Toybota
14 Renault Espace (Not exactly JC's favourite)
15 James
16 Top of the NatWest Tower
17 Japan
18 Suzuki
19 British Leyland Challenge
20 Toyota
21 b) Rag soaked in fox urine
22 a) Edinburgh
23 The parachutist
24 Twickenham

25 Richard Briers
26 Brit Awards
27 Jeremy
28 James
29 Richard Hammond
30 c) Fiat Panda
31 Scum class
32 a) Eric Clapton
33 Italy
34 b) A safari park
35 True
36 b) Middlesbrough
37 It was an active volcano
38 An ice cream van
39 True
40 It was agreed that no one was a winner
41 c) Lowestoft
42 Richard's
43 a) 24 hours
44 Sheep
45 A letter (travelling by the Royal Mail)

59 The Supercar Part 3

Things are getting a bit silly in Supercar world. We are in the midst of a global depression the likes of which hasn't been seen since the original Wall Street Crash when bankers were throwing themselves out of windows, but every week a new 200mph, £250k sports car appears and people are still buying them. Ferrari and Lamborghini continue to take chunks out of each other with upstarts like Pagani doing as much damage to both of them. Meanwhile McLaren is keeping the British end up and we're all left wondering if it's ever going to stop. And hoping it won't.

1 The limited edition Mercedes McLaren SLR speedster bears the name (and the signature) of which racing legend?

2 Which Hennessey model is also known as the hypercar as it reaches 100 km/h in 2.4 seconds?

3 The Suzuki XL7 Pikes Peak bears which name on its side – the nickname of its creator Suzuki's Nobuhiro Tajima?

4 Which manufacturer trades under the banner 'Always different'?

5 Which 21st-century Bentley shares its name with a legendary venue in racing in the early decades of the previous century?

6 Whose first supercar was the R8?

7 The Noble M600 can do 0–60 in 3 seconds dead! True or false?

8 How many seconds did it take the Mitsubishi Lancer Evo VIII FQ-400 to reach 60mph? Clue: It probably took you longer to say the car's full name!

9 Which was the last Aston Martin built at its Newport Pagnell production line?

10 The Mercedes Benz SLR was powered and financed by Mercedes Benz and was made in Hockenheim. True or false?

11 Which supercar was the first to have a one-piece carbon fibre body?

12 At the end of the first decade of the 21st century Belgian Luc Donckerwolke was head of design with which manufacturer?

a) Porsche
b) Audi
c) Lamborghini

13 Name the year
- The Dagenham production line produced the last Ford to be made in the UK
- Aston Martin made just 99 DB7 Vantage Zagoato models
- The Ferrari Enzo appeared

14 What was special about the roof of the Spyker C8 Laviolette?

15 What does VED stand for in the name of the BMW VED?

16 At which motor show did the Morgan Aeromax concept cause jaws to drop, triggering a limited production run of just 100?

17 In 2013, who introduced the Veneno with a $3.9 million price tag?

18 How many wheels did an all-new 2011 Morgan have?

19 The Lotus 340R had no windscreen or doors. True or false?

20 Which make of engine powered the Ariel Atom?
a) Honda
b) Renault
c) McLaren

21 The Mark IV Supra was a 170mph twin turbo V6 from which manufacturer?

22 How was the Nissan GT-R previously known?
a) Skyfall
b) Skyline

c) Skywards

23 Why is the BAC Mono so called?
a) It has one seat
b) It has one door
c) It has one window

24 The Lotus Evora emerged from which project?
a) Project Condor
b) Project Eagle
c) Project Kestrel

25 The Lamborghini Sesto Elemento (Sixth Element) is so called because it travels faster than the speed of sound. True or false?

26 Name the year
- A self confessed white van man won £56 million in the Euro millions lottery
- Gordon Brown left 10 Downing St for the last time as Prime Minister
- The SSC Ultimate Aero replaced the infamous Bugatti Veyron as the fastest car on the planet

27 The Morgan three wheeler has a motor bike engine. True or false?

28 The Pagani Huayra is made in Italy but its designer is from which country? Clue: He's the same nationality as Pope Francis!

29 What is distinctive about the doors on the Mercedes SLS?

30 The Ferrari 458 Italia can get from 0 to 60 in under four seconds. But how far under?
a) 3.4

b) 3.6
c) 3.8

31 In their first encounter, who was the winner when the Ascari A10 took on the Gumpert Apollo on the *Top Gear* track?

32 The four-door Aston Martin is still a supercar contender. What name did they give it to underline the point?

33 Who made the mouthful that is the MP4-12C?

34 Why was the Aston Martin One-77 so called?
a) It cost £77,000
b) Only 77 were built
c) It will deliver 777bhp

35 The MG SV was never road tested as it exploded on one of its first track test drives. True or false?

36 The Pagani Huayra has a carbon fibre body reinforced with what?

37 Where was the engine in the Ariel Atom 500?
a) In front of you
b) Beneath your feet
c) Behind your head

38 Which of the following is not a BMW – the M1, the M5 or the M25?

39 Which Honda supercar became a Type R towards the end of its period of manufacture?

40 Only five Pagani Zonda Cinque Roadsters were ever built. True or false?

41 Name the year
- Ellen MacArthur broke the record on the *Top Gear* track
- George W Bush became US President for the second time
- Maserati unveiled the Birdcage as homage to a 1960s racing car of the same name

42 By the middle of the first decade of the 21st century supercar maker Maserati was owned by which Italian company?
   a) Lamborghini
   b) Alfa Romeo
   c) Fiat

43 Which member of the *Top Gear* team almost came to grief in the Koenigsegg CCX?

44 The Ferrari FF has a five speed gearbox. True or false?

45 Which company described its LFA as 'the supreme supercar'?

The Answers

1 Stirling Moss
2 Venom GT
3 Monster
4 Lamborghini
5 Brooklands
6 Audi
7 True
8 Three
9 Vanquish
10 False (It was made in Woking)
11 Invicta S1
12 c) Lamborghini
13 2002
14 Clear glass
15 Vision Efficient Dynamics
16 Geneva
17 Lamborghini
18 Three
19 True (You'd think they could have added those for an asking price of £35,000)
20 a) Honda
21 Toyota
22 b) Skyline
23 a) It has one seat

24 b) Project Eagle
25 False (It's made of carbon, the sixth element on the periodic table as all you chemistry boffins will know!)
26 2010
27 True (But it was a Harley Davison)
28 Argentina
29 Gullwing doors
30 a) 3.4
31 Gumpert Apollo
32 Rapide
33 McLaren
34 b) Only 77 were built
35 False (They ran out of money when they were making it so it was never really finished)
36 Titanium
37 c) Behind your head
38 The M25
39 NSX
40 True (With a £1.1 million price tag it was a bargain!)
41 2005
42 c) Fiat
43 The Stig
44 False (Seven speed)
45 Lexus

60 Where to Next?

The car industry is in a state of flux, with energy and emissions taking precedence over performance and styling for the first time in history. Every time we get a sneak preview of some radical new idea we scoff in disbelief and a year or two later your grandmother has got it fitted as standard. In cars like nothing else, tomorrow gets here today. The future is unwritten, but it's already in some mad car designer's head.

1 As a sign of things to come, the new Volkswagen Beetle was launched in New York, Berlin and which other city?

2 In 2013 cars travelled around 65.4 billion miles on Britain's roads. What is the Department of Transport prediction for 2035?
   a) 75.4 billion
   b) 82.3 billion
   c) 89.5 billion

3 Bioethanol is fuel produced from what?

4 What does V stand for in the VTOL car?

5 Goggles developed in the Netherlands in the 21st century are able to do what, at night, making them useful to the emergency services?
   a) See things in colour
   b) See things invisible to the naked eye
   c) See things where thermal imaging is ineffective

6 In 2013 Audi announced that all its 2014 models other than the R8 and TT will have what as standard?
   a) DAB radio
   b) A hybrid option
   c) Night drive sensors

7 Which 2012 Ferrari boasted a transmission system called 4RM that was developed by Ferrari themselves?

8 On the M6 toll road which facility (perhaps surprisingly) is one of the most used on the motorway network?
   a) Hard shoulder
   b) Cafe

c) Roadside telephones

9 What colour were the fleet of hybrid buses introduced in London?
a) Red
b) Silver
c) Green

10 Which manufacturer announced its Hybrid Air model in 2013?

11 Hopefully James May will never enter politics. But is it true that David Cameron's first Home Secretary, Theresa May, is our James's cousin?

12 Which US state was the first to pass a law about autonomous or self driving cars?
a) California
b) New York
c) Nevada

13 Who am I?
- I was constructed in the *Top Gear* Technology Centre
- I have the chassis of an old TVR and the motor of a milk float
- As an electric eco car the boys wanted an impressive name… sadly Jeremy decided what to call me!

14 In a hybrid car, the fossil fuel powers the car in non urban driving and also generally fulfils which other role?

15 E10 is a petrol which contains 10% what in order to be more environmentally friendly?

16 Which car's S60 model will stop if a pedestrian is in its path?

17 The CLEVER is a Compact Low Emission Vehicle for which

sphere of travel?
a) Urban transport
b) Country transport
c) Air transport

18 The BMW Gina will be able to change its shape to what the owner wants. What is the model made from?
a) Plastic
b) Fabric
c) Aluminium foil

19 There were fewer cyclists in London in 2011 than there were 10 years previously. True or false?

20 According to a 2013 survey, the average motorist will spend how much on their cars from passing their test until they stop driving, not including buying vehicles?

21 The Electric Blue car, which reached a record speed of 175mph, uses what percentage of the energy from its batteries to power its wheels, resulting in very little power loss? Is it
a) 85%
b) 90%
c) 93%

22 Cars of the future will have the technology to eliminate which annoying, and potentially dangerous, motoring activity?
a) Parking on a double yellow line
b) Tailgating
c) Hogging the middle lane of the motorway

23 Which roads are getting busier than any other type of road, with this trend set to continue?
a) Motorways

b) Rural A roads
c) Rural minor roads

24 What shape is the futuristic car the Peugeot Ozone?
a) Cube
b) Sphere
c) Cylinder

25 The Bufori Geneva sports a thermal imaging camera for night time identification of obstructions. True or false?

26 Name the year
- Volvo announced it expects its cars will be unable to crash due to the number of sensors they will have on board
- The Post It note will celebrate its 40th birthday
- This year marks the 100th anniversary of the advent of the turning right hand signal

27 By 2020 it is expected that emergency vehicles, will not only persuade you to get out of the way with warning sirens and flashing lights, they will be able to make you do what else?

28 What name is given to the motor racing series designed for electric cars?

29 The first all electric Rolls Royce, the 102 EXis based on which model?
a) Silver Ghost
b) Silver Cloud
c) Phantom

30 Cars of the future will be able to reposition themselves so that a collision is less damaging to the vehicle and its occupants. True or false?

31 Back in the 1950s cyclists cycled over 12 billion miles. How much pedal power was spent in 2010, with a prediction that the decline will be even greater in the years to come?
   a) 10 billion miles
   b) 5 billion miles
   c) 3 billion miles

32 The controversial high speed rail link leaves London heading north, south or east?

33 Who sponsors London's eco friendly bikes?
   a) An electricity company
   b) A bank
   c) A solar panel manufacturer

34 The British Steam Car which reached a record speed of 140mph in 2009 was nicknamed what?
   a) The flying rocket
   b) The flying pressure cooker
   c) The flying kettle

35 In series 19 Jeremy tried to make the world's smallest car. Was he thinking about his future employment prospects when he named it? What was it called?

36 What is the General Motors Hydrogen car called?
   a) Hy-power
   b) Hy-wire
   c) Hy-lite

37 Which German manufacturer developed the Turbosteamer which could increase fuel efficiency by up to 15%?

38 What name is given to the hypersonic aircraft which will herald the arrival of much faster travel?
  a) Zoomjets
  b) Scramjets
  c) Hyperjets

39 What is the name of the revolutionary tank on the Hybrid Air?
  a) Oxygen tank
  b) Magic tank
  c) Scuba tank

40 By 2020 it is expected that car parking places will be able to tell you when they are available so you don't have to keep cruising around to find a space. True or false?

41 The Detroit Electric SP:01 can transfer its electric power to another car and also to what, in the event of a power cut?

42 Government figures suggest that the largest increase in road use in the next 20 years will be from vans. But why?
  a) High cost of rail transport
  b) Online shopping
  c) More people self employed

43 Which south west city was marketed as a 'cycling city' and is a rare area of the country where cycling is on the increase?

44 Where did the UK's first public refuelling station for hydrogen powered vehicles open?

45 Guess the year
- There will be an Olympic Games
- It will be 50 years since Lord Lucan disappeared
- *Top Gear* would be putting out its 300th episode. God help us.

The Answers

1 Shanghai
2 c) 89.5 billion
3 Sugar or starch
4 Vertical (Vertical Take Off and Landing)
5 a) See things in colour
6 a) DAB radio
7 FF
8 b) Cafe – why pay a toll to get there more quickly and then stop for tea?
9 a) Red
10 Peugeot
11 False
12 c) Nevada
13 Geoff
14 Recharges the battery
15 Ethanol
16 Volvo
17 a) Urban transport
18 b) Fabric
19 False (The number has more than doubled)
20 £200,000
21 c) 93%

22 b) Tailgating (A sensor will stop the car from getting too near the one in front)
23 b) Rural A roads
24 c) Cylinder
25 True
26 2020
27 Slow down and stop
28 Formula E
29 c) Phantom
30 True
31 c) 3 billion miles
32 North
33 b) A bank
34 c) The flying kettle
35 The P45
36 b) Hy-wire
37 BMW
38 b) Scramjets
39 c) Scuba tank
40 True (Imagine the time we will all save!)
41 Your home – for up to two days
42 b) Online shopping (Increase in home deliveries)
43 Bristol
44 Swindon
45 2024